Pocahontas's Daughters

Pocahontas's Daughters

Gender and Ethnicity in American Culture

MARY V. DEARBORN

OXFORD UNIVERSITY PRESS
New York   Oxford

Oxford University Press

Oxford   New York   Toronto
Delhi   Bombay   Calcutta   Madras   Karachi
Petaling Jaya   Singapore   Hong Kong   Tokyo
Nairobi   Dar es Salaam   Cape Town
Melbourne   Auckland

and associated companies in
Beirut   Berlin   Ibadan   Nicosia

First published in 1986 by Oxford University Press, Inc.,
200 Madison Avenue, New York, New York 10016

First issued as an Oxford University Press paperback, 1987

Oxford is a registered trademark of Oxford University Press

Library of Congress Cataloging in Publication Data
Dearborn, Mary V.
Pocahontas's daughters.
Bibliography: p. Includes index.
1. American literature—Women authors—History and criticism.
2. American literature— Minority authors—History and criticism.
3. Women in literature. 4. Minorities in literature.
5. Ethnic groups in literature. 6. Love stories, American—History and
criticism. 7. Miscegenation in literature. I. Title.
PS147.D43   1986   810'.9'9287   85-5093
ISBN 0-19-503632-8
ISBN 0-19-505182-3 ppbk.

9 8 7 6 5 4 3 2 1

Printed in the United States of America

To the memory of my mother,
and to my father

Acknowledgements

I have had a great deal of support while writing this book. The staff at the Columbia University Libraries was very helpful, and financial help from the Mrs. Giles F. Whiting Foundation freed me to devote my time to my work.

Many individuals read earlier drafts of this manuscript. Sacvan Bercovitch, Nancy Goulder, Jack Salzman, James Shenton, and Cornel West all provided helpful comments. Ann Douglas, Carolyn Heilbrun, Karl Kroeber, and Joseph V. Ridgely were thoughtful and generous advisers. Pamela Nicely and Sheldon Meyer of Oxford University Press provided excellent editorial advice. The staff of Columbia University's Department of English and Comparative Literature, especially Joy Hayton and Doris Getzler, untangled bureaucratic knots with grace and generally made life easier for me.

I am very grateful to Meryl Altman and Nat Austern for their invaluable intellectual contributions to this book, and to Warren Johnson and Beth Langan for sustaining me during its writing. The intelligent guidance of Allan M. Brandt, as well as his continued friendship and support, is deeply appreciated. Finally, my greatest debt is to Werner Sollors, my teacher and friend.

Contents

Pocahontas's Daughters

INTRODUCTION

Gender and Ethnicity in American Culture

A favorite story in American ethnic historiography is that of Oscar Handlin's realization that the story of America's immigrants was the story of America. "Once I thought to write the history of American immigrants," wrote Handlin at the outset of his classic 1951 study *The Uprooted*. "Then I discovered that the immigrants *were* American history."[1] Handlin meant that immigrants or the children of immigrants had shaped or indeed "made" American history; his statement, however, is suggestive in further ways, reminding us that the central feature of American identity is the experience of migration, that Americans are in fact all descended from immigrants and that American selfhood is based on a seemingly paradoxical sense of shared difference. As Americans we partake of a national identity, a communally determined and accepted sense of self; at the same time, as Americans and ethnics all, we define ourselves ancestrally. This inherent tension in American identity accounts for the richness and complexity of our national literature and culture, which simultaneously reflects and questions notions of national and individual identity, interrogating the relationship of the self and society, the private and the public, or, to borrow a term from the feminist movement, the personal and the political. This understanding of ethnicity, which makes literal this special and crucial aspect of American identity, enables us to read American literature in new ways, alert to such insistent and important thematic concerns as, for instance, inheritance or the lack of it (the American hero as bastard or orphan), social marginality (the American hero as outcast), marriage and romantic

love (the American hero as social being), alienation and participation (the American hero as divided self). In short, ethnicity allows
us to see in a new light the ways in which difference or "otherness" has always been an integral part of American culture.

Moreover, readings of American culture that begin with the concept of ethnicity as a determining factor in American identity also
begin to explain some of the notorious problems associated with
defining the unique qualities of American literature. There has
been a persistent sense, among literary critics, historians, and writers, that the outsider can best represent what it means to exist
within American culture. It is possible to trace this insistent intui-
tion in such observations on the literary scene as those made by
William Dean Howells and others at the turn of the century—a
period in which there was much investigation of the concept of
a national literature. Edward Eggleston suggested in his 1892
regionalist novel *The Hoosier School-Master* that the great American novel was destined to come out in bits and pieces; Robert
Herrick in 1914 issued a call for a national literature that would
reflect our mixed blood. Howells, reflecting on the increasingly
multiethnic and multiregional nature of American life, supported
regionalist or "local color" writers and ethnic writers like Abraham Cahan and Charles Chesnutt in their efforts to define and
partake of an American literary tradition. Calling for a "decentralized literature," Howells recognized that a national literature must
reflect our national diversity.[2] In doing so he acknowledged the
premise with which I began: that literature by and about those
who seem to be on the edges of American culture can perhaps best
represent what happens within that culture.

This understanding of ethnicity as acknowledged diversity demands a reading of the American literary tradition as one that consists not only of those writers commonly thought of as writing
within the mainstream (many of whom in fact wrote as outsiders
and explored what might be called outsiders' or "ethnic" themes)
but also of those often overlooked—women writers and those
commonly described as ethnic. Werner Sollors has recently argued
that ethnic literature *is* American literature. Echoing Handlin, he
writes, "Ethnicity as a tenuous ancestry and the interplay of different ancestries may be the most crucial aspect of the American
national character."[3] If this is so, a study of ethnic women writers

in America can reveal the female version of the American "national character"; in fact, it is necessary to look to factors of "otherness" just such as those of gender and ethnicity in order to understand American identity. If we consider again Handlin's famous statement, alert to the factors of gender and ethnicity in American culture, it is hardly surprising that the "first" American woman in our national cultural imagination is also the first American ethnic woman: Pocahontas, the Indian princess whose meeting with America's first settlers has become part of American legend. Indeed, her presence seems as remarkable a cultural comment on the history of women in America as Handlin's rhetorical observation on the history of immigrants. It suggests that ethnicity can provide a particularly persuasive means toward understanding the history of women and the workings of gender in American culture.

How is gender a factor in "otherness"? Simone de Beauvoir, whose *The Second Sex* (1952) is as much a landmark in feminist thought as Oscar Handlin's is in ethnic historiography, first suggested that women have always been culturally defined as "other." "Woman," wrote de Beauvoir, "is defined and differentiated with deference to man and not he with reference to her; she is the incidental, the inessential as opposed to the essential. He is the Subject, he is the Absolute—she is the Other." Acknowledging that the "category of the *Other* is as primordial as consciousness itself," de Beauvoir suggested, in an argument that has important ramifications for the concept of ethnicity, that it is inevitable that the self—and, in turn, culture—be defined in terms of "otherness."[4] The factors of gender and ethnicity bring together the concept of "otherness" as it exists within our culture. Carolyn Heilbrun has suggested that the ethnic woman is an outsider twice in America; the nexus of "otherness" her existence represents can explain much about the workings of the culture that purports to but cannot exclude her.[5] Literature produced by American ethnic women presents in dramatically high relief aspects not only of the female or ethnic experience in America, but of American culture itself. Moreover, if we reexamine traditional concepts of ethnicity and understand the stuctural workings of ethnicity in American society, it becomes clear that many American women not considered ethnic in the usual sense in fact wrote as ethnics, treating "ethnic" themes and applying "ethnic" strategies of authorship. Under a broad definition of ethnicity, one that recognizes the essentially ethnic quality of American life, it is possible to uncover connections between the female and ethnic experiences in America that go far beyond easy equations of the sort that Gunnar Myrdal, for instance, provides between blacks and women in his 1944 *The American Dilemma*.[6]

Do women understand or represent ethnicity in a gender-specific way? Is it possible or profitable to consider gender and ethnicity as marginalizing factors in American life? Taken together, what can they tell us about American culture? The kind of approach a study of such questions demands is necessarily interdisciplinary, drawing on the contributions of ethnic, women's, and American cultural studies. The groundwork for such an approach has been laid by important work within these disciplines, but few scholars have worked toward the synthesis needed for an understanding of gender and ethnicity in our culture. Moreover, as the claims of revisionism among the disciplines have made us aware, ethnicity and gender have long been overlooked as crucial features of American identity. In recent years this has begun to change, and it is in fact possible to gather scholarly information on ethnic women by reading around in the various disciplines and piecing together what has been said. For an understanding of the historical role of immigrant women, for instance, one might turn to John Higham's *Send These To Me: Jews and Other Immigrants in Urban America* (1975) and *Strangers in the Land: Patterns of American Nativism 1860–1925* (1963), both classics of immigrant history that provide valuable incidental information about ethnic women. If one wants to learn more about women of particular ethnicities, one might turn to Irving Howe's popular *World of Our Fathers* (1976), which has two sections on Jewish women: "The Girls and the Men"—about women and labor, and "Girls in the Ghetto"—about growing up Jewish and female; or to Debra Dash Moore's *At Home in America: Second Generation New York Jews* (1981) or Virginia Yans McLaughlin's *Family and Community: Italian Immigrants in Buffalo, 1880–1930* (1977), both extremely suggestive historical studies of small segments of the ethnic population, roughly half of which are female. If one shifts the focus to black women, historical analyses are more readily available, but are again compartmentalized by discipline, so that one turns to historians of black culture like Eugene Genovese and Herbert Gutman for insightful information about black women during discrete historical periods, or a historian of the family like Carl Degler, who devotes a chapter in his *At Odds: Women and the Family from the Revolution to the Present* (1980) to the families of blacks and immigrants, and thus to ethnic women. What these important studies seem to indicate is that primary sources tell us relatively little about ethnic women—a fact that, if it is true, would seem to suggest that scholars might consider more closely what ethnic women have written. Two excellent recent collections that exemplify approaches designed to study ethnic women through relevant documents are Gerda Lerner's *Black Women in White America: A Documentary History* (1972) and Maxine Schwartz Seller's *Immigrant Women* (1981): volumes that contain brief selections from oral histories, documents, autobiographies, and fiction, these works give the impression that the ethnic woman's story, like Eggleston's great American novel, is coming out in bits and pieces.

The historical sophistication of works such as those noted above is paralleled by the literary sophistication that has recently been brought to bear in the field of literary criticism on both ethnic and women's texts. Many of the ethnic women considered in this study have received considerable attention from such scholars as Robert Hemenway, who is Zora Neale Hurston's biographer, or Richard Bridgman, who is a Gertrude Stein critic. Feminist critics are writing about these women in growing numbers. Yet only in the field of what might best be called cultural history have the factors of gender and ethnicity been studied congruently, and the barriers between disciplines broken down. Something of the synthetic approach that is needed is supplied by the fact that, for instance, the most insightful literary criticism about Anzia Yezierska, an important Jewish-American writer, has been written by Alice Kessler-Harris, a feminist labor historian. Other useful approaches look at literature in a cultural context, as do those of Werner Sollors, Jules Chametzky, and Leslie Fiedler, or study ethnic history with an eye to popular culture, as do those of historians Philip Gleason, Lawrence Levine, and Nathan Huggins.[7] In this study, I have integrated several critical methodologies in order to gain as complete a picture as possible of gender and ethnicity in American culture. I have used a number of historical sources to clarify my understanding of ethnic women's roles in specific historical periods, but this study in no way claims to be a history of American ethnic women. While it does contain a good deal of textual criticism and biographical information about women authors, it is not literary biography; rather, I have attempted to draw from a wide range of sources, literary and otherwise, in order to create a sense of ethnic women's literature and its place in American culture, and, at the same time, to reach a broader understanding of American culture in terms of gender and ethnicity. My goal is not only to draw attention to a neglected area of American culture studies but to suggest that we cannot talk about American culture without attention to these issues.

The organization of this study, then, is thematic and arguably episodic, divided not in terms of chronology or of ethnic group. It is almost impossible to provide a coherent history of American ethnic women's writing, because to do so would require forced definitions of authorship and of ethnic group. It would be useful indeed to possess such a blueprint of American female ethnicity and authorship: one that tells us, for instance, that "x" number of novels were published by Italian-American women between 1920 and 1940, or that ethnic women's writing "began" with the 1859 publication of black Mrs. Harriet E. Wilson's *Our Nig*. Such a blueprint, however, would mandate troubling distinctions between ethnicities and literary forms. Bibliographical work of this sort is needed, to be sure: it is interesting to note and important to know that there have been few if any novels written by Italian-American or Greek-American women, for instance, until contemporary times—though such a statement again involves arbitrary and forced distinctions of ethnic group and chronology. Rather than provide such a blueprint, then, I have attempted first to identify a broad outline of the ethnic female literary tradition and the problems surrounding it, then to explore some of the themes and concerns shared by this body of writing, and, finally, to address whether there is value in reclaiming a distinctly female ethnic literary tradition and examining its place in American culture.

Why is it, in fact, that there seems to be no ethnic female literary tradition? Is there any value in locating or defining such a tradition? My first three chapters attempt, albeit indirectly, to answer these questions and to address some of the problems outlined above. My first chapter discusses, first, fiction by American Indian women, the scantiness of which is perhaps best reflected in the ironic fact that our most famous Indian woman, and a favorite heroine of American culture, Pocahontas, left no authentic record of herself. Her story was first "written" by John Smith, the man whose life she saved and who "discovered" her. Smith left for us the first erotic version of Pocahontas—a woman whom culture was persistently to eroticize—reminding us that he could have "done what he listed" with her, and complaining of his sexual harassment at the hands of this 12-year-old and her friends: "all these Nymphes more tormented [me] than ever, with crowding, pressing, and hanging about [me], most tediously crying, Love you not me?"[8] Pocahontas was not an author: what can this tell us about gender, ethnicity, and authorship? Indian women who have been "authors" have often retold legends, written autobiographies, or been the subjects of biographies. Does gender or ethnicity affect genre? Mourning Dove, the "first" Indian woman author, seems to have produced *Co-ge-we-a* (1927) with considerable help from a male friend—how then do we study her autobiographical novel?

The aim of this chapter and the second is to reclaim ethnic women's authorship, and to understand why it is so tenuous a condition in the first place. Chapters 2 and 3 look more closely at the writings of other ethnic women, and particularly black women, exploring the strategies of authorship available to women writers. If the ethnic woman sets out to mediate between her culture and the one that seems to her oppositional, what does she gain and what does she give up? In the black genteel tradition, in which black writers attempted to show white readers that blacks were fundamentally "like" whites, women like Reconstruction novelist Frances Harper and Harlem Renaissance writer Jessie Fauset have long been critically slighted, in part for the weaknesses of their fiction, but more so for the problems associated with their politics. In the heavily charged climate of the Harlem Renaissance, when the issue of black art became overtly political, Jessie Fauset and her contemporary Nella Larsen were criticized for their presentations of middle-class blacks with middle-class concerns, with the result that their portrayals, their historical significance as black women writers, and, in Larsen's case, her considerable literary

achievement, have been largely overlooked. The work of Zora
Neale Hurston, roughly their contemporary, is generally acknowledged to be outstanding, but Hurston had her own struggles with
authorship that are instructive for a study of this sort.

For ethnic women, authorship is always at issue; my first three
chapters necessarily reclaim it. In my fourth chapter, I begin to
look at what they do with the language they have adopted. This
chapter, "Fathers and Founding Fathers: The Making of Little
American Women," addresses the meanings of the ethnic woman's
acculturation and her "conversion" to the American self. The
generational conflicts engendered by the Americanization experience are the obsessive subjects of Jewish-American writers Anzia
Yezierska and Elizabeth Stern, and of Norwegian-American writer
Martha Ostenso, whose works I discuss in some detail. Mary Antin's *The Promised Land* (1912), an immigrant classic, details the
immigrant daughter's renunciation of her own Old World father
for the rhetoric of America's Founding Fathers. Participating in
what Werner Sollors has pointed out is a typologically familiar
rhetoric of New World regeneration and rebirth, ethnic women
often vigorously adopt myths and rhetoric provided them by the
culture in which they wish to be included.[9] Toni Morrison's very
recent *Song of Solomon* (1977) questions women's interaction
with and adoption of myths and rhetorics offered by a culture that
is, she seems to argue, for the most part only by adoption the ethnic woman's own.

Chapters 5 and 6, both on what I have called "the Pocahontas
marriage," return to the figure of Pocahontas in order to examine
how women writers have responded to one of America's most
ideologically potent myths: that of the mixed marriage between
a native-born white male and an eroticized and exoticized ethnic
woman—of which Pocahontas's marriage to John Rolfe is the pro-
totype. The first of these chapters, "America is a Lover's Land,"
takes its title from an Anzia Yezierska story; Yezierska's insistent
subject is the promise of romantic love held out by the American
experience, and specifically the marriage of a stereotypically passionate and fiery ethnic heroine to an equally stereotypically rational and coldblooded WASP—a relationship that had its biographical equivalent in Yezierska's lifelong obsession about her
relationship with John Dewey. Most of the writers discussed in

this chapter—Yezierska, Mourning Dove, Nella Larsen, and Tess Slesinger, among others—to varying degrees endorse the Pocahontas story, endowing the ethnic heroine with an erotic power that is perhaps different from that John Smith and his followers attributed to Pocahontas herself. Chapter 6, "Miscegenation and the Mulatto: Inheritance and Incest," explores what might be called the darker side of the Pocahontas marriage. Miscegenation, because it effaces clear distinctions of inheritance while it literalizes genealogy in the figure of the mulatto, is a persistent subject for ethnic women's fiction; such black writers as Gayl Jones, Frances Harper, and Nella Larsen, and such white writers as Gertrude Atherton, Kate Chopin, and Lillian Smith have turned to miscegenation and the mulatto as a locus for concerns about the meaning of inheritance in the American identity.

All of these concerns come together in my last chapter, in which I read Gertrude Stein's *The Making of Americans* as an ethnic text. In considering Stein as an ethnic author, I want less to remove her from the ranks of "the modernists" and place her among those of "the Jewish-Americans" than to investigate the relationship between ethnicity and modernism, to question whether there exists an awareness of and relationship to language and the literary tradition, or indeed to culture itself, that we might call ethnic. Stein's classic American novel addresses issues of American identity that I have identified as classically ethnic; the meaning of generations in the life of the individual, women's relationships to their fathers and to America's founding fathers, the tension between ancestrally derived and individually created versions of selfhood. Moreover, Stein's considerable artistic achievement in *The Making of Americans* suggests some resolution to the perplexing problems of authority and authorship raised at the outset of this study. Just as it is important to reclaim authorship of important texts by ethnic women, so it is equally important to reclaim Stein as an ethnic American author, because by doing so we can reassess the claims of gender and ethnicity on the American identity. Stein's novel asks and begins to answer the questions posed by all writers considered here, the questions with which I began: what it has meant to be a woman, an American, and an outsider, what the myths and symbols of American female ethnicity have been and what they ought to be.

CHAPTER 1

Pocahontas's Sisters:
A Case Study of American
Indian Women Writers

Pocahontas, the obliquely rendered heroine of my introduction and a favorite heroine of American culture, has achieved that status only through representations. The only means by which her story can be told is by piecing together the accounts of others, by studying interpretations of her image in literature, history, and cultural iconography. To study Pocahontas is to study these representations. Only through dimestore calendars and a portrait painted in London can we guess at how she looked; only through John Smith's accounts and imaginative reconstructions can we guess at how she lived. Illiterate and unphotographed, Pocahontas left no authentic record of herself.[1]

Judging from historical and literary scholarship until the last few years, the ethnic woman in America has been as mute as Pocahontas. She has been studied largely through representations: from unemployment statistics and ships' records to the novels of Abraham Cahan and William Faulkner. With the revolution in the last two decades in the historiography of women and the tools it has provided, it is possible to study women not only through representations of them provided by others, but through their own representations of themselves.

As I have argued in my introduction, this implies study of all American women's writing, but it particularly demands readings of writings of women from ethnic groups whose literary output has been thought to be so marginal and minor that they have been read only scarcely. If, for instance, Pocahontas is our culture's favorite ethnic heroine, a national symbol with different meanings for men and women, it is important to study the ways in which women of all ethnicities have responded to her as a symbol, but it is essential to look first at what Pocahontas—or her Indian sisters—wrote. For this reason, and because the body of literature by American Indian women emerges as paradigmatic for ethnic women's writing generally, I would like to consider the "case" of Indian women's writing first, looking to determine the nature of ethnic female authorship in American culture.

The literary critic who turns to literature by American Indians looking for a novel by an Indian woman is confronted, usually exclusively, with Leslie Marmon Silko's 1977 *Ceremony*. Silko's critically praised novel is about the readjustment of a World War II veteran, Tayo, who has been emotionally damaged by his service in a white man's war and the continued tensions of being Indian in a white society. The novel, a stylistic tour de force that incorporates poetry and Indian legend in an aggressively non-linear narrative, examines the role of tradition in twentieth-century Indian life, suggesting the need for "ceremony" as a redress for the ills both of society and the individual, white and Indian.

Silko's "authorship" seems to be under no debate. She wrote the novel; indeed, Edith Blicksilver, in her entry on Silko in *American Women Writers,* identifies Silko as "the first Native American woman to publish a full-length novel."[2] The reviewer for the *New York Times Book Review,* in a praiseful review, calls Silko "the most accomplished Indian writer of her generation." The components of the equation, a writer and an Indian and a woman and a novel, seem to add up to our sense of Silko's authorship. On the other hand, several factors, some in Silko's control and others beyond it, seem to militate against such a sense.

The *Times* reviewer who so admires her book, for instance, points out in the last paragraph that Silko is half Laguna Pueblo, half white, and reminds us of her gender:

> Her dual sensibility has given her the strength to blend two forms of narrative into a single work. It may also have given her the perspective, as a woman, to write so movingly about her male characters.[3]

Frank MacShane seems to imply that "the most accomplished Indian writer of her generation" achieves that status only by virtue of her marginality, both as a woman and a half-blood Indian. The fact of Silko's authorship is not threatened, but the identity of the author becomes blurred. Her Indianhood is compromised (she is only half that) as is her gender (a woman cannot write with sensitivity about men unless she is in some other way marginal). Her identity as an Indian woman author is granted only with compromise. Similarly, Indian critics have questioned Silko's authority to write a novel about Indians by virtue not of her half-blood status but because Silko is an academic, presumably too far from the reservation to understand it. Can an outsider—or in Silko's case, half an outsider—authentically author works about ethnic culture? And, as I will show, Silko's authorship is often questioned in bibliographic inquiry, in which other, prior novels authored by Indian women are cited.

Furthermore, Silko's *Ceremony* questions the very nature of authorship in interesting and important ways. The incorporation of legend and poetry into the narrative invites us to question our notions of the novel as a definable genre. The implicit defense of an oral storytelling tradition asks us to rethink our idea of the "story." Is the woman who sets down stories an author or a transcriber? Silko suggests that authors do not own stories, that stories belong to the tellers. She prefaces her text with a poem based on Indian legend, a poem that in effect denies Silko's authorship and establishes her as a teller of stories:

> Ts'its'tsi'nako, Thought-Woman
>   is sitting in her room
> and whatever she thinks about
>   appears.
>
> She thought of her sisters,
>   Nau'ts'ity'i and I'tcts'ity'i,
> And together they created the Universe
>   this world
> and the four worlds below.
>
> Thought-Woman, the spider,
>   named things and
> as she named them
>   they appeared.
>
> She is sitting in her room
>   thinking of a story now
>
> I'm telling you the story
>   she is thinking.[4]

The inclusion of this poem as a prefacing statement by virtue of its placement within the text questions authorship and creation; the poem itself asks whether language—thought, naming, story-telling, literature—is in fact inextricable from the act of creation. It also establishes a matrilinear structure to storytelling, associating women with language and the act of creation. Later in the novel Silko writes, "That was the responsibility that went with being human . . . , the story behind each word must be told so there could be no mistake in the meaning of what had been said; and this demanded great patience and love."[5] The responsibility that goes with being an Indian woman novelist, for Silko, is to tend language and authorship with infinite care.

For the ethnic woman writer, language and authorship are indeed very fragile entities. The case of Silko's novel, the "first" "novel" by an "Indian" woman writer, suggests the complexity of the act of writing by an ethnic woman. Authorship is always at issue for the ethnic woman writer. Sometimes this is literally so, and the authenticity of the ethnic woman's writing is questioned by bibliographers and critics on grounds of ethnicity and authorship. Indeed, many ethnic women's novels are not *by* ethnic women; they are "as told to" stories, anthropological narratives, collections of letters, biographies. If authorship is determined by ownership of copyright there are, for instance, indeed few if any novels by Indian women before Leslie Marmon Silko's *Ceremony*. If authorship is determined by genre, it is again difficult to designate ethnic female novelists. Folktales are not fiction, but what about fiction built around folktales? Autobiographies and biographies are supposedly not fictional—or are they? In studying ethnic women's fiction, we need at times to accept a collectivity of authorship seemingly antithetical to literary study, to be alert to evidence of compromised authorship, and to relax our standards and expectations of genre itself.[6]

Ethnicity, too, can become a troubling factor in defining ethnic female literature. Silko, who is half Laguna Pueblo, is considered Indian, but is granted special sensitivity by at least one critic because she is not fully white. The woman with less Indian blood is less likely to be defined as ethnic. For other ethnicities, the distinction is no less troubling. Is the great-granddaughter of Russian Jewish immigrants considered an ethnic writer? Only if her grand-

parents and parents married other Russian Jews? Only if she identifies herself as Russian Jewish? Only if she attends synagogue?
Knows Russian? Yiddish?

In determining the authenticity of the author's ethnicity, it is
best, I think, to posit a continuum or sliding scale of ethnicity.
Here it is useful to recall the origins of the word itself. Werner
Sollors notes that the noun "ethnicity" derives from the Greek
word for "nation" or "heathen," used in the Greek Bible to describe non-Israelites, or Gentiles:

> [T] he word "ethnic" . . . recurred, [however,] from the 14th
> through the 19th centuries, in the sense of "pagan, heathen, non-
> Christian." Only in the mid-19th century did the more familiar
> meaning of "ethnic" as "peculiar to a race or nation" reemerge.
> However, the English language has retained the memory of
> "ethnic" as "heathen," often secularized in the sense of ethnic as
> "other". . . .[7]

In this light, it is interesting to recall Pocahontas, who until the arrival of the English was not "ethnic," in a number of senses. First,
she was a member of an Indian race, and only Indians peopled
the continent at that time (already mixed, however, with European explorer strains). In comparison to the Europeans, the
Jamestown Indians were the more "American" in that they had
"immigrated" far earlier, at a point too distant to pinpoint. Furthermore, Pocahontas's religion, language, and customs were presumably those of the dominant culture in her land. Of course, in
relation to other tribes, Pocahontas might have been seen as ethnic, but persumably the Powhatans were in contact with only one
tribe at a time, in various skirmishes in which one would be
tempted to describe the outnumbered tribe as "ethnic." In this
sense, an important point emerges: only in relation to other groups
can a group be defined as ethnic. Ethnicity has always been defined as otherness; the other is always ethnic. The Indians of
North America became ethnic only when European settlers appeared, who, first by gunpowder and goods and later by sheer
numbers emerged as dominant, i.e. nonethnic. Whether or not ethnicity is related to class—in the vehement contemporary debate of
the issue, the two are seen as structurally different, and certainly
an equation of the two has difficult political and social consequences—ethnicity *is* related to power, however broadly defined.

When gender is introduced, the relationship becomes more clear. Pocahontas, a sexually and culturally colonized woman, reminds us that, in effect, white males exist as a dominant group only insofar as there are other entities whom they can perceive as ethnic and female, or colonizable. When John Smith—an immigrant, after all—arrived in Jamestown, Pocahontas began to be ethnic.[8]

Did Pocahontas know that she was an ethnic woman? We cannot know, because she did not write, and in some ways that is in fact the point. If female ethnicity is in the sense discussed above an unbounded condition, a shifting concept on a sliding scale, it becomes meaningful when the ethnic woman, in writing, fixes her place on the continuum, when, that is, she enters culture. Paradoxically, however, the odds are against her authorship.

Because of the problems surrounding ethnic female authorship, the very question of defining a body of fiction produced by ethnic women presents, in the words of two bibliographers of American Indian writing, "bibliographic nightmares."[9] Bibliographers are unsure how to classify—or whether to include—works like Helen Sekaquaptewa's *Me and Mine: The Life Story of Helen Sekaquaptewa* (1969), an as-told-to story "edited" by Louise Udall; or Polingaysi Qoyawayma's *No Turning Back: A Hopi Indian Woman's Struggle to Live In Two Worlds* (1964), a biography of Qoyawayma by Vada S. Carlson, which at least one student of American Indian literature has discussed as an "autobiography."[10] Gretchen Bataille and Kathleen Mullen Sands, for instance, in their very recent *American Indian Women: Telling Their Lives* (1984), are careful to distinguish between autobiography and biography, and another critic claims his field of study is "Native-American Bi-Autobiography."[11]

Many of the problems posed by American Indian bibliography can, of course, be answered with common sense. Answers to all questions of authorship can also be obtained in semiotic analysis, by which all texts are merely significations, authors becoming irrelevant entities. While I do attempt to use common sense in making necessary bibliographic determination in this study, a semiotic approach to questions of the sort raised here seems counterproductive, negating the achievement and even the existence of the ethnic woman who produced the text. While such an approach might well be employed on the texts considered here, it seems

more important first to reclaim authorship than to look beyond
it.[12] In the interest of doing so, and of further clarifying the complex notion of ethnic female authorship, I would like to consider
the case of the "other" first novel by an American Indian woman,
Mourning Dove's 1927 *Co-ge-we-a: The Half Blood: A Depiction
of the Great Montana Cattle Range*. The case of this remarkable
novel raises with some thoroughness each troubling question related to ethnic female authorship.

The name of *Co-ge-we-a*'s author is one of the first questions
raised in a consideration of the text. The title page of *Co-ge-we-a*
says the book is "by Hum-Ishu-Ma"; the preface of the novel refers always to "Mourning Dove," presumably the English translation of Hum-Ishu-Ma. On the other hand, this "author" is referred
to by a variety of names in the papers of Lucullus McWhorter, a
man to whom I will turn in a moment. Sometimes, for instance,
she is Cristal McLeod. In this context, Cristal McLeod seems to
be the "social" translation of her name, what she is called within
the white world. Then again, McWhorter refers to Cristal Galler,
whom the cataloguer of his papers also identifies as Mourning
Dove; at some point "Cristal McLeod" must have married and
taken her husband's name. (It is not known whether he too was
Indian and might thus have had other names of which she might
partake.) This secondary social translation of her name at some
point underwent a further transformation, and her first name was
changed: McWhorter writes also to Catherine Galler and Mrs.
Fred Galler, both of whom his cataloguer identifies as Mourning
Dove. Presumably she might also have used the name Catherine
McLeod, if McLeod was her maiden name. To complicate matters
further, McWhorter often makes an understandable mistake and
refers to Mourning Dove as Morning Dove. All tallied, "Mourning
Dove" went by at least eight different names.[13] Of course, many
women who marry are possessed of more than one name, as are
many Indians; mathematics imply that Indian women will indeed
have many names. Mourning Dove's case, however, seems rather
remarkable. To the extent that names define identity—and the
concept of naming in Indian culture is central—and to the extent
that identity defines authorship, Mourning Dove's authorship is
already obscure.

The details of Mourning Dove's life are less difficult to trace, though much information is provided by McWhorter in a bio-graphical sketch accompanying the novel, and McWhorter is a friendly but not always reliable source. She was born in Bonner's Ferry, Idaho, around 1888, a "Colville Indian woman."[14] McWhorter writes that she also had a "remote strain of good *Celtic* blood, dating back to the earlier advent of the Hudson Bay Company into the Northwest" (McWhorter's emphasis).[15] At age seven, she went to the Sacred Heart Convent in Washington state; at thirteen her mother died, and she was entrusted to her grand-mother's care. In 1908 she became involved in issues surrounding the Indian's right to Northwestern cattle ranges, and worked in Indian schools, rendering, McWhorter relates, "signal and telling service to the dependent tribesmen."[16] In 1912 and 1913 she at-tended Calgary Business College. After these years the facts of her life must be pieced out from the books she "authored." In 1927 her novel, *Co-ge-we-a,* was published by the Four Seas Publishing Company in Boston. In 1933, Mourning Dove, with Dean Guie, collected some Okanogan legends which were published as *Coyote Tales.* (This volume raises questions of authorship of its own: did Mourning Dove give the tales narrative form? Who titled the tales? What was Dean Guie's role?) Mourning Dove's marriage and death can be inferred, but not the details of them.[17]

On the other hand, if we accept McWhorter's designation of *Co-ge-we-a* as "a semiautobiographical novel," it is perhaps legiti-mate to refer to the text itself for details of Mourning Dove's life.[18] Cogewea, Mourning Dove's heroine, certainly does many of the same things her author did. She has been away to school, spends time associated with the cattle ranges, and is raised by her grandmother. She is, like Mourning Dove, an Okanogan, and has an Anglicized last name of Scottish origin, MacDonald. Cogewea, significantly, is a "half-breed"; her father was white. Here her story diverges from that of Mourning Dove in significant ways, as her half-blood status takes fictional expression.

Cogewea, as a half-breed, feels herself very much torn between two cultures. She loves her worthy half-breed suitor, but is at-tracted to Alfred Densmore, a villainous Easterner who comes to the Montana cattle ranges looking for wealth, adventure, and titil-lation. Similarly, Cogewea takes seriously the legends and lessons imparted by her Indian grandmother, the Stemteemä, and main-

tains such customs as ritual sweats, but at the same time she
is given to reading extensively and orating grandiloquently on the
Indian cause. To the Stemteemä, Cogewea intones, "I do not forget your counseling of other suns" (104). In another, quite different, linguistic flight, Cogewea denounces the Indian Bureau to
Alfred Densmore:

> A nasty smear on the Government escutcheon. . . . A stagnant
> cesspool swarming with politically hatched vermin! Stenchful
> with the fumes of avarice and greed; selfishly indifferent to the
> Macedonian cry of its victims writhing under the lash wielded by
> the hand of Mammon! (145)

Perhaps the best expression of Cogewea's double status is her
entry, in the Fourth of July races, in both the squaw's and the
lady's races. Characteristically, she wins both, but is offered the
twenty-five dollars due her as the squaw's prize and not the forty-
five dollar lady's prize: she refuses the judge's "tainted money."
Cogewea's experiences are fictional representations of Mourning
Dove's divided selfhood. Both the writer and her heroine seem to
have suffered from an interesting form of cultural schizophrenia.

Co-ge-we-a, it should already be clear, is a slightly schizo-
phrenic book; more than that, it is a text gone crazy. For added to
what might be called the Indian plot, in which Cogewea is a romantic spiritualist, and to the genteel, melodramatic plot, in which
Cogewea is a lady in distress, is a western plot, in which Cogewea
romps with cowboys and Indians. Cogewea, squaw and lady, is
also a cowgirl, " 'a bepistoled woman who can swear a little on
occasions' " (81). In this guise, Cogewea is capable of yet another
sort of discourse, and is given to remarks like the following:
" 'Now don't start throwing me that hot air stuff. . . . I was born
farther west than Montana, and you can't make anything like that
stick with this squaw. Savey?' " (195). In Cogewea's cowboy
world, eyes are "optics," Frenchmen are "frog-eating fools," and
obnoxious people had better "skedaddle" or "skiddo." A significant part of the text is given over to descriptions of cowboy activities and episodes in the life of the ranchers, most notably
scenes in which outsiders—in one case two wealthy Parisians
"struck by the American craze" for the West—are farcically undone by their "authentic" cowboy hosts.

In a variant of the genteel, melodramatic personality of the novel, Cogewea, taking on a spiritualized and sentimental air, is much given to reflecting on the land. To Densmore, Cogewea urges,

> See, Alfred! the leaves have fallen and are returning to dust. The beauty of their present life has passed forever. Youth gone, seared and lifeless, they lay at our feet—lopped and cast down— as a love discarded for another of fairer hue. (231)

She addresses Alfred at another point in the language of knighthood in full flower: " 'Sir Shoyapee! From whence, my gallant knight-errant of the wilderness way?' " (142). At her most annoying in this guise, Cogewea, or her author, usually cuts short such nonsense. After reading an offensive book on the half-breed and much lamenting ruination, Cogewea finds "solace in consigning the maligning volume in the kitchen stove" and is off for more cattle roping and ritual sweats (94).

Less a novel than a bizarrely textured pastiche, *Co-ge-we-a* contains a variety of discourses, all of which are available to the book's versatile heroine. Several chapters are given over to transcription of legends told by the Stemteemä. Other chapters, as I have pointed out, describe cowboy jollity. To each chapter is attached an epigram, the sources of which reflect the confusion of the novel. Longfellow's *Hiawatha* is heavily quoted, as is Western writer Badger Clark's "The Passing of the Trail," a mournful ballad about the demise of the Wild West. Byron's "The Giaour," Scott's "The Lady of the Lake" and "The Lay of the Last Minstrel" reflect the novel's romantic elements. As I will argue, these epigrams are often used ironically, but my point here is the remarkable variety of influences brought to bear on the writing of *Co-ge-we-a*. At one point I believe Mourning Dove even paraphrases Horace.

This brings the analysis again to the question of authorship. Could one person be responsible for such a pastiche? In Charles R. Larson's useful study, *American Indian Fiction,* Mourning Dove's novel is discussed in the appendix rather than the text of the book. With some regret—though he finds the effect of the novel artificial, stilted, and clichéd, he also senses its charm— Larson concludes that Mourning Dove's novel was not only hers but Lucullus Virgil McWhorter's.[19]

It is important to state at the outset that McWhorter never

claimed authorship of the book. He is on record only as Mourning
Dove's editor, biographer, annotator, promoter, and friend. A review of the catalogue of McWhorter's papers indicates that he
maintained a lifelong personal and professional relationship with
Mourning Dove: his personal correspondence with her covers such
matters as her health and her "domestic concerns" as well as the
sales and reviews of her books. A longtime friend of the Indian,
Lucullus Virgil McWhorter—his name and that of his brother
(Ovid) suggest a possible source for the Horace—is an interesting
figure in his own right. Born in 1860 in West Virginia, McWhorter,
the cataloguer of his papers relates, was steeped in the frontier
tradition, well-versed in the romantic poets and English history. A
midwestern farmer for a time, McWhorter moved to Washington,
and, interested in the Yakima Indians, took up the cause of Indian
rights. With brief forays into other fields—he was an active advocate of Prohibition, a crusader against cruelty to animals; he also
tried and failed to cultivate the Pawpaw tree—McWhorter worked
to further interest in Indian culture and Indian rights. The author
of *Yellow Wolf: His Own Story,* about the Nez Perce wars,
McWhorter, in an activity reminiscent of George Eliot's Casau-
bon's, labored all his life on a comprehensive "Field History" of
the North American Indians, which he never finished. Apparently
well-loved by the Indians, McWhorter, like Mourning Dove, used
other names. He was adopted into the Yakima tribe as He-mene-
Ka-Wan, or "Old Wolf," and liked to sign his letters with this
name. Among his many activities, McWhorter also encouraged,
promoted, and perhaps co-wrote *Co-ge-we-a.*[20]

It is impossible to be certain how much of *Co-ge-we-a* was
written by Mourning Dove and how much by McWhorter. One
charitable interpretation could conclude that McWhorter influenced Mourning Dove, making suggestions and editing heavily;
at the other extreme an equally reasonable assessment could conclude that Mourning Dove talked and McWhorter wrote. There is
simply too much in the novel for it to be the work of a single
mind. Such speculation, however, obscures the real point, which
is the way in which McWhorter translates, transcribes, and anno-
tates the experience of Mourning Dove, and how each of them
seems to have viewed their respective roles. *Co-ge-we-a* is representative of an important tradition in ethnic literature in which

the relationship of author to audience, and the transmission of the author's work to the audience, is mediated by a midwife figure. As I will argue, "midwiving" of this sort took various forms; my point here is that McWhorter to a certain extent was responsible for the "birth" of Mourning Dove's novel, and that her authorship within this structure necessarily became compromised.

Mourning Dove wrote, McWhorter tells us, in order to preserve the legends and traditions of the Indians, and to build a bridge between the Indian and white worlds.[21] This theme is echoed within the text, when Cogewea expresses admiration for Indian writers who attempt mediation between the two cultures, but more so within the writings of Mourning Dove's various male editors. Donald Hines, who in 1976 reprinted Mourning Dove's *Coyote Tales* as *Tales of the Okanogans,* speculates that Mourning Dove "must have been a remarkable woman; poorly educated, working under impossible conditions, she sought to bridge two cultures."[22] This concept of the ethnic woman as herself a mediator, an "ambassador between two cultures," as Hines describes Mourning Dove, will surface again both within and surrounding the writings of ethnic women. If the ethnic woman is a mediator or ambassador, her writing is legitimized but also to some extent defused. Her mission is peaceable, and the dominant culture can understand ethnic female identity in a way that is not threatening if it is presented in a work written with a mediating purpose. In such a context, the ethnic woman's voice and identity are ultimately compromised, and as I will argue, her writing is more interesting when it struggles against the concept of mediation than when it succumbs to it.

In this sense the notion of Mourning Dove as a mediator is a kind of red herring that merely throws us off the scent. For Mourning Dove's two purported goals, to preserve the traditions of her people and to bridge the gap between Indians and whites, are in some ways mutually exclusive, or at least competitive. Within the text Cogewea translates the Stemteemä's oral legends for Alfred Densmore (and the reader), and is constantly called upon to deliver laborious explanations of concepts like the smoking of a peacepipe. In so translating or explaining rituals she deritualizes them, or in fact reinvents them as inauthentic rituals in the white audience's mind. An analogue to this process can be found in the construction of the text of *Co-ge-we-a;* it is heavily, and unevenly, annotated—presumably by McWhorter. Many things must be *explained.* This continues to be a significant feature of ethnic women's writing; to cite just one example, often, as in Mary Antin's 1912 *The Promised Land,* a glossary is affixed to the text, translating not only non-English words but "foreign" concepts.

Moreover, such annotation or translation is more often than not inaccurate, especially if performed by the "midwife" figure, be he or she publisher, editor, or promoter. Cogewea, for instance, is particularly offended by a white-authored novel called *The Brand,* which purports to describe half-breed life. The novel's half-breed hero falls in love with a white woman and becomes her emotional slave, cursing his mother for the stigma of his Indian heritage. Cogewea is offended, first, by the hero's denial of his heritage, which she finds unbelievable, and, second, by the stigmatization of Indian blood. She rails at the way Indians have been victimized through the writing of outsiders:

> Cogewea reflected bitterly how her race has had the worst of every deal since the landing of the lordly European on their shores; how they had suffered as much from the pen as from the bayonet of conquest; wherein the annals had always been chronicled by their most deadly foes and partisan writers.

What really excites Cogewea's contempt, however, is the novelist's misuse of Indian words. She remarks to Jim LaGrinder, her half-breed suitor, " 'It contains a few tribal phrases, supposedly the names of birds and animals. These have been conferred on some of the characters, or pet saddle horses; which, if properly translated, would shock the public immeasureably' " (91–93).

In Cogewea's objection to the white author's wrongful translation, however, lies the means by which the ethnic writer *can* both preserve the traditions of her culture and mediate with the white world; here lies one solution to the problem of ethnic female authorship; here lies, so to speak, the trick. Who provided the white author of *The Brand* with these dirty Indian words? In doing so, the author's Indian "informant" (as the Indian is commonly described in many of these texts) participates in authorship of the text, in effect writing a subtext to *The Brand,* a subtext that functions as an inside Indian joke and that does preserve Indian language and culture.

Jim LaGrinder explains to Cogewea that he had had some contact with the white lady who wrote *The Brand,* and offers another story that explains the workings of ethnic authorship:

> I was there when the boys was a stuffin' one poor woman. It was at the first buffalo roundup when lots of people come to see the sight. A bunch of us riders was together when this here lady come up and begins askin' questions 'bout the buffaloes; and Injun names of flyin', walkin', and swimmin' things and a lot of bunk. Well, you know how the boys are. They sure locoed that there gal to a finish; and while she was a dashin' the information down in her little tablet, we was a thinkin' up more lies to tell her. We didn't savey she was writin' a real book, or maybe we would a been more careful. Yes, *maybe!* Why, them there writin' folks is dead easy pickin' for the cowpunchers. (93–94, Mourning Dove's emphasis)

If this strategy is available to the Indian, a good deal of his or her power is preserved. The constant comments in *Co-ge-we-a* on strategies very like this one, indeed on authenticity itself, argue that the authenticity of the finished text is in fact compromised by McWhorter's "authorship," and that there exists a subtext within the novel that is wholly Mourning Dove's. In a world in which whites are perceived as, and reveal themselves to be, treacherous authors, one must lie to them, and in lying, after all, one authors fictions.

In this light, incidents within the novel, such as the cowboys' farcical sendups of effete Easterners, can be interpreted as expressions of the insider's possession of authenticity. Only the insider knows the language, and language is an important weapon. This can be briefly illustrated by the example of Alfred Densmore, lured to the West by Western novels, disillusioned by the reality behind the romantic rhetoric: he expresses "vexation and disgust for the wirters who had beguiled him to the 'wild and woolly'" (44). As Jim LaGrinder says, "'Well, you know how the boys are.'" They cannot resist playing on Densmore's ignorance of right language and bet him that he cannot ride a bronc. Densmore goes along, thinking that "bronc" is "a western phrase for donkey" (49), and promptly gets thrown by a very real unbroken horse. Knowledge of authentic language is a prerequisite for survival in a West that is "wild and woolly" in quite another way than Densmore understands.

If concerns about authenticity and explanations of inside texts so abound in the text, we might expect that Mourning Dove would indulge in some joking of her own. And, in fact, the text is riddled with tricks, some of which are, quite suitably, forever inaccessible to outsiders not well-versed in Okanogan culture, and which I can only guess at. Others are more easy to locate. Mourning Dove's hand is evident, for example, in the use of epigrams and chapter titles, some of which militate rather violently against the contents of the chapters. This is particularly true of chapters given over to the oral legends provided by the Stemteemä—which are, after all, close to authentic texts. The Stemteemä's story of the disastrous coming of the white man is related in a chapter titled "The Superior Race." The epigram is from Scott's "Lay of the Last Minstrel"; of course in this chapter the Stemteemä, or Mourning Dove herself, is the "last minstrel" singing a "lay" of a supposedly vanishing race. Longfellow's romanticized and inauthentic *Hiawatha* is similarly subverted. While in *Hiawatha* the male Nawadoha relates legends and visions, in *Co-ge-we-a* this is the Stemteemä's province. In affixing—or allowing McWhorter to do so—Longfellow's lines about Hiawatha's courtship to a chapter that describes the story of Green Blanket Feet, an Indian woman who married a white man with tragic consequences, or in affixing lines from "The Giaour" to a chapter in which the treacherous Densmore courts Cogewea, Mourning Dove turns a trick, inserts her own voice into McWhorter's didactic narrative, and creates an alternative text available to the insider. Indirectly, she claims authorship.

Mourning Dove's novel is in many ways an extreme case, in the sheer exaggeration of its plot, and a slippery object, in the overwhelming uncertainty surrounding its authorship. As a case, however, it functions accurately as a paradigm for writing by ethnic women, as the following chapter should finally make clear. Many features of the case of *Co-ge-we-a*, or, in fact, of the case of Indian women's writing in general, seem to appear with regularity around other texts by ethnic American women. Before turning to these, however, I would like to discuss the strategy of Mourning Dove's authorship by which she maintains or reclaims her authorship by telling inside jokes, or, in effect, turning tricks. The trickster, an important figure in American folk culture, bears significant resemblance to Mourning Dove as an author.

While the trickster figure has a long tradition, particularly in African and Afro-American folk culture, it is possible to remain for a moment within the framework of American Indian culture to explain the workings of this figure. Mourning Dove's *Tales of the Okanogans,* in fact, provides an interesting representation of the trickster hero. These tales, Mourning Dove explains in her preface, are animal tales, specifically, part of the coyote cycle. The animal-tale tradition, she explains, preserves the time when human life was "in the intermediate stage between man and animal. It seems that [animals] were somewhat in the form of humans, but were able to transform themselves into animals at will. . . . These half-animal people knew all the time that at some later date the creation of man would come. When that day came, the Great Spirit created man, and the speech of animals was forbidden." Coyote, however, as the "ancestor" of the Indian, presumably preserves this forbidden speech; he is, Mourning Dove relates, also called the "Trick Person."[23] One of the tales collected, "The Great Spirit Names the Animal People: How Coyote Came by His Name," explains the evolution of Coyote as follows: The Great Spirit calls all his animal people together, announces that everyone will be named, and that the animal people will henceforth rule. Coyote determines to wake at dawn in order to collect the name Grizzly Bear, but oversleeps, only to find all the names taken but Coyote, which nobody wanted. The Spirit Chief takes pity on Coyote and makes him father of all tribes; in addition, he adds, "because you are so hated, degraded, and despised, you will be known as the Trick-Person."[24] Another tale, "Coyote as a Beautiful Woman," shows Coyote's powers as a trickster. Because his family is out of food, Coyote transforms himself into a beautiful woman in order to marry Badger, a warrior in another encampment, and thereby obtain food. The trick works, and the tale explains that the badger's discovery of it makes him a humble animal.

These tales reveal some important points concerning the trickster figure, including the implicit power of the word and of naming. Margot Astrov, in "The Power of the Word," in *American*

Indian Prose and Poetry, a collection that introduced Indian legend to a wide audience, explains that the word in Indian cultures
had literal power; the singing of healing songs, for instance, would
heal the singer. Moreover, language was implicitly tied to creation;
she writes, "The Word is believed to perceive the creator, . . . in
the beginning was the thought, the dream, the word." If Coyote is
the "ancestor" of the Indians, the persistence of his "forbidden
speech" ties language implicitly to the function of the trickster.
The trickster can, through language, assert the ultimate authority
of language against authorities that forbid it.[25]

It is this link between the trickster and language that I want to
emphasize here, rather than the trickster figure himself or herself.
Undeniably important in Indian and black folklore, and however
important to the structure of Brer Rabbit tales and Philadelphia
street gangs, ethnic women's fiction presents few trickster characters. Rather, the notion of ethnic female authorship often hinges
on the notion of playing a trick within language, of subverting authority while seemingly endorsing it.

And, in fact, the trickster as an analogue for the ethnic writer
has real problems if the trickster is taken as a weak figure who
must revert to the childlike in order to accomplish his ends. In this
sense he becomes, especially for male critics, a difficult figure to
account for. In Roger Abrahams's insightful analysis of Philadelphia street culture, for instance, the trickster hero represents an
emasculated and childlike response to an emasculating matriarchy
and an anxious adolescence, the only means by which a "severely
stunted ego" can regain a feeling of power or manliness. Such an
interpretation obviously leads to problems: the trickster is a difficult hero.[26] In fact, a heated debate between Stanley Edgar Hyman
and Ralph Ellison in 1952–1953 centered precisely upon Hyman's
suggestion that the ethnic writer, like the "darky entertainer," was
a trickster. Ellison responded, interestingly, by claiming the universality of the trickster figure: "America is a land of masking
jokers."[27]

If, on the other hand, we reconsider the trickster in terms of
power, the concept retains value for ethnic female authorship.
Abrahams, while overestimating the psychological malaise the
trickster represents, adds that the figure also reflects "a veiled revolt against authority in the only terms available."[28] The trickster

is, as Karl Kerenyi points out, "the spirit of disorder, the enemy of boundaries."[29] As such, the trickster/author can rebel without seeming to, writing, for instance, within a genteel literary tradition and with the express purpose of mediating between her culture and the dominant one, but maintaining a posture of rebellion by weaving subversion into her text. Lawrence Levine, whose study of black culture in America contains the most thorough and insightful discussion of the trickster, writes that the trickster tale in American slave life provided a "mechanism . . . by means of which psychic relief from arbitrary authority could be secured, symbolic assaults against the powerful could be waged, and important lessons about authority relationships could be imparted."[30]

Similarly, the ethnic woman writer who wrote as a trickster could gain some relief from her feelings of anonymity or powerlessness within the dominant culture and could wage assault against it by subverting authority within her text, passing along to alert readers messages of strategies for protest. As I have said, few ethnic women present trickster heroines, or tell trickster tales, but many use the authorial strategy of the trickster, purporting to tell one story and project one persona and actually implying another message, setting out to mediate but only pretending to do so. Elizabeth Janeway, in her 1980 *Powers of the Weak,* a study of women's relationship to a hierarchy of strong and weak and the mechanism of power that structures that hierarchy, discusses the trickster hero in a related but slightly different fashion, one that does not relate the trickster's trick to language but to power and taboo. Drawing on Laura Makarius's analysis of American Indian tales in "The Crime of Manabozo," Janeway identifies the taboo-breaking, antisocial quality of the trickster's work, and the ways in which the trickster suffers from and gains from his or her actions. As Janeway points out, the trickster, whose "natural sphere is boundlessness," is the equivalent of the *id* in Freudian terminology, acting instinctually and scornful of taboo.[31] While this interpretation of the function of the trickster might seem rather far afield at this point from the concept of woman writer as trickster, the connections Janeway makes regarding power and taboo will prove to be relevant in particular instances of female-authored novels. As a trickster, covertly maneuvering for power, the woman writer often exploits the realm of taboo — as, for instance, when she writes about miscegenation or incest — while seeming to endorse nontabooed versions of American myths.

Because so many factors militate against the ethnic woman's authority and authorship, however, her tricks are slight, and must be considered within the fuller context of her compromised authorship. In fact, the study of ethnic women's fiction requires that authorship be established before its workings can be understood. The case of American Indian women's writing is instructive, for it suggests the complexity of that very task. It is necessary to turn from Indian women's writing to the ethnic female tradition in general, in order to understand how the ethnic woman came to write and to examine what she was able to write in a culture that so strongly stacked the odds against her authorship.

CHAPTER 2

Strategies of Authorship in American Ethnic Women's Fiction: Midwiving and Mediation

On 8 November 1982, the *New York Times* reported that a "black literary landmark" had been uncovered: an 1859 novel, *Our Nig,* by a black woman, Mrs. Harriet E. Wilson. "Discovered" by Henry Louis Gates, Jr., a literary critic, *Our Nig* had been previously unrecorded with its author correctly identified in bibliographies of black-authored fiction; the first novel by a black woman has always been thought to be Frances E. W. Harper's 1892 *Iola Leroy, Or Shadows Uplifted.* Of undeniable importance, Gates's discovery raises interesting questions about the nature of ethnic literary scholarship. How is it that the first novel by a black woman should have been obscured for all these years? The novel is, Gates's assertions aside, listed in such bibliographies as the Dictionary Catalogue of the New York Public Library's Schomburg Collection of Negro Literature and History and the Cumulative Author Index to the Microfilm Collection of American Prose Fiction 1774–1900 (the Wright Series). True, none of these compilations identify the author as black, but any attention to the book would have revealed this fact since, as Gates points out, Wilson announces it in her preface.

Gates astutely points out some features of the novel that might have contributed to its obscurity: first, because it describes racism in the North, and because it relates the story of a "fake" fugitive slave, abolitionists were not likely to promote the book. Second, the novel begins with an interracial marriage between a white woman and a black man, which presumably made it troublesome—though why not sensational?—for a pre-Civil War audience. In fact, the obscurity of *Our Nig* for over one hundred years raises questions not only in the realm of literary scholarship and bibliography, but questions regarding ethnic female authorship as well. Here it might be useful to consider the text itself, to determine what forces might have been at work in constructing its "cover."[1]

Our Nig relates the story of Frado, a mulatto child who has been abandoned by her white mother and delivered to brutal indentured servitude in the Bellmont household; while the bulk of the novel describes Frado's mistreatment and her own will to survive, the last chapters briefly describe her independent life, which is narrowly less bleak than her previous existence, including a bad marriage and failing health. Like many novels by ethnic women, *Our Nig* addresses issues of inheritance and kinship; Frado is "orphaned" and parodically "adopted" by the Bellmonts—whose child is she? Like many a mulatto heroine, she experiences the legacy of a divided self. Frado's tale seems to parallel that of her author—the story is written in the third person, but a typical chapter title is "A New Home for Me"—and *Our Nig* once again raises questions of genre and authorship.

Our Nig is a novel that was brought into being, in effect, twice, once by friends of Mrs. Wilson, whose authenticating documents close the original text and who seem to have arranged for the book's publication, and, again, one hundred and twenty-three years later, by a black literary critic. Harriet E. Wilson appears in the physical text through her voice as it is heard in the tale: *Our Nig*'s author is given on the title page as "Our Nig." Mrs. H. E. Wilson is identified as holding the copyright, and a preface, signed "H.E.W.," explains the author's reasons for publishing the book:

> Deserted by kindred, disabled by failing health, I am forced to some experiment which shall aid me in maintaining myself and my child without extinguishing this feeble life.[2]

To the text are appended three notes: the first by "Allida," the second by "Margaretta Thorn," and the third by "C.D.S.," all of which urge the public to buy the novel to alleviate Wilson's plight. By such devices—prefaces, appendices, explanations and authentications—the ethnic text makes its way into the world. As Gates discovered, the child whom Wilson wrote the book to aid died six months after the publication of the novel; just as the child died, so too did the novel. In fact, because *Our Nig* did not thrive, presumably, the child did not. With Gates's discovery, however, the novel has in effect been born again, and Gates has acted as a second midwife in bringing this book into being again. The novel now exists in a new edition published in 1983, with an excellent long introduction by Gates, a "Note on the Text," "Notes to the Text," "Chronology of Harriet E. Adams Wilson" (by David A. Curtis), and a "Select Bibliography."[3]

As I have suggested, the ethnic female text is often introduced in similar ways, eased into the world by midwives—editors, publishers, friends, authenticators. In such a process a text is produced, but in many instances, the identity of the author—and, as in the case of *Our Nig,* the existence of the text—can be obscured. The tradition of ethnic female authorship is a tradition of mediation, by which novels are introduced and sometimes produced by agents other than the ethnic woman. It is to this complex tradition of mediation that I would first like to turn in considering ethnic female authorship.

On the one hand, the mediating process is direct, characterized simply by a structure of mentor and pupil, and sometimes literally of teacher and student. In the case of immigrant women, this structure can be seen most clearly, because some immigrant women learned English as a second language, and because these women were often at distant remove from a literary or in fact literate context in which they could generate texts. The case of Mary Antin, a Jewish-American writer whose 1912 autobiographical novel *The Promised Land* became a best-seller, is particularly illuminating in this regard. Born in Polotzk, Russia, in 1881, Antin immigrated with her family at the age of thirteen. In *The Promised Land,* Antin relates that she authored her first "text" in her first months in America: a series of letters to her uncle in Russia, written in Yiddish, describing the family's passage. Antin was later to translate these reminiscences into English and publish them in 1899 as *From Plotzk to Boston;* she also quotes them at length in *The Promised Land.*[4]

The Promised Land is in some ways about authorship, and Antin describes at length her efforts at writing during her school years. Her fervent belief in the Americanization of the immigrant through public schooling I will discuss in another chapter; here I

would like to stress the importance Antin attributes to her teach-
ers' encouragement of her writing. Miss Mary Dillingham, a grade-
school teacher, becomes the heroine of this part of *The Promised
Land;* lending Antin the works of Longfellow, she encourages the
child's poetry writing. In fact, Antin's first appearance in print was
engineered by Miss Dillingham, who sent Antin's essay, "Snow,"
to *Primary Education,* along with an accompanying "preface,"
which reads as follows (Antin reproduces the "document" in *The
Promised Land*):

> EDITOR "PRIMARY EDUCATION":—
>   This is the uncorrected paper of a Russian child twelve years
> old, who had studied English only four months. She had never,
> until September, been to school even in her own country and has
> heard English spoken *only* at school. I shall be glad if the paper
> of my pupil *and the above explanation* may appear in your paper.
> Chelsea, Mass.   M. S. Dillingham[5]
> (second emphasis added)

Seldom, in fact, was Antin's work to appear without an "above
explanation"; her next "text," a poem about George Washington,
appeared in the Boston *Herald* with, Antin tells us, "a flattering
biographical sketch,"[6] and *From Plotzk to Boston* is legitimated by
a preface written by Israel Zangwill. Her stories only attain that
status by virtue of the story of her life. Moreover, Antin, a great
believer in pupilhood, was to find many successors for Miss Dillingham: she was taken up by members of the Boston literati Edward
Everett Hale and Barrett Wendell, both of whom encouraged her
to read and write, Hale telling her "never [to] study before break-
fast," and Wendell providing her with a library card to the Boston
Atheneum.[7] *The Promised Land* staggers under the weight of
Antin's gratitude to such mentor figures.[8]

The tradition of the mediated text, to which Antin's work belongs, is central in the history of the immigrant novel, as critic
Jules Chametzky has pointed out. Discussing the friendship between William Dean Howells and Abraham Cahan, a Jewish-
American writer who was Antin's contemporary, Chametzky concludes that the mediation process worked both ways; Cahan
introduced ethnicity to Howells, and Howells introduced Cahan to
the reading public, encouraging, promoting, and favorably reviewing Cahan's 1896 *Yekl.* But compromises were effected in the inter-

change, so that Howells came to see Cahan as "thoroughly natural-ised," and was momentarily distressed by Cahan's decision to publish the novel first in Yiddish.[9]

Though Cahan and Howells remained friends, the structure of their alliance, which is that between mediator and author, and which characterizes that between many ethnic women writers and their promoters, is implicitly uneasy. Though Antin did not express or did not feel this potential conflict, another important Jewish-American woman writer, Anzia Yezierska, made mentored author-ship the subject of her fiction and the obsession of her life. The relationship between Yezierska and John Dewey, which led to Yezierska's becoming a novelist and which I discuss in some detail in Chapter 5, resembled that of Antin and her various mentors, Cahan and Howells, and Mourning Dove and Lucullus McWhorter. Yezierska's fictional accounts of their friendship suggest that she began to write at Dewey's urging; Dewey's poetry, much of it to or about Yezierska, suggests that he saw in her a passionately com-mitted writer, as in fact she was. Their relationship, however, could not bear the weight each seems to have given to the opposing nature of their personalities, and Yezierska was in some senses to write "against" Dewey in her novels, using relationships similar to theirs as the bases for her romantic plots.[10] In Yezierska's case, the struc-ture of mediated authorship becomes extremely complex.

I do not mean to give the notion of mediation or midwiving an authority it does not possess: that of being unique to the ethnic female literary tradition. The example of Howells and Cahan is instructive, for Howells also encouraged and promoted writers as diverse as Henry James, Mark Twain, and Sarah Orne Jewett. An-other important example, that of the tireless promoter Carl Van Vechten, commonly described as "midwife" to the Harlem Renais-sance, and also the "life-time American agent—without pay" of one of America's greatest ethnic women writers, Gertrude Stein, is similarly instructive, for the example of Stein in turn reminds us that a vast body of influences can be brought to bear on an author's work:[11] Stein was, for instance, influenced intellectually by figures like William James and Picasso, motivated to write perhaps by childhood reading, Alice B. Toklas, or forces unknown. Indeed, the issue of influence is a complicated one, and the concept of mediation inextricable from it. Nor do I want to claim primacy for

this aspect of female authorship, because to do so at length diverts
attention from that which has been so steadfastly obscured: ethnic
women's texts. I do want to emphasize, however, the extent to
which both ethnic women *and* their promoters have perceived the
necessity of mediation for their fiction.

To return, in fact, to the texts, I would like to discuss some of
the devices by which mediation is signaled in ethnic women's
novels. Among these devices are prefaces and appendices that
authenticate the text, and glossaries, annotations, and what would
today be called "blurbs." All of these devices serve to "translate"
the foreignness of the ethnic experience for the dominant culture,
to guarantee the author's ethnicity, and often, in the last analysis,
to make the text more accessible to the reader.

Some of these devices are more intrusive than others, becoming
almost appendages obtruding from the text; others are modest,
calling little attention to themselves. McWhorter's annotations—
for presumably they are his—to Mourning Dove's novel are long
and discursive, telling stories of their own. He footnotes her novel
both at the bottoms of its pages and at the back. To Mary Antin's
The Promised Land is affixed an extensive glossary, with a "Key
to Pronunciation" and "Explanations" that explain the nature of
the definitions that follow ("The religious customs described pre-
vail among the Orthodox Jews of European countries. In the
United States they have been considerably modified, especially
among the Reformed Jews."). Definitions either translate Hebrew
or Yiddish words ("Dayyan," "Fetchke,"), identify places ("Polotzk") or explain Jewish customs or historical events ("Earlocks,"
"Pogrom"). Curiously, many of the glossarized items, particularly
Jewish customs, do not appear in Antin's text, so that the glossary
functions as further reading, and *The Promised Land* as a kind of
guide to Jewish culture.[12]

The provision of a glossary or annotations also authenticates
the author's ethnicity, proving that she is foreign and must be explained or translated. This purpose is also served by the authenticating preface or appendix, written usually by a "non-ethnic" man,
which attests to the author's "ethnicity." The second female-
authored black novel, Frances Harper's 1892 *Iola Leroy,* is
prefaced by a note by William Still, which identifies Harper as
black and goes on to provide her "credentials" in temperance
work and oration.[13] Such a tradition has persisted, and is in fact

encouraged, by certain conventions of contemporary book publishing. The 1977 Bantam edition of Margaret Walker's 1966 *Jubilee,* for instance, is promoted on the page inside the cover not by review blurbs or copy about the contents but by an unsigned authenticating biographical sketch that attests not only to Walker's blackness but also to her erudition, popularity, respectability, and the authenticity of her experience. It begins, "Dr. Margaret Walker Alexander is one of America's most popular and respected black writers. *Jubilee,* she says, was based on the true story of her great-grandmother."[14]

Not simply a bibliographical accident, the authenticating preface purports to bolster and proclaim the authorship of the text, if by authorship is meant the identity of the writer as an ethnic woman and her act of writing. In reality, however, authenticating devices like prefaces and glossaries have a strangely opposite effect, so that the text staggers under and is nearly submerged by their weight. The story of the story or the story of the author threatens to become the story itself. The ethnic woman's novel is always in danger of becoming an historical event or, like *Our Nig,* occasion for an article in the *New York Times.* Mary Antin's name, for instance, is found far more often in the indexes of history books than in books of literary criticism, and the title of her novel is even more rarely found.

The case of ethnic women's fiction presents an intensification of a process that critics of ethnic literature have recently begun to foreground. Texts by male ethnic writers are subject to similar patterns of overlaid authentication. Frederick Douglass's 1845 *Narrative of the Life of Frederick Douglass an American Slave Written by Himself* is accompanied by a preface, a prefatory letter, and an appendix; Robert Stepto, in an essay on narration and authentication in the *Narrative,* analyzes the way in which all slave narratives are similarly authenticated, but to varying degrees, so that Douglass's narrative becomes remarkable, an "integrated narrative," in that there is "an energy between the tale and each supporting text."[15] A very interesting dynamic of authentication, authorship, authority, and authorial control could also be studied in the case of Alex Haley, who as the as-told-to "author" of *The Autobiography of Malcolm X* (1964) writes one of the most significant parts of Malcolm X's "story," his death; who became the author of the phenomenally best-selling 1977 *Roots;* and who was subsequently plagued by plagiarism suits, one of which, incidentally, claimed that he borrowed from Margaret Walker's *Jubilee*.[16]

The phenomenon of authentication, and the issues of authority and authorship related to it, are gender-specific only in degree. The ethnic woman's text is more heavily mediated than is the ethnic man's. The simplest evidence for this is the fact that ethnic literary scholarship studies predominantly male-authored texts, in part for this reason.[17] Ethnic women's novels have been so heavily and variously mediated that they have often, like *Our Nig,* disappeared. If this is true, however, it is necessary to understand why it is true, and to do so it is in turn necessary to look beyond the mediation to the author, and examine ethnic women's variously successful strategies of authorship.

An appropriate place to begin is with the concept of mediation, but in this case with the author's perception of *herself* as a mediator, working between two cultures. Here again it is useful to consider Mary Antin, who seems to have made a career of mediation—in the very real sense that it was her life's profession and that she made money from it. Antin, whose *The Promised Land* actually contains the phrase "Three cheers for the Red, White, and Blue!"[18] and whose favorite hero was, unequivocally, George Washington, was often held up as a model of Americanization, a walking advertisement for relaxation of immigration restriction laws. In fact, Antin was to become a potent force in the movement to relax restriction, not only through her exemplary conduct, but also because her 1914 *They Who Knock At Our Gates* became, as its subtitle indicates, "A Complete Gospel of Immigration."

This remarkable book, which contains the memorable statement, "What we get in steerage is not the refuse, but the sinew and bone of all the nations,"[19] best exemplifies Antin's authorial stance, which is that of mediation. Her favored strategy is comparatism or equation. As Werner Sollors has pointed out, she recasts the immigrant experience in terms of the Puritan migration, participating in a familiar typological drama of descent and rejuvenation. Under the terms of this scheme, the immigrants are "like" the Puritans, who are in turn "like" God's chosen people. She writes,

> Those who are excluded when our bars are down are exiles from Egypt, whose feet stumble in the desert of political and social slavery, whose hearts hunger for the bread of freedom. The ghost

of the Mayflower pilots every immigrant ship, and Ellis Island is another name for Plymouth Rock.

For Antin, Jefferson is another version of Moses, Washington of Joshua, and the Declaration of Independence an analogue for Mosaic Law. The immigrant shares the Puritan's devotion and civic sensibility, argues Antin, pointing to immigrant enthusiasm for education and public libraries. Always comparative, she equates the daring of the immigrant in the jungle of the city with the pioneering spirit of the first settlers in the forest of the New World, likening the intensity, nerve, and commercial daring of the new settlers to the hardiness and muscle of the old. What is most remarkable about Antin's "gospel" is her pointed use of the first person plural, the way in which the Declaration of Independence is *our* Declaration of Independence, and *our* "mission among nations" is to accept the immigrant, because it is in keeping with the democratic system generated by "our particular quarrel with George of England."[20]

Mary Antin wrote at a time in which, as her insistent comparatism suggests, immigrants were perceived as significantly *different* from native-born Americans. A contemporary of Antin's, *Atlantic Monthly* essayist Agnes Repplier, is a representative member of the anti-immigration forces. Though Repplier, a practicing Catholic, insisted that she was of French heritage, downplaying her German immigrant mother and German immigrant grandparents on her father's side, she argued vigorously for immigration restriction and against voting rights for immigrants. In "The Modest Immigrant," Repplier takes particular issue with Mary Antin, whom she classes with those foreign commentators on American life James Russell Lowell had criticized in his "On A Certain Condescension in Foreigners" fifty yars before. Repplier writes,

> Why should the recipient of so much attention be the one to scold us harshly, to rail at conditions she imperfectly understands, to reproach us for our ill-mannered children . . . , our slackness in duty, our failure to observe the precepts and fulfill the intentions of those pioneers whom she kindly, but confusedly, calls '*our* forefathers.' (Repplier's emphasis)

Repplier's conclusion is that Antin's is "the hopeless old story of opposing races, of people unable to understand one another be-

cause they have no mutual standards, no common denominator."[21]
Mary Antin's lifelong task was to point out mutual standards and
common denominators between the supposedly opposing "races."

The Promised Land indicates that Antin felt the desire to mediate between two cultures even as a child, when she was abused in
Polotzk by Gentile children. Oppression, to Antin, is based on lack
of understanding: "Vanka [a Gentile child] abused me only because *he did not understand*. If he could feel with my heart, if he
could be a little Jewish boy for one day, I thought, he would
know—he would know" (Antin's emphasis).[22] Antin's insistence
on the commonality and mutuality of Jewish and Gentile experience motivates her pleas for understanding. She comes to feel that
it is her responsibility to promote such understanding, to make it
possible for native Americans to feel with immigrant hearts. Authorship accordingly becomes a highly charged issue, one that
she returns to repeatedly in *The Promised Land*. The following
representative passage from that book indicates the complex responsibility of a writer who is "speaking for thousands":

> Should I be sitting here, chattering of my infantile adventures if
> I did not know that I was speaking for thousands? Should you be
> sitting there, while the world's work waits, if you did not know
> that I spoke also for you? I might say 'you' or 'he' instead of 'I.'
> Or I might be silent, while you spoke for me and the rest, but
> for the accident that I was born with a pen in my hand, and you
> without. We love to read the lives of the great, yet what a broken
> history of mankind they give, unless supplemented by the lives
> of the humble. . . . It is well now and then that one is born
> among the simple with a taste for self-revelation. The man or
> woman thus endowed must speak, will speak, though there are
> only grasses in the field to hear, and none but the wind to convey
> the tale.[23]

Though Antin seems to suggest otherwise in the last sentence of
this passage, the mediating text of the American ethnic woman is
written very much with a sense of an audience; that audience, in
fact, is the ethnic text's professed reason for being. As she un-
covers similarities between her culture and the dominant American
culture, she feels that mediation is not only possible but impera-
tive. Anzia Yezierska, in an autobiographical essay called "America
and I," recounts a story that is paradigmatic of the operation of this

kind of mediation. She reads about the Pilgrims, a group that she elsewhere calls "dissenters and immigrants like me."[24] The common fact of American life—that we are all immigrants or children of immigrants—has for Yezierska the weight of a religious revelation:

> Fired up by this revealing light, I began to build a bridge of understanding between the American-born and myself. Since their life was shut out from such as me, I began to open up my life and the lives of my people to them.[25]

Another writer of the same period, Elizabeth Stern, the author of two autobiographical works, both important texts of ethnicity and Americanization, describes in her 1917 *My Mother and I* and her 1926 *I Am a Woman—and a Jew* how she comes to feel, as a child of two cultures, that she must mediate between them. Stern is told on her graduation from high school by the school's Yankee principal: " 'You must be the interpreter of the old to the new world, and of the new to the old.' "[26] Stern's two books describe the painful generational conflicts engendered by Americanization; she was to marry a Gentile, which significantly altered her relations with her parents. By and large not a successful author, Stern turned eventually to ghostwriting. It is interesting to note that *My Mother and I,* a moderate best-seller, was criticized by the *Nation* reviewer for its representation of thoroughly successful Americanization. Stern shows, complains the reviewer, "a predominance of pride over tears in the countenance of the narrator as she shakes the dust from her feet and goes to dwell in the tents of the Americans.[27] The ethnic woman who mediates too successfully, who writes from the perspective of the dominant culture (which has insisted on her Americanization and conversion to its values) rather than that of what the *Nation* reviewer implies is "her own" culture, is roundly scolded.

Obviously, this strategy of authorship is not without problems, as the case of Stern's critical reception makes clear, and as does the example of Yezierska's writing career. Yezierska, who believed utterly in the promise of the melting pot, held to her promise to open up her culture to native-born America. Because she was to take this promise of the melting pot to heart, attempting to realize it fictionally by promoting marriage between her immigrant heroines and unresponsive white Anglo-Saxon men, her plots are repetitive and her passionate prose eventually tiresome. Initially, however, the reading public responded with enthusiasm to Yezierska's portraits of passionate immigrant women striving to find expression and success in the new world. In fact, the story of Yezierska's changing literary reputation sounds not unlike a familiar Yezierska plot in which a native-born male is initially attracted to the immigrant heroine for her passionate exoticism and later rejects her for the very qualities he once sought in her, as Yezierska critic Babette Inglehart has pointed out. In her semiautobiographical *Red Ribbon on a White Horse* (1950), Yezierska describes how the public had propelled her to Hollywood on the basis of her 1920 story collection *Hungry Hearts*. Like her heroines, Yezierska was called a "sweatshop Cinderella"; widely admired, she was a "Sunday supplement heroine." In Hollywood, however, she felt cut off from her culture, as if she were "part of a stage-set," and was unable to write. After this point, her reputation began to fall off; reviewers of her 1927 *Arrogant Beggar* criticized her "highhanded impatience at the existing order of things" and her ignorance of the gentile mind. No longer charmed by her "fresh foreigner's perspective," reviewers ironically likened her *Salome of the Tenements* (1923) to a cheap movie. Finally, Yezierska's Hollywood success backfired in the Depression years, when the legend of her Cinderella success dissuaded employers from hiring her for the menial jobs she was then forced to seek. She lived out her life in relative obscurity, and only recently have her works been rediscovered and reprinted.[28]

Stern, Antin, and, to a lesser extent, Yezierska, all wrote by casting their experience in the terms of the dominant culture, allowing that culture to prescribe modes of narration, stances toward authority, and plots and morals for their stories. By writing in the language, so to speak, of the dominant culture, they could mediate between that culture and their own. Antin is today not widely read at least in part because she thoroughly internalized the dominant culture's vision of the ethnic and the foreign. More interesting as a text of American patriotism and as revealing of American values and typologies, *The Promised Land* seems to lack any alternative, protesting voice. Elizabeth Stern's work, which I will discuss later, contains an interesting subtext that preserves the ethnic woman's oppositional stance to the dominant culture as it asserts the value of assimilation; like the best ethnic texts, her work sets forth the ethnic American's double allegiance to ancestry and to the American community. Yezierska's work, recently praised for its expression of female independence and ambition, portrays the ethnic woman at war with the dominant culture at the same time as she wishes to join it—because within it she can find expression and success. Yezierska's fiction borrows conventions of the dominant culture, particularly the movies, with the result that her plots are overly schematized and melodramatic; at the same time, her own voice is preserved in the intensity of her prose.

The ethnic woman writer as mediator effects a number of trade-offs. By writing too thoroughly in the language of the dominant culture, her work can become dated as that language changes. Moreover, when the ethnic woman does not write about her ethnicity, her work is usually ignored. Zora Neale Hurston's *Seraph on the Sewanee* (1948) and Ann Petry's *Country Place* (1947), for instance, both novels by important black women writers about white characters, are usually overlooked by ethnic literature scholars.[29]

A similar set of conditions is brought to bear in consideration of an important body of ethnic women's fiction: those novels, of various periods, that have been characterized as belonging to the black genteel tradition. This body of fiction, which includes novels by Reconstruction writers Frances Harper and Pauline Hopkins, Harlem Renaissance writers Jessie Fauset and Nella Larsen, and such later writers as Dorothy West and Ann Petry, has characteristically been considered by scholars of ethnic literature with some embarassment. In recent years, this has begun to change, as readers of ethnic literature have recognized that a text can reveal its ethnicity in terms other than those of form and subject matter. Genteel conventions do not always bespeak gentility, just as the language of the dominant culture can be used to express ethnicity. In fact, novels of this tradition, because they seem not to question the values of white middle-class culture, can question that much more forcefully the black woman's place in that culture, and address with frankness the psychological problems of white middle-class culture. The trickster creeps into much of this fiction, as the author seeks to subvert what she so vigorously seems to support, criticizing the culture she seems to clamor to enter.

Moreover, the apparent gentility of these novels must be considered in light of the historical conditions under which they were written. This is particularly true of the Reconstruction novels of Frances Harper and Pauline Hopkins, which I would like to turn to briefly first. As Barbara Christian points out in her survey, *Black Women Novelists,* these novels are in the tradition of *Uncle Tom's Cabin, or Life Among The Lowly* and *Clotel, or the President's Daughter;* that is, they are first and foremost protest novels, in which, writes Christian, "the concepts of good and evil, salvation, are pitted against each other."[30] Melodramatic in form, these novels sought, first, to protest the social and economic conditions of Reconstruction blacks, their exclusion from white institutions, and the disruption of inheritance engendered by those conditions under slavery that produced the mulatto. To dismiss these novels as simply accommodationist expressions of a community eager to join the ranks of the middle class, as Robert Bone seems to in his important study of black fiction, is to overlook the political intent behind these works. In such a context, these novels become historical events, losing their status as texts.[31] While it is true that the form of these novels is often marred by the author's attempt to generate inspirationally a success-oriented assimilationist ideology among Reconstruction blacks, it is important to emphasize also the author's attempt to explore the possibility of expression of that protest through fiction.

Reconstruction novels, written largely for white audiences, are mediating texts in that they work to generate sympathy and understanding for black suffering; like Mary Antin, Harper and Hopkins are comparatists, attempting to prove that blacks are like whites, rather than to stress differences. This is one of the many reasons that their characters are often mulatto, and usually well-educated, middle-class, and Northern. Harper and Hopkins are not content, however, merely with generating sympathy; in fact, the discussions and *conversaziones* on the race problem that appear throughout their novels allow the authors indirectly to criticize whites for the injustices they have visited upon blacks, and ultimately to work to effect change.

These novels, moreover, go beyond mediation in interesting and important ways. Robert Bone writes that "the early novelist attempted to arouse a passion for justice among whites, and for property among Negroes."[32] In making this statement, Bone implies an important point: that Reconstruction novels were actually written for a dual audience, composed of both blacks and whites. If this is true, it seems unlikely that the only message these novelists attempted to impart to other blacks was a passion for property. Just as the concept of mediation, in which the ethnic writer writes for her white audience, has a more complex goal than arousing a passion for justice, so too does the ethnic woman novelist develop a more complicated relationship with her ethnic readers.[33] This is not to deny that within the terms of that relationship the author's primary goal might be to impart didactic messages. But such messages are often less assimilationist or accommodationist than analyses like Bone's would allow. A representative novel of Reconstruction, Frances Harper's 1892 *Iola Leroy, Or Shadows Uplifted,* presents in this sense an implicitly subversive message to black readers, while it attempts simultaneously to mediate black experience for white readers, and to perform all the other genteel functions Bone and other critics claim for it.

Frances Harper, who states she hopes to awaken a "stronger sense of justice" and "a more Christlike humility" in the hearts of her countrymen, embeds within her text not only trickster motifs but explanations of the workings of the trickster figure. If tricksterism in slave life consisted of subversive communication, southern blacks also used coded language to pass on news of the war in which they had such stake. Slaves, writes Harper, "invented a phraseology to convey in the most unsuspected manner news to each other from the battle-field. . . . In conveying tidings of the war, if they wished to announce a victory of the Union army, they said the butter was fresh, or that the fish and eggs were in good condition."[34]

Implicit in the notion that communication is subversive is the fact that language itself can be a means to power. It is by now a commonplace in Afro-American scholarship that literacy, the central subject of Frederick Douglass's slave narrative, is also a subject of all black fiction, particularly that about slavery. Whites, of course, recognized to varying degrees the power of literacy; more to the point, however, is the insistence of black novelists on its value. Hopkins describes a white mistress's "gift" of literacy to a male slave with thinly disguised triumph:

> Mrs. Johnson taught him to read on the same principle she would have taught a pet animal amusing tricks. She had never imagined the time would come when he would use the machinery she had

put into his hands to help overthrow the institution to which she
was so ardently attached.[35]

Iola Leroy contains a double message: on one level, Harper urges
race pride in the complicated context of Reconstruction life, under
the terms of which blacks aspired to attain middle-class status and
to gain acceptance in the white world, by, in effect, being good
citizens. On another level, the novel urges other blacks, by Harper's example, and by her explicit direction, to write.

These twin and arguably competing goals shape the ending of
the novel, both the last chapter and Harper's closing "Note." In
the last chapter, Iola and her family are invited to a *conversazione*
at which the topic under discussion is, of course, the "race question." While options for response are discussed, such as migration
to Africa, the consensus of the group is a jeremiadic call to renewed patriotism. Miss Delany, the intended of the heroine's
brother, delivers a representative speech:

> "I would have our people . . . more interested in politics. In-
> stead of forgetting the past, I would have them hold in ever-
> lasting remembrance our great deliverance. Hitherto we have
> never had a country with tender, precious memories to fill our
> eyes with tears, or glad reminiscences to thrill our hearts with
> pride and joy. We have been aliens and outcasts in the land of our
> birth. But I want my pupils to do all in their power to make this
> country worthy of their deepest devotion and their loftiest pa-
> triotism. I want them to feel that its glory is their glory, its dis-
> honor their shame."[36]

While the thrust of this consensus is inherently conservative, in
that it urges good citizenship and patriotic devotion, it also con-
serves the memory of a tragic past. Moreover, the very idea of
"working within the system," the single most available option to
blacks in Reconstruction years, is, of course, sometimes akin to
"infiltration from within." Harper's novel is no Trojan horse, but
it is clear that she senses that "race pride" is founded not only on
good citizenship but on shared anger, and to some extent her novel
endorses this.

Harper's stance becomes more clear in her endorsement of literacy, or, more precisely, her urging of blacks to write. The *conversazione* of the last chapter closes, significantly, with Iola Leroy,
the novel's heroine, resolving to write a novel. And in her "Note,"

Harper acknowledges three goals in her writing the novel: first, to awaken a "stronger sense of justice" in the hearts of her countrymen, i.e. to reach whites; second, to inspire blacks to "determine that they will embrace every opportunity, develop every faculty, and use every power God has given them to rise in the scale of character and condition, and to add their quota of good citizenship to the best welfare of the nation." Harper's third professed goal, also aimed at blacks, is to inspire blacks to write. Recognizing the implicitly subversive power of language, Harper writes:

> There are scattered among us materials for mournful tragedies and mirth-provoking comedies, which some hand may yet bring into the literature of the country, glowing with the fervor of the tropics and enriched by the luxuriance of the Orient, and thus add to the solution of our unsolved American problem.[37]

Reminding blacks of an audience eager for details of the "fervor of the tropics," Harper senses that the "mournful tragedies" and "mirth-provoking comedies" black writers might produce would alleviate their oppression not only by legitimating black existence but also by developing a means of literary expression that could lead, ultimately, to power.

CHAPTER 3

Black Women Authors
and the Harlem Renaissance

In advocating literacy, or literature, as a strategy by which the free black could gain power in white society, Frances Harper not only participated in an ongoing black literary tradition with its roots in slave narratives and slaves' acquisition of literacy, but also looked forward to the Harlem Renaissance, an important phase in the black literary tradition, in which black artists saw and to some extent realized the possibility of gaining acceptance, equality, advancement, and power through cultural expression. As Nathan Huggins points out in his important study of the Harlem Renaissance, American society has commonly looked to culture—visual arts, literature, and music—as "the true measure of civilization. Harlem intellectuals," writes Huggins, "sharing in that belief and seeing themselves as living out of the moment of their race's rebirth, naturally marked off their achievement by such artistic production. Thus they promoted poetry, prose, painting, and music as if their lives depended on it."[1] Economic, political, and social advancement were seen by blacks as tied to cultural expression in a remarkable and meaningful fashion. By and large, participants in the Harlem Renaissance were correct in formulating such a link, and successful to the extent that they were able to capitalize on it.

In a climate in which cultural expression is so gravid with promise, aesthetics of such enormous importance, in which art becomes a premise on which the future of the race rested, expression itself can become extremely difficult, and evaluation of that expression even more so. David Levering Lewis, in his recent cultural history of the Renaissance, *When Harlem Was In Vogue*, insightfully characterizes "the double-edged nature of the material of the Renaissance" as "the ever-present problem of the right thing said by the wrong person or the wrong thing well said by the right person."[2] The Harlem Renaissance was characterized by a proliferation of black- and white-authored novels about black life and a proliferation of responses to them. It mattered terribly if the wrong person said the right thing, or vice versa, and everyone was quick to say so. Did Van Vechten "cash in" on his black connections and misrepresent Harlem life with his 1926 *Nigger Heaven*? Was Jean Toomer a white in blackface? What *was* Africa to Countee Cullen, or to twentieth-century black followers of Marcus Garvey? "The Negro in Art: How Should He Be Portrayed?" asked a 1926 symposium sponsored by the *Crisis*. As like whites, or very different? Should Harlem be presented as a genteel world of libraries, teas, and drawing rooms, or as a primitive jungle of crime, sex, and riots? Questions like these held enormous significance for Harlem artists in the 1920s, and continue to trouble contemporary scholars to the extent that American society continues to equate artistic expression with civilization.

In such a context, the value of the ethnic text can be based largely on its meaningful contribution to an overall effort rather than on its intrinsic worth. Some novelists transcended the debate on propaganda and art either through sheer artistry, because their art portrayed black life in a way offensive to no one, or both. Jean Toomer's *Cane* (1923), probably the single most lasting artistic effort of the period, is one such work. On the other hand, critical reception of new works in such a climate is so heavily dependent on current theories of propriety regarding the politics of aesthetics that energy can be expended on formulating those theories at the expense of production or fair reading. It is remarkable how quickly books came into public favor and left it over the course of the Renaissance years, how quickly allegiances and alliances shifted and reformed. Van Vechten's *Nigger Heaven,* to cite just one example, was, for the most part, heralded at first appearance, then largely scorned by the black community. Another, more relevant example is the critical reception of the novels of Jessie Fauset. Her work seemed to carry the official stamp of approval of the Harlem Renaissance, yet nobody, black or white, admitted personally to liking her work very much.

Of the three women novelists who were part of the Harlem Renaissance, whom I would like to consider in some detail, only Zora Neale Hurston negotiated this terrain with any lasting success. Jessie Fauset and Nella Larsen wrote novels that were widely read in the Harlem Renaissance but not widely remembered. The case of each of these writers is instructive, for each case shows the difficulties associated with ethnic female authorship in America. Fauset, whose novels were widely acclaimed and who was acknowledged as a figure of some stature in the period, was and is virtually dismissed as an important writer; a critical reading of her work supports such a judgment but does not explain the dismissal of the significant fact of her authorship. Nella Larsen's novels rank next to Toomer's *Cane* in their sensitivity of expression and psychological depth, yet none of her contemporaries seem to have given her much credence; even today, the facts of her life remain largely unknown and her novels largely unread. Hurston, in the context of the Harlem Renaissance, was considered a controversial and difficult creature.

Jessie Fauset, of these three writers, presents the most extreme and most instructive example of ethnic female authorship, because she seems to have given the sensitive issue of black cultural expression the most careful thought, and at the same time to have missed the mark the most widely. Fauset, a Phi Beta Kappa graduate of Cornell, from an old Philadelphia family, served as literary editor for the *Crisis* from 1919 to 1926; she published a number of poems, stories, and articles in that magazine, and wrote as well four novels, *There is Confusion* (1924), *Plum Bun* (1929), *The Chinaberry Tree* (1931), and *Comedy, American Style* (1934).[8] Black and white audiences hailed her work; among her enthusiastic critics were Mary White Ovington, W. E. B. DuBois, George Schuyler, and William Stanley Braithwaite. Fauset's novels, all of which portray middle-class American blacks in middle-class professions striving for middle-class goals, were welcomed as providing proof to white readers that blacks shared values similar to those held by whites, a goal that Fauset explicitly acknowledged. On the other hand, Fauset's mediating purpose met with considerable sharp response. Claude McKay, for instance, commented, "Miss Fauset is prim and dainty as a primrose and her novels are quite as fastidious and precious."[4] After her removal from the literary scene following her last novel, critical reaction intensified, and Fauset remains in critical disfavor. Robert Bone's aptly dismissive remark about Fauset—that *The Chinaberry Tree* "seems to be a novel about the first colored woman in America to wear lounging pajamas"—has functioned as a kind of critical death sentence, quoted by every reader of black literature looking for something to say about Fauset.[5]

This critical response is not entirely unjustified. Fauset's novels disappoint, however, not because they present genteel blacks with genteel concerns like lounging pajamas, but because they are poorly constructed and sketchily populated. It is misleading to dwell negatively on the genteel texture of Fauset's world; in fact, Fauset's novels have implicit value because they present this world with loving accuracy, and because they document a facet of black culture in which the author's predominant aim is to convince whites that blacks are like them.[6] Fauset is an important writer in that her novels provide the fullest expression of one of the most attractive and most treacherous authorial stances available to the ethnic woman writer—that of a mediator, bringing two cultures together by asserting their samenesses rather than their differences.

Like Mary Antin, Fauset employs the techniques of a comparatist. DuBois, in his enthusiastic review of *The Chinaberry Tree,* wrote that "her attitude is to emphasize the similarity between the blacks and the whites, rather than the differences."[7] Fauset acknowledges this in her foreword to that novel, in which she compares the black's history to the white's, virtually dismissing slavery as a factor in that history:

> [The black man] started out as a slave but he rarely thinks of that. To himself he is a citizen of the United States whose ancestors came over not along with the emigrants in the Mayflower, it is true, but merely a little earlier in the good year, 1619. His forebears are to him quite simply the early settlers who played a pretty large part in making the land grow. He boasts no Association of the Sons and Daughters of the Revolution, but he knows that as a matter of fact and quite inevitably his sons and daughters date their ancestry as far back as any. So quite as naturally as his white compatriots he speaks of his "old" Boston families, "old Philadelphians," "old Charlestonians." And he has a wholesome respect for family and education and labor and the fruits of labor.[8]

A representative Fauset heroine, Joanna Marshall in *There Is Confusion,* plays out a drama that makes explicit Fauset's comparatist approach. Joanna, overcoming prejudice to become a Broadway dancer, is called upon to dance the part of black America in a pageant in which the parts of red and white America are also danced. Eventually, because of her talent, Joanna is asked to dance all three parts, but is made to wear a white mask as white America. After she dances this part, Joanna removes the white mask, speaking for Fauset as she challenges the startled audience:

> I hardly need tell you that there is no one in the audience more American than I am. My great-grandfather fought in the Revolution, my uncle fought in the Civil War, and my brother is "over there" now.[9]

Fauset's concern is not to remind white audiences what the Civil War was fought for, but to remind them that her ancestors fought in it.

In *The Chinaberry Tree,* Laurentine Strange, the mulatto heroine, is ostracized by the small town in which she lives because of her mother's liaison with a white man. Laurentine is determined to marry Phil Hackett, a respectable black community member, in order to prove her worth to the town. Her motivation is not unlike Fauset's own: " 'Oh God,' " Laurentine prays, " 'you know all I want is a chance to show them how decent I am.' "[10] In trying to prove the decency of blacks to whites, Fauset in a sense confused civilization with civility, believing that the civilization of blacks could be proved by their civility. In doing so, Fauset responded to what Huggins points out is an inevitable cultural requirement in America: American society's idea of art has usually been that which measured society's excellence, so black art in the twentieth century was in this way expected to prove black civilization on the grounds of black civility. The phenomenon of black art, writes Huggins, "was forced to signify far more than poetry, art, and fiction are ordinarily required to do."[11]

Huggins acknowledges that Harlem Renaissance writers wrote in a context of social reform entirely consistent with American progressive thought, in that a belief in the efficacy of reform was built into all reform efforts.[12] Something of this sense informs Fauset's fiction, which is marked by a certain naiveté in its social protest.

Fauset's novels are, in fact, extremely critical of white society, and white treatment of blacks, far more critical than they are of culturally backsliding blacks. Implicit in Fauset's criticisms, however, is a belief that they will be acknowledged by white readers. William Stanley Braithwaite, in a 1934 *Opportunity* essay on Fauset's fiction, in which he calls Fauset "the potential Jane Austen of Negro literature," asserts that the philosophy of her work is *rebuke,* rebuke "to an inhuman principle, elevated to an institution and safeguarded by both law and public opinion."[13] The notion of rebuke, something given to naughty children or set forth formally in ritualistic protest, characterizes Fauset's stance. Protest was not her primary concern, and protest that went beyond rebuke would have been counterproductive to Fauset's mediating aims.

Fauset's authorship is interesting in other important ways. As Lewis makes clear in his study of the Harlem Renaissance, Fauset was one of the leading forces in the promotion of black art in the 1920s. From 1919 to 1926, acting as literary editor of the NAACP magazine the *Crisis* and close friend of editor DuBois, Fauset virtually ran the *Crisis,* as well as *The Brownies' Book,* DuBois's magazine for children. As Lewis points out, she recognized the talent of such writers as Jean Toomer and Langston Hughes before practically anyone else. Under her management, the *Crisis* was to strive to be an organ that, like *Opportunity,* represented the arts as well as political viewpoints—a shift that indirectly led to Fauset's departure from the magazine and her eventual estrangement from DuBois. Langston Hughes, in *The Big Sea,* was the first to dub Fauset a "midwife" of the Harlem Renaissance; Lewis places her among the ranks of "The Six"—a group that included Charles Johnson, Alain Locke, Walter White, Casper Holstein, and James Weldon Johnson. The Six, writes Lewis, were responsible for the widely felt impact of Harlem art: "there would have been no emergency loans and temporary beds, professional advice and Downtown contracts, prizes and publicity without the patient assemblage and management by a handful of Harlem notables of a substantial white patronage."[14] Midwiving, of course, leads often to the assemblage and management of patronage, with all that implies; this was to have substantial ramifications for the Harlem Renaissance in general and for such women writers as Zora Neale Hurston in particular. On the other hand, it is important to read

Fauset's novels and pronouncements of literary standards against her encouragement of black writers whose work was very different and often antithetical to her own. Fauset, who volunteered evenings at the important 135th Street branch of the New York Public Library (with all *that* implies), was, first and foremost, like Frances Harper, an advocate of literacy.

The Harlem Renaissance is commonly thought of as a period in which white artistic traditions were challenged and a new black artistic tradition established. Yet, as Huggins shows definitively, though a black tradition may have been solidified in those years, few black artists were truly innovative in technique. In fact, writes Huggins, "except for Jean Toomer and, in a very special way, Langston Hughes, there was no evidence of literary inventiveness in Harlem."[15] Just as Claude McKay and Countee Cullen used the Romantics as stylistic models, so novelists like Fauset and Nella Larsen turned to models of genteel realism in their writing. Artistic inventiveness seems possible only in a context of artistic tradition. Few blacks recognized a black artistic tradition within and against which they could work; Zora Neale Hurston was something of an exception, drawing on such traditions as sermons, call-and-response patterns, dialect, and folk culture in her work. Jessie Fauset realized the void left by the past in the life of the twentieth century black. In a 1921 *Crisis* essay called "Nostalgia," she again likens blacks to immigrants, citing the homesickness of these groups for their native lands. The black, however, is doubly burdened:

> It is from this spiritual nostalgia that the American Negro suffers most. He has been away so long from that mysterious fatherland of his that like all the other descendants of voluntary and involuntary immigrants of the seventeenth century—Puritan, pioneer, adventurer, indentured servant,—he feels himself American. The past is too past for him to have memories. Very, very rarely does he have a backward reaching bond, be it never so tenuous.[16]

As Fauset well knew, however, twentieth-century black identity was not only shaped by a lack of sense of the past but at the same time by a tangible history of oppression and, in fact, slavery. I will try to show that it is with this sense of a divided self, of being both determined by ancestry and entirely self-made, that the ethnic woman writes, and that the dominant theme of her fiction is the tension between ancestral and communal definitions of self. The consequences of this kind of double consciousness for the form her writings have taken has often been a curious and varied alliance with the literary tradition. Literary tradition, like ancestry, is inevitable; the ethnic woman writer can, like Fauset and Nella Larsen, write within it, or like Gertrude Stein, the subject of my last chapter, simultaneously within and against it.

Nella Larsen, Fauset's contemporary, raises two sets of interesting questions for a study of ethnic female authorship. The first set concerns the quality and reputation of Larsen's work, which seem to be at odds with each other. Larsen's work, in any context and by any set of standards, emerges as extraordinary; in more particular contexts, such as that of the Harlem Renaissance or that of women's writing, she becomes a particularly important figure as a black, a woman, and a writer. Her two novels, *Quicksand* (1928) and *Passing* (1929), were praised by her contemporaries and are almost always cited as outstanding by critics of ethnic literature. Yet Larsen's novels have been scantily reprinted. She is not widely read, and critical treatment of her remains largely perfunctory. The vagaries of academic interest and the reading public aside, it seems curious that Larsen is so militantly underacknowledged as a major novelist of ethnic and female identity. This underacknowledgment is related to the second set of questions, which concern the mystery of Larsen's life. Like the first, this set has partial answers in the realm of scholarship and its vagaries. Yet what we know of Larsen's life, and the evidence of her fine novels, suggests that the story of her life would be of considerable interest in the history of ethnic women.

Larsen was the daughter of a white Danish immigrant mother and a black West Indian father; after her father's death, Larsen's mother married a white man and had another daughter. The conflicts this engendered were to reappear in Larsen's fiction. Raised as black, Larsen studied at Fisk University, and, like Helga Crane, the heroine of *Quicksand,* spent some time in Denmark with her mother's relatives, in Larsen's case attending the University of Copenhagen. In America Larsen graduated from the Lincoln Training School for Nurses in 1915; she was to work as a nurse supervisor in a Brooklyn hospital in the years after her disappearance from the literary world in 1930. During the years of the Harlem

Renaissance, during which she wrote her two novels, Larsen worked as a children's librarian. In 1929 she won the bronze medal of the Harmon Foundation for distinguished Negro achievement, and in 1930 she traveled to Spain as the first black female recipient of a Guggenheim fellowship. She never completed her third novel, lapsing instead into a thirty-year silence that lasted until her death in 1963.[17]

Larsen's silence seems, significantly, to have been motivated by a problem of authorship: she was accused of plagiarism. The incident is worthy of consideration, because it has never been fully understood, and because it suggests problems implicit in ethnic female authorship. In January 1930 Larsen published a short story called "Sanctuary" in *Forum* about a woman who shelters a fugitive after he reminds her that he is a friend of her son's, only to have it revealed to her that he is in hiding for having shot her son. In the April letters column, Marion Boyd wrote to *Forum* suggesting that Larsen's story bore striking resemblance to a story by Sheila Kaye-Smith, "Mrs. Adis," published in *Century* in 1922. The editors, in the same column, acknowledge the resemblance, but they stand by Larsen, reminding their readers that "the theory of natural selection was worked out independently, and at precisely the same moment, by Charles Darwin and A. R. Wallace." A letter from Larsen also appears, in which she pleads that the resemblance is so striking that "anyone who intended to lift a story would have avoided doing it as obviously as this has been done."

In fact, though resemblances between "Sanctuary" and "Mrs. Adis" are very strong, differences proliferate, and Larsen's defense is convincing. She writes that she had heard the story from a black patient in a black-staffed hospital who was distressed by the need for blacks to report on each other to white officials. In this "informant's" tale, as in Larsen's, the point is that blacks must band together (the woman tells the fugitive that his "black face" kept her from turning him in)—a message that is entirely absent from Kaye-Smith's story of white laborers in Sussex. Moreover, Larsen writes that "in talking it over with Negroes," she found the tale was so old that it was really a folk tale:

It has many variations: sometimes, it is the woman's brother, husband, son, lover, preacher, beloved master, or even her father, mother, sister, or daughter who is killed. A Negro sociologist tells me that there are literally hundreds of these stories. Anyone could have written it up at any time.

Finally, Larsen says that she wished she had placed the story in the city, in the context of her interchange with the old black woman patient, but that the "little old Negro country woman was so vivid" before her that she set it down as it was told.[18]

Whether Larsen plagiarized from "Mrs. Adis," was influenced by or unconsciously borrowed from it is not the point—in fact, the evidence supports Larsen, and her story is at any rate far superior to Kaye-Smith's. Rather, it is significant that Larsen's choice of material left her open for such a charge in just this way. Again, ethnic authorship seems to hinge on the ownership of stories. Does the woman who sets down a folk tale then own the tale? Are folk tales fit matter for fiction? Because Larsen set down a story told to her by another woman, is she then the author of that fiction? If Larsen had set it all down as it happened—recounting her meeting with the black patient, then the story—would "Sanctuary" be fiction? These questions may seem trivial, but they seem to surround ethnic female authorship with some impenetrability; we have seen how the fiction of American Indian women raised similar questions, and they arise again around the work of Zora Neale Hurston, a folklorist and novelist who was also accused of plagiarism.

Moreover, the issue is significant in Larsen's case, for it seems to have contributed to her abandonment of a writing career. The sense one gets of Larsen is that she was never exactly comfortable with authorship; her letters to Carl Van Vechten indicate that she found the process of writing annoying and nerve-wracking.[19] In general, Larsen's life seems to have been difficult. As a mulatto, who felt that any contact with her now all-white family would upset her mother and half-sister so much that she never saw them, Larsen felt the legacy of a divided self, one that was to inform her sensitive novels about mulatto heroines.[20] Larsen, like Helga Crane, *Quicksand*'s heroine, seems to have felt wholly part of neither the black or the white world; unlike Helga, Larsen saw internalization of this conflict as inevitable, and was able to maintain a certain perspective on it. While she could be indignant or enraged when oppression made itself felt, she was realistic in choosing

the battles she would fight. Many of her remarks to Van Vechten
indicate the shrewd good humor with which she viewed the ideological terrain of the Harlem Renaissance. About DuBose Hey-
ward, the white author of *Porgy* and *Mamba's Daughters* (a figure
of considerable controversy), Larsen wrote, "I hate all Southerners
'as a matter of principle,' but in fact I have never met one I didn't
like." Clearly, Larsen would speak out against Southerners in an
appropriate forum; her honesty dictated, however, that she be
pragmatic about principle among friends. (Whether Van Vechten
was an appropriate forum for her confidence remains a matter for
debate.) She could analyze the politics of race with a clear eye,
asking Van Vechten whether he noticed that when whites talked
about the admission of blacks to their homes it was rank prejudice,
"but when we take the same attitude about white people it is race
loyalty?" Black critics might have liked to see this clear eye turned
more steadily on the hypocrisy of whites, as in the following remark, in which Larsen assumes the pose of ethnic woman as
trickster:

> I went to lunch the other day with some people I knew very
> little (ofays). In the course of our talk it developed that they
> would have been keenly disappointed had they discovered I was
> not born in the jungles of the Virgin Isles. So I entertained them
> with quite a few stories of my childhood in the bush, and my
> reaction to the tomtom undertone in jazz. It was a *swell* luncheon.[21]
> (Larsen's emphasis)

Larsen attempted to transcend the battles about art and politics
then raging through Harlem by privileging aesthetics; she could
not fully do so, and was the subject and sometimes the participant
in some nasty ideological quarrels.[22] Larsen was, for instance, able
to recognize an outstanding artistic triumph that went beyond politics, writing to Gertrude Stein to commend her for her brilliant
portrait of a mulatto woman in Stein's 1909 *Melanctha*. Larsen
wrote, with characteristic honesty, "I never cease to wonder how
you came to write it and just why you and not some one of us
should so accurately have caught the spirit of this race of mine."[23]
    Larsen's difficulty was that the climate of the twenties in Har-
lem was not entirely sympathetic to honesty of this sort; indeed,
a black author's praise of a white author's portrayal of blacks was
just the kind of issue that was so often to divide the ranks of

Harlem artists. Not surprisingly, Larsen's fiction troubled her contemporaries and continues to puzzle critics today. Some critics,
like Bone, have tried to dismiss Larsen as a member of what David
Levering Lewis calls, in a revealingly combative metaphor, the
"genteel letters team."[24] Larsen's novels, however, contain severely ironic comments about genteel middle-class life that even
unsympathetic critics cannot overlook. In *Passing*, for instance,
when three middle-class passing black women drink tea in the
presence of one woman's blatantly racist husband, who is unaware
of their racial status, Irene Redfield can barely contain her "leap-
ing desire" to shout, "And you're sitting here surrounded by three
black devils, drinking tea."[25] Because of complications like this,
Larsen is given a slight critical nod by Robert Bone and Nathan
Huggins for her "psychological depth."[26] In recent years, feminist
criticism has made it possible for critics to ignore troubling dimensions of race and claim her novels as documents of sexism; such
attempts have proven equally reductive.[27] Her work remains an
ideological problem.[28] Barbara Christian, in her study of black
women novelists, makes a criticism that is representative in its attitude toward Larsen's politics, or lack of them. Christian takes
Larsen to task because her realistically portrayed heroines are not
happy: "The urban, sensitive, light-skinned heroine of the twenties is not free either in conventional, urban, upper-class society
or in 'primitive,' rural America. Given her options, she is doomed
in Larsen's novels to become a self-centered, oppressed neurotic
or a downtrodden, half-alive peasant."[29] Christian seems to call
for a black writer who can present "the smiling aspects of life"—
like Jessie Fauset?

Larsen's novels cause critical difficulty because they are written
from the point of view of a woman; the heroine's mulatto status
contributes to her feelings of marginality as a woman, so that in
the end her novels are reducible more to gender than they are to
race. The problems Larsen's heroines suffer derive from their identities as women; race functions symbolically in her novels rather
than realistically, so the mulatto condition is, for instance, a metaphor for a divided self—a condition Larsen feels all women share.
Helga Crane cannot come to terms with her sexual identity in a
society that either debases women sexually (Helga is accused of
prostitution by a man whose proposal she rejects) or impregnates

them relentlessly (*Quicksand* closes with Helga married to a black
preacher and locked into a squalid deep Southern existence by per-
petual pregnancy). For Helga, blackness becomes a symbol of
sexuality that cannot be repressed; her black "half" is her sexual
self. Similarly, in *Passing,* Irene Redfield's horror at her friend
Clare's successful passing is clearly a horror of repressed sexuality
unleashed. Clare, in passing successfully and at the same time en-
joying black life in Harlem when she wishes, is possessed of a
freedom Irene both fears and envies; moreover, Clare as a kind of
id figure is able to voice thoughts that prim Irene can never admit
to, telling, for insance, an ambivalently maternal Irene that " 'children aren't everything' " and shocking Irene with her laughter.
Irene herself cannot pass without horrible anxiety; a scene in
which she is uncomfortably doing so opens the novel, and inevitably, Clare arrives on the scene, upsetting Irene's world. The
mulatto condition in *Passing* is a symbol, in Irene's case, for a
female identity in which sexuality is repressed and considered dangerous, and in Clare's, for an identity in which the woman can find
freedom in her very marginality.

If this is indeed Larsen's point, it is not surprising that she has
been found difficult. Larsen bought fully into the *Zeitgeist* of the
twenties, when Harlemites agonized over whether the black should
be presented as an exotic, warm-natured, creature of the flesh, or
as an educated and proper citizen of the intellect; Larsen insisted
that the black was obviously both. She dramatized the split that so
worried Harlem artists, creating heroines who represent proof
that such a split is an integral part of the psyche, particularly the
female psyche. Such a split, she seems to have felt, was felt in
blacks and whites and in men and women; in the case of the mulatto woman, it was only that much more manifest. With *Quicksand* and *Passing,* Larsen achieved that much-maligned and problematic goal: she showed that black experience was like white experience, or, more accurately, that certain aspects of black female
experience presented in high relief aspects of the human experience. Larsen unsettles readers in a profound way, insisting on
the uneasiness implicit in the human condition.

I have discussed at length the authorship of Jessie Fauset and
Nella Larsen because the problems that surround their authorship
emerge as representative and persistent in ethnic women's writing.
Indeed, to stay with the case of black women, similar problems

plagued the black writers who followed Larsen and Fauset, at least until recent years. A novel like Dorothy West's 1948 *The Living is Easy* is, as Bone rightly points out, a savage satire of black and white middle-class Boston, but is often dismissed as another genteel novel in the Fauset mode. The lesson to be learned from *The Living is Easy* is that such novels must be read with care. The novel's heroine, Cleo, is a snobbish, race-conscious woman who warns her dark daughter not to show her gums when she laughs; on the other hand, Cleo rivals Larsen's heroines in complexity and is an ingenious and sympathetic strong woman, proud of her ethnic female identity.[30] Black writer Ann Petry, whose first novel *The Street* (1946) is a deterministic protest novel of what Bone calls "the Wright school" and also, significantly, a novel about possibilities for female autonomy in a hostile environment, is positively chameleonlike in the way in which she changes genres and voices; she is a difficult novelist to discuss because of her very range. Her 1947 *Country Place* is a novel about whites in a small Connecticut town and is narrated by a man who confesses his hatred of women in the opening pages; her 1953 *The Narrows* is a novel about interracial love; to complicate matters, Petry then turned to writing historical children's books about such black heroines as Tituba and Sojourner Truth.[31]

In fact, only in recent years does it seem that a tradition of black female authorship has become solidified and therefore explicable; indeed, a second black literary Renaissance, in which women are taking significant part, seems well under way. To understand how this has come to pass, I would like to trace black female authorship until the present through the person of Zora Neale Hurston. Hurston's career is instructive, first, because it spans both "Renaissances" in that she was part of the Harlem Renaissance and remains, despite her death in 1960, an important force in black literature today, with many black women acknowledging her influence on their work.[32] Second, Hurston's authorship was as compromised, threatened, and tenuous as that of many of the writers I discuss, and yet she produced a novel, *Their Eyes Were Watching God* (1937), which most critics recognize not only as the best novel thus far written by a black woman but as an American literary classic. The controversy and difficulty that surrounded Hurston's authorship during and after her lifetime creates a striking backdrop for the emergence of this brilliant

novel of black female independence. As a writer, Hurston confronted each of the factors that have so often complicated ethnic
female authorship: because she was an important folklorist, her
work raises considerable questions of *genre;* as a struggling black
woman looking to make something of herself she was provided
for by a succession of white patrons, and her work affected by the
conditions of *patronage;* because she was a black artist working
in the context of the 1920s and 1930s, she participated in the ongoing *political/aesthetic debate* about the nature of black art,
usually to no one's satisfaction; and finally, her sense of identity
as a writer provides one of the richest examples of the interrela-
tionship of *identity and authorship* in ethnic women's lives.

Hurston came to Harlem in 1925 after two of her stories,
"Drenched in Light" and "Smoke," attracted the attention of
Harlem literati and earned prizes collected at the 1925 *Opportunity* awards dinner that Lewis posits as the opening scene of the
literary Renaissance. Although she was indisputably part of the
literary Harlem Renaissance, she began her career as a folklorist.
Her first major work was *Mules and Men* (1935), a collection of
folk tales gathered from blacks in the region of Eatonville, her
Florida home town, and Hurston devoted most of her time until
the writing of her first novel, *Jonah's Gourd Vine* (1934), to the
collection and study of folklore. The distinction between folklore
and fiction, however, was never for Hurston to be as clear as this
account implies. The fiction Hurston worked at during this early
period, for instance, is shaped by the use of folklore, and *Mules
and Men* is shaped fictionally. Indeed, Hurston's ongoing struggle
was to accommodate the two, which she rightly saw as inseparable,
to each other. Among her Harlem contemporaries, Hurston was
known as a great teller of stories, especially tales of exaggeration
that she called "lies," many of which she seems to have brought
with her from Florida. As an aspiring folklorist and writer, Hurston was confused by the distinction between lies, folktales, and
fiction. Robert Hemenway, Hurston's biographer, asks a set of
critical questions that Hurston may have confronted during this
time:

> She had grown up in an oral-aural tradition, where one's ability to
> entertain and hold an audience with metaphorical imagination
> and colorful language defined the role of artist. The folk artists

on Joe Clarke's porch [in Eatonville] had no need to write down
their tales, for they did not realize they were creating literature.
Why was it so important for Zora Hurston to create *written* literature? . . . how could she capture the Eatonville essence in fiction and drama? How did one express the viability of black traditions? (Hemenway's emphasis) [33]

In such a context, a writer's work can attain a certain fluidity
that makes it possible to confuse distinctions between fictions.
Looking at a story in Hurston's folklore collection "Hoodoo in
America," published in the *Journal of American Folklore* in 1931,
Hemenway detects resemblances to an earlier Hurston story,
"Black Death." Wondering whether "Hurston's informant for the
variant [later] text was not Zora Neale herself," Hemenway asks,
"Was Hurston lying in 1931, passing off her own creative work as
folklore? Or had the 1925 version been simply a redaction of a
folktale remembered from Eatonville, and given a special telling
by the young short-story writer?"[34] When there is confusion as to
the point at which fiction leaves off and folktales begin, authorship
itself can become tenuous.

During the years Hurston spent collecting folklore in the South
and in Haiti, she became increasingly troubled by this distinction,
a distinction complicated by the terms of her patronage, which
stipulated that she "use" none of the folklore she collected but
said nothing about the "use" of folklore in fiction. Moreover, during the Harlem Renaissance, folklore was valorized as preserving
an inherent black dignity and tradition. At the same time, however, fiction shaped by folklore was vulnerable to criticism on the
grounds of insufficient artistic form, or of presenting a condescending portrayal of black life. Like Larsen and Fauset, Hurston
suffered from these ambivalences. By the time *Their Eyes Were
Watching God* appeared, the influence of the Communist Party
had further complicated the debate about black art; Richard
Wright felt that the novel was counterrevolutionary in portraying
simple, minstrel-show blacks. The wording of Wright's criticism
suggests the confusion of such debate: he complains that Hurston's
characters exist in "that safe and narrow orbit in which America
likes to see the Negro live: between laughter and tears"; one
wonders how he would expand that orbit.[35] Sterling Brown responded similarly, seeing the novel as slight and condescending

toward black culture. Alain Locke thought the novel's "main point" was folklore, and therefore dismissed it. The reception of *Their Eyes were Watching God* was representative. In the context of the debate between propaganda and aesthetics, Hurston was criticized, variously, because she, for instance, "opened up" to whites too easily (by Alain Locke for her essay "How It Feels To Be Colored Me"), for practicing cultural colonialism by collecting folklore (by white radical Harold Preece in a *Crisis* article), for not being bitter enough about the black condition (by Sterling Brown in his review of *Mules and Men*), for using folklore too obtrusively in her fiction (by the *Crisis* in a review of *Jonah's Gourd Vine*).

Partly in response to problems of these sorts, Hurston confined herself in the early part of her career to the collection of folktales, occasionally leaking what she called "juicy bits" to friends like Langston Hughes for artistic use.[36] Especially attracted to the idea of using folklore dramatically, Hurston gave a good deal of thought to the choice of the best medium for the use of her folk material.

However much Hurston might puzzle over the relation of folklore to fiction, in the important years between 1927 and 1932 the terms of her patronage obviated some confusion in that they simply did not allow Hurston to publish. Mrs. Rufus Osgood Mason, the Park Avenue matron who supported Hurston in these years, held the technical rights to all folklore Hurston collected; in fact, until 1932, Hurston wrote and published scantily, and only after the severance of her ties to Mrs. Mason was she able to turn to the writing of what was to become her first novel, *Jonah's Gourd Vine*.

Hurston is a unique figure in American literary history because of the extent to which her career was based on her dependence on the support of others. In one form or another, this independent woman existed in a state of financial dependency most of her life. The sources of support included Annie Nathan Meyer, the Barnard trustee who encouraged Hurston's Barnard education; Jewish-American novelist Fannie Hurst, who employed her as a secretary in her early New York years; Franz Boas, who directed Hurston's folklore collection in graduate school; the Guggenheim and Rosenthal foundations; and the WPA Federal Writers Project. As late as 1936, Hurston wrote, "I find myself tied to money matters like a grazing horse to a stake."[37] The most formidable and generous source of support was Mrs. Mason, whom Hurston was to dub "godmother."

The terms of Hurston's relationship with Mrs. Mason have largely been misunderstood. Patronage in general is a difficult issue to understand; in the context of the Harlem Renaissance, when many black writers were inundated with prizes and grants, funded from "downtown," the issue was often confused with the debate surrounding black art. A scenario in which art and politics were already intertwined became even more complicated by, for instance, a black artist who had the friendship and support of a Carl Van Vechten or Mabel Dodge Luhan. Generally, historians of the period have perpetuated the terms of the general debate by viewing this scenario and the issue of patronage in a predominantly negative light; the conclusion of David Levering Lewis's *When Harlem Was in Vogue,* for instance, seems to be that black art was compromised by white money.

Of course, it would be equally reductive to posit an alternative scenario in which white money made black art possible. In fact, consideration of patronage must be grounded in specifics, with generalizations avoided. The specifics of Zora Neale Hurston's relationship to Mrs. Mason provide a compelling example of the complexity of the issue and go a long way toward explaining the dynamics of authorship in such a climate.

Hurston's relationship with Mrs. Mason has usually been considered in light of what Lewis calls Mrs. Mason's "court," with Hurston the court's jester. Included in this court were Langston Hughes, Aaron Douglas, and Alain Locke; Mrs. Mason, by all accounts, liked "primitives." (She had already played an important role in generating a collection of Indian folklore, traveling with Natalie Curtis to the Southwest to gather material for Curtis's *The Indian Book.*) In fact, Mrs. Mason, with Alain Locke, demanded of her black artists an allegiance to folk culture and African traditions that they often did not fully feel. Lewis points out that figures as various as James Weldon Johnson, DuBois, Roland Hayes, and Wallace Thurman were criticized for their involvement with the white world. White culture, Mrs. Mason told Locke, was to be "slough[ed] off," used "only to clarify thoughts that surged in [his] being."[38]

Hurston, with her ties to the folk, was a ready candidate for the

support of a woman with Mrs. Mason's avid interest in black culture. Indeed, Hurston's behavior with Mrs. Mason is usually re-
counted in a way that throws the comic aspect of Mrs. Mason's
interest in high relief. Nathan Huggins writes that Louise Thomp-
son, another artist sponsored by Mrs. Mason, remembered Hurston calling herself a "little darky" before Mrs. Mason, winking
to her friends. Wallace Thurman's portrayal of Hurston as Sweetie
May Carr in his *Infants of the Spring* (1932) endorses this image.
Sweetie May entertains white audiences with "darky stories," re-
marking to her black friends, "Being a Negro writer these days is
a racket and I'm going to make the most of it while it lasts. Sure
I cut the fool. But I enjoy it too. . . . Thank God for this Negro
literary renaissance. Long may it flourish!"[39]

In classic trickster fashion, Hurston was able to turn her dependence on Mrs. Mason to her own advantage, maintaining her integrity while appearing to please. This was a pattern with which
Hurston was very familiar; one of her favorite folk figures was
High John de Conquer, the all-time master of "hitting a straight
lick with a crooked stick." She presented a formulation of the
derivation of this classic trickster figure in an article published in
the *American Mercury* in 1943:

> Old Massa met our hope-bringer all right, but when Old Massa
> met him, he was not going by his right name. He was traveling,
> and touristing around the plantations as the laugh-provoking
> Brer Rabbit. So Old Massa and Old Miss and their young ones
> laughed at Brer Rabbit and wished him well. And all the time,
> there was High John de Conquer, playing his tricks of making a
> way out of no-way. Hitting a straight lick with a crooked stick.
> Winning the jack pot with no other stake but a laugh. Fighting
> a mighty battle without outside-showing force, and winning his
> war from within.[40]

Hurston clearly saw the potential of tricksterism as an authorial
strategy for the black woman; in her version of Moses and the
Israelites, *Moses, Man of the Mountain* (1939), her heroine is
Miriam, Moses' sister, who, Hurston writes, "can hit a straight lick
with a crooked stick."[41]

Familiar though she was with the role of the trickster, Hurston
was well aware of its complexity and of the compromises implicit
in ethnic authorship. She once commented, "Rather than get

across all of the things which you want to say you must compromise and work within the limitations [of those people] who have the final authority in deciding whether or not a book shall be printed."[42] It is misleading to present a woman of Hurston's intelligence as alternately exploited or muzzled by a wealthy white patron. In fact, the exchange implicit in Hurston's "contract" with Mrs. Mason was, for the most part, remarkably clear to both women. It was, however, complicated by an emotional component that deeply affected Hurston's sense of her identity as an author.

The appellation used by both Hughes and Hurston for Mrs. Mason, "godmother," suggests the complexity of their emotional exchange. As a "god," Mrs. Mason could be a stern taskmaster as well as a bestower of gifts. Hurston made this point explicitly when she wrote to Hughes that Godmother disapproved of their dream of creating a "new Negro theatre" with Alain Locke: "She trusts her three children never to let those words pass their lips again until the gods decree that they shall materialize."[43] A god can also be a censor, as well as a protector or a guard. Hurston once described Mrs. Mason as "A guard-mother who sits in the twelfth heaven and shapes the destinies of the primitives."[44] In this guise, Mrs. Mason sometimes terrorized and sometimes irritated Hurston, often hurting her deeply, as when she refused to allow her to participate in a prestigious research project with Boas. Mrs. Mason's prohibitions about publishing must have particularly rankled with an incipient writer; when she did write, Hurston told Hughes, Godmother "toned down" the dirty words.[45]

On the other hand, Mrs. Mason's role as a god*mother* was tremendously important to Hurston, who had lost her own mother at the age of nine. During an especially close period, Hurston addressed Mrs. Mason as her biological mother:

> Flowers to you—the true conceptual mother—not just a biological accident. To you of the immaculate conception where everything is conceived in beauty and every child is hovered [covered?] in truth. . . . I have taken form from the breath of your mouth. From the vapor of your soul am I made to be.[46]

In fact, Mrs. Mason's belief in the value of folk culture may have been particularly compelling to Hurston because of the circumstances of her mother's death. Denying the value of folk ritual on her deathbed, Hurston's mother asked her daughter not to perform the rituals attendant to death. Hurston's inability to carry out her mother's wishes—her father and family friends conducted the proscribed rites over Hurston's protests—affected her deeply. She wrote in her autobiography, "If there is any consciousness after death, I hope that Mama knows that I did my best. She must know how I have suffered for my failure."[47] In Mrs. Mason's encouragement of Hurston's reembracing folk culture, Hurston must have seen a persuasively maternal act. In fact, Mrs. Mason did function as a "conceptual" mother to Hurston, one from whom Hurston had to separate in order to write fiction.

Conditions worked out so that Mrs. Mason engineered this essential separation. In April 1932, Mrs. Mason gave Hurston money to return to Eatonville, her home town. During her stay there, Hurston wrote the draft of *Jonah's Gourd Vine,* a novel about her parents. One of the most moving chapters in the book, in fact, reenacts Hurston's mother's deathbed scene. From this moment Hurston's authorship derived. Because of the acceptance of the novel by Lippincott, and because of its good reception, Hurston was able to find a publisher for her folktale collection *Mules and Men.* Because *Mules and Men* contained that material over which Mrs. Mason had control, the terms of their mutual contract were over.

In her autobiography, *Dust Tracks on a Road* (1942), Hurston acknowledges the significance of this moment. She describes a series of "visions" she had as a child, culminating in a vision of Mrs. Mason. She writes that upon the realization of this vision, "then I would be at the end of my pilgrimage, but not at the end of my life."[48] In fact, Hurston was, at this moment, beginning her life as a writer. It was not without regret that Hurston moved beyond Mrs. Mason toward establishing her identity as a writer; at the beginning of her publishing career she wrote to Alain Locke, "Instead of feeling less need of godmother and more independent as success approaches me, I need her more and feel her great goodness to me more deeply. If I am acclaimed by the world and make a million in money, I would still feel that she was responsible for it."[49]

In 1937 Hurston, in the wake of this struggle, published her masterpiece, *Their Eyes Were Watching God.* The story of Janie

Crawford, who comes to independence through a series of marriages, the last to an exuberant and vital younger man named Tea Cake, whose exuberance turns into a case of rabies for which Janie must kill him, *Their Eyes Were Watching God* masterfully integrates folklore story-telling traditions and elements of Hurston's autobiography with a sophisticated narrative: during Janie's marriage to Joe Starks, she lives in a black town very similar to Eatonville, and tends a store in which the men gather to spin long tales about, for instance, a neighbor's meanness to his old mule; when Janie and Tea Cake farm in the Everglades they entertain their coworkers with elaborate gambling rituals that Hurston describes in detail. The narrative form itself reflects the midwiving aspect of the ethnic female tradition; Janie relates her story to her friend Phoeby, and the novel is "framed" by their discussion. Janie returns to the black town after her adventure with Tea Cake, finding her friends and neighbors gossiping about her running off with a younger man and returning husbandless; to Phoeby, her best friend, Janie says, " 'Phoeby, we been kissin'-friends for twenty years, so Ah depend on you for a good thought. And Ah'm talking to you from dat standpoint.' "[50] When Janie finishes her story (having soaked her feet in the meantime), Phoeby "breathe[s] out heavily, 'Ah done growed ten feet higher from jus' listenin' tuh you, Janie. Ah ain't satisfied wid myself no mo'. . . . Nobody better not criticize you in mah hearin'.' "[51] The telling of Janie's story has done both teller and listener good; what the reader must remember is that the bulk of this powerful novel is meant to be a simple transcription of Janie's story. Stylistically sophisticated, the novel is dependent on an oral tradition, and in it are preserved many of the folk tales and stories Hurston collected earlier in her life.

It was from an extraordinary complex of circumstances that emerged not only Janie Crawford, the independent and indomitable heroine of *Their Eyes Were Watching God,* but also Zora Neale Hurston, the independent heroine so important to black women writers today. In Hurston's case, we see the extraordinary forces brought to bear on the making of an ethnic female author. Questions of mediation, authentication and authority, influence, patronage, and politics all fall away when the reader confronts Hurston's important novel. It is something of a relief, in fact, to emerge from this consideration of ethnic female authorship with a text as wholly self-sufficient and unmediated as *Their Eyes Were Watching God*. Because many novels by ethnic women have been so heavily mediated, compromised by circumstances, or textually fragmented, it has been necessary to analyze those circumstances at work in obscuring these texts, and to reconstruct the dynamics of their authorship. In the following chapters, I would like to return, at last, to the texts.

CHAPTER 4

Fathers and Founding Fathers: The Making of Little American Women

Ethnic women writers attain the authority we associate with authorship within a context not always conducive to their self-expression. Their sense of familiarity with the language varies according to the ease with which they take on this authority. The ethnic literary tradition implies, of course, the acquisition of the English language; at some point, ethnic writers or their ancestors learned to read, write, and speak a new language. Moreover, they learned a common language, a way of speaking, that was inevitably imposed on them by the dominant culture and the structure of language itself. They learned American rhetoric and acquired an American identity. That identity implied both an awareness of the ethnic woman's past and her ancestors and membership in the American community or "family." Often, she responded to the demands of acculturation by vigorous renunciation of her foreign or slave ancestors; born anew, she saw herself as a child of America rather than of foreign parents. A descendant now of America's founding fathers, she wrote her experience in terms of an American rhetoric that expressed particular features of American ideology: a struggle for self-expression and success, whether through independent enterprise or a prudent marriage, usually to a native-born American; a sense of personal and public mission; and a pervasive yearning for self-improvement and acceptance.

In the "early" writing of ethnic women—in novels by women like Anzia Yezierska, Mary Antin, and Mourning Dove—the novelist's lack of familiarity with the common language of America leads her to attempt to reproduce it vigorously, to insert herself within American rhetoric. At this "stage" in the ethnic literary tradition, received myths, heroes, and modes of discourse are endorsed. The ideologically important story of Pocahontas, for instance, is not questioned and is often obsessively rewritten. For writers like Zora Neale Hurston and Gertrude Stein, on the other hand—whose authority, authorship, and use of language are less compromised, and, in Stein's case, highly complex—ideological features of American myth and discourse are questioned, sometimes subverted, and sometimes transcended. Moreover, conflicts endemic to the ethnic experience but inevitably glossed over by ideological myth-making—like the emotional weight of miscegenation attached to the Pocahontas story—are increasingly the subjects of these women writers.

It is possible to understand the nature of this development of a self-conscious use of the common language of America by examining how ethnic women write about or reproduce the acquisition of an American identity. In the making of their American selves, ethnic women partake of an ahistorical and often typological rhetoric of rebirth. Fathers of the Old World are to be replaced by the fathers of the New: George Washington, Ben Franklin, Abraham Lincoln. The common language of America seems to the "early" ethnic woman writer to be capable of including her. Increasingly, she will come to see that only with careful attention to a more particular and less public language can she insert herself within, or, sometimes, write against American rhetoric.

The story of Pocahontas's acquisition of an American or a non-ethnic identity is, for the ethnic woman, an important feature of the common language of America. When Pocahontas laid her head over John Smith's to prevent her father's men from clubbing him to death, she simultaneously defied Powhatan and rejected her own ethnic and familial identity. After her marriage to John Rolfe, Pocahontas converted to Christianity, was renamed Lady Rebecca and led to England in triumph, her Indian selfhood apparently renounced. Pocahontas's story implies renunciation and rebirth, a rechristening in the dominant culture's language, and the rejection of a private family for membership in another, more public family. Through her own generational rebellion, she became part of what we might call the American "Jamestown generation."

Generational conflict, the struggle between parents and children by which an adult self is formed, is—in spite of, or perhaps because of—its universal relevance, often held out as the predominant feature of American identity, and, more particularly, of ethnic identity. Not only psychohistorians, but literary critics, politicians, clergymen, and American writers as diverse as Nathaniel Hawthorne and Gertrude Stein have found in the idea of generational conflict a rhetoric of American identity so compelling that the notion of children struggling against their parents as a way of describing American life has attained the status of an ideological force. It is not surprising that what has often been thought of as a subheading of American identity—ethnic identity—should partake of this rhetoric as thoroughly as it does, to the extent that in the rhetoric of ethnic identity one can locate a compressed and intensified version of a larger American rhetoric of generational conflict.

In fact, generational conflict is felt by many historians of ethnicity to be the most striking feature of ethnic American identity. The language of ethnicity refers bewilderingly, often inaccurately, and always insistently, to generations. Marcus Lee Hansen's statement, "what the son forgets the grandson wishes to remember," has attained the status of a "law"; Margaret Mead's assertion that we are all third generation is taken as a metaphorical truth. Such generalizations are puzzling because the definition of "generations" remains elusive and is applied with insistent ahistoricism. If Americans are the "children" of the "founding fathers," for instance, what happened to intervening generations? On the other hand, in studying the rhetoric of Americanization, it is impossible to deny the sense that something familial is going on here. And, because American experience is defined in familial or kinship language, the ethnic woman must come to terms with a generational rhetoric to become part of the American family.[1]

Not only is generational rhetoric ahistorical, it is also, at first consideration, asexual. Granddaughters wish to remember, it seems, as much as do grandsons. On the other hand, the gender specificity of the language of "fathers and sons" cannot be written off merely as linguistic shorthand. This is less to suggest that the rhetoric deliberately excludes women—though in important cases it does and must—than that it focuses on a particular conflict that has a gender-specific psychological structure. Daughters have different kinds of generational conflicts from those of sons. While it is not necessary to stress this structural difference unduly, it is important to remember that the ethnic woman who inevitably partakes of the rhetoric of generational conflict is just as inevitably speaking of a private, particular, and different generational conflict of her own. The term "generations" has an abstract, metaphorical, public meaning, so that we can speak of a "lost generation," a "beat generation," or say with Margaret Mead that we are all "third generation," but it also has a specific, familial, and personal application. In studying ethnic American identity, it is important to consider both of these aspects.

Generational conflict is a recurrent theme in ethnic fiction, and male ethnic writers have compellingly presented its role not only in the development of American sons (as in Michael Gold's 1930 *Jews Without Money*) but also in that of American daughters (as in John Brougham's 1850s Indian drama, *Metamora; or the Last of the Pollywogs*). In ethnic women's fiction, a predominant motif is generational conflict of a highly specific sort: the heroine's rebellion against her Old World father. Some of the strongest novels by American ethnic women are those that explore the apparent necessity for vigorous renunciation of the heroine's father. Norwegian-American author Martha Ostenso's *Wild Geese* (1925) and Russian-American Anzia Yezierska's *Bread Givers* (1925) both depict second-generation immigrant heroines who struggle for self-expression, come to realize that achievement of that goal is only possible through rebellion—often violent—against their tyrannical and rigid Old World fathers, and find that their goal has only been partially realized. While the overwhelming message of these novels is that American identity for the daughters of immigrants is contingent on defiance of foreign fathers and ancestral identity, American identity is never defined or achieved in any way beyond this. The heroines of these novels, struggling to learn and often to write, exist in a state of insistent yearning and, as one critic has suggested, hunger, which is only partially satiated.[2]

For the ethnic heroine, the generational conflict inherent in becoming an American simultaneously shaped identity and threatened to destroy it. Acculturation seemed to demand the rejection of her family and her culture. The father, rigid and unbending in his treatment of his wife and children, represented all that had to be cast off. For the Jewish heroine, he was often associated with an intense religiosity distinctly inappropriate in the new world.[3] Anzia Yezierska's fictional fathers are often Talmudic scholars (as was her own), in the Old Country supported by the largesse of the community, but in America often forced to depend on the extradomestic labor of their wives and children. The Yezierska heroine comes to question the practical value of her father's religious system, while he maintains that " 'the real food is God's Holy Torah.' "[4] Furthermore, the patriarchal nature of Jewish culture her father maintains forces the heroine to look elsewhere for self-definition and fulfillment. The father of the heroine of *Bread Givers* instructs his daughter Sara, " 'It says in the Torah, only through a man has a woman an existence. Only through a man can a woman enter heaven' " (137). Where she might once have accepted this and similar dictates (as Yezierska's fictional mothers often do), the social and economic realities of her New World existence force the second-generation immigrant heroine to question the nature of the religious values that inform her ethnicity.

Bread Givers is subtitled "A Struggle Between a Father of the Old World and a Daughter of the New": the very confusion of syntax (does the New World possess the daughter, or she it? or did it parent her?) reflects the confusion of parentage that results from the Americanization experience. Reb Smolinsky allows his family to bring with them no baggage from the Old World save his books; he insists that the baggage of Judaica is all that is necessary for adjustment in the New World. " 'Woman!' " Reb Smolinsky instructs his wife,

> What for will you need old feather beds? Don't you know that it's always summer in America? And in the new golden country, where milk and honey flows free in the streets, you'll have new golden dishes to cook in, and not weigh yourself down with your old pots and pans. But my books, my holy books always were, and always will be, the light of the world. You'll see yet how America will come to my feet to learn. (9)

Of course, America doesn't, but Reb Smolinsky believes and preaches otherwise throughout his family's calamity-ridden experience in the New World.

Adopting the language of promise purveyed by his native-born male counterparts, Reb Smolinsky ignores the realities of immigrant life, and as such must be rejected by the heroine, whose sur-

vival depends on her practical and realistic vision: until she can
express her experience in her own terms, she must translate it
literally. To her husband's Talmudic illustration of the superior
value of "wine in heaven" to gold on earth, Shenah Smolinsky
sighs, " 'If he was only so fit for this world, like he is fit for
Heaven, I wouldn't have to dry out the marrow from my head
worrying for the rent' " (16). Reb Smolinsky shares with the
dominant culture of native-born America a belief in and a pro-
pensity for promises. Driven to matchmaking, he advertises, " 'Put
your future in my hands and I'll settle you with good luck for
life' " (91). Sara Smolinsky becomes increasingly disillusioned as
the false nature of her father's promises—the ones he makes and
the ones he believes in—is brutally revealed. The diamond-dealer
he forces on his daughter Mashah is only a salesman in a jewelry
store, who loses his job the day after the wedding because he has
borrowed the diamonds with which he impresses the Smolinskys.
Reb Smolinsky's tyrannical wrong-headedness is unrelenting; his
response to Mashah's tearful return is " 'Empty-head! . . .
Couldn't you see he was a swindler?' " (83).

In another of Reb Smolinsky's unlucky business ventures, he
buys a grocery store in New Jersey, endorsing again the dominant
culture's rhetoric of the success story. " 'In America, there is no
need to be poor, if you only got brains and money,' " he asserts
("as though Rockefeller's millions were already burning in his
pockets," adds the narrator) (112–13). The promises of consu-
merism are hollow: the store is a fake—oatmeal boxes are filled
with air and sugar barrels with sawdust. The family's unsuccessful
attempts to run the store after they have been swindled drive Sara
from her home in anger and frustration.

In the heroine's rejection of her father following this debacle,
Yezierska introduces a notion that will prove insistent in ethnic
women's fiction: "This is America, where children are people"
(135). Sara Smolinsky announces her independence by renouncing
her parentage: " 'You made the lives of the other children! I'm
going to make my own life!' " (138). In her struggle to do so, the
ethnic heroine finds herself alone. Sara reflects,

> Knowledge was what I wanted more than anything else in the
> world. I had made my choice. And now I had to pay the price.
> So this is what it cost, daring to follow the urge in me. No father.

No lover. No family. No friend. I must go on and on. And I must go on—alone. (208)

In Yezierska's autobiography, *Red Ribbon on a White Horse* (1950), she describes her Hollywood success and her own sense of alienation from her own culture. She confides to Sam Goldwyn her desire to write an "expiation of guilt," a novel with the syntactically significant title, *Children of Loneliness,* about children who lose their heritage in their struggle to become Americans. She explains:

> I had to break away from my mother's cursing and my father's preaching to live my life; but without them I had no life. When you deny your parents, you deny the sky over your head. You become an outlaw, a pariah.[5]

This is, finally, the central dilemma in Yezierska's life and work. Her immigrant heroines often attempt to solve it by reembracing the fathers they have rejected. Sara Smolinsky, after her successful marriage to a fellow immigrant, comes upon her scholar father peddling chewing gum on the streets of the Lower East Side. After several stormy reconciliation scenes, she and her husband invite her father to live with them. "How could I have hated him and tried to blot him out of my life?" Sara asks. "Can a tree hate the roots from which it sprang?" (286). Neither the narrator or the reader is wholly satisfied with the conclusion reached. The novel closes as Sara and her husband hear her father chanting, " 'Man born of woman is of few days and full of trouble.' " Yezierska writes, "Hugo's grip tightened on my arm and we walked on. But I felt the shadow still there, over me. It wasn't just my father, but the generations who made my father whose weight was still upon me" (296–97).

The story of Yezierska's Sara Smolinsky, overcome by the weight of generations, struggling to resist an ancestrally imposed identity, is echoed in a novel written in the same year by Martha Ostenso, *Wild Geese.* Ostenso's story of the midwestern Gare family, ruled by a tyrannical father who keeps his wife and children beaten down and tied to the bleak farmland, is a harsh naturalistic portrayal of generational conflict at its most violent. Caleb Gare lords it over his wife Amelia by means of his knowledge of her illegitimate son; Amelia, who defeatedly claims that she wishes that her family could stop eating once in a while because " 'it gets tiresome,' "[6] is no ally for her daughter Judith, the only one of her children who shows any signs of independence and life. *Wild Geese* is characterized by a structure shared with Yezierska's *Bread Givers,* Ostenso's later novel *The Waters Under the Earth* (1930), and a derivative proletarian novel by German-American writers Hope Sykes, *Second Hoeing* (1935), in which the struggle of the heroine to resist the forces that threaten her growth is set off by cautionary tales of her sisters and mother who, to varying degrees, succumb to the patriarch's wishes. Just as Reb Smolinsky's daughter is inspirationally horrified by the fate of her sisters, so is Judith Gare driven to struggle by the example of her sister Ellen who, like Bessie Smolinsky, rejects a lover who promises escape in deference to her father's wishes. Ellen Gare feels "a contorted sense of loyalty that had been inbred in [her and] had overrun every other instinct like a choking tangle of weeds. She reasoned only as Caleb had taught her to reason, in terms of the advantage to the land and to him" (96).[7] The Ostenso heroine's quest involves the rejection, sometimes violent, of the models of selfhood offered by her sisters' and mother's example. Judith Gare, one of the angriest of ethnic heroines, watches her sister bleeding from a splinter with furious detachment: "Judith found herself viciously glad that it had happened. There was nothing admirable in Ellen's suffering. It had no purpose" (20).

Judith's rebellion against Caleb Gare is made possible by the arrival of a schoolteacher, Lind Archer, in the Scandinavian community. Lind's presence in the Gare household acts as an impetus for Judith's flight. Lind does what she can for the Gares, trying to get Ellen a pair of glasses and arranging meetings between Judith and the lover who wants to take her away. The narrator writes, "Lind Archer had come and her delicate fingers had sprung a secret lock in Judith's being. . . . There was no going back now into the darkness" (67). Judith Gare, however, is so overcome by her father's tyranny that violence is the only means by which she can escape. Confronted by her father, who has witnessed her assignation with her lover, Judith flings an ax at him. The ax misses and is lodged in the barn wall, where Caleb leaves it as a reminder to his daughter that she is now totally under his control because he can turn her in to the law or accuse her of insanity. Judith, now pregnant and furious, understands the elemental nature of her struggle with Caleb, and her difference from Lind:

> Lind would not have [committed so violent an act]. Lind was fine, and controlled. She, Judith, was just an animal, with an animal's passions and sins, and stupid, body-strength. And now she held an animal's secret, too. She was coarse, brutal, with great beast-breasts protruding from her, and buttocks and thighs and shoulders of a beast. (275)

Ostenso emphasizes the violently sexual nature of the overly determined heroine's revolt against her father. Judith escapes because she is pregnant and has to, and escapes only narrowly. Caleb, finally, is himself beaten—a fire springs up in the brushy swampland he so loves, and in an ending reminiscent of naturalistic novelist Frank Norris's *The Octopus,* he is swallowed up by a horribly feminized swampland, "[t]he earth . . . closing ice-cold, tight, tight about his body" (352).

Lind Archer, the idealistic schoolteacher possessed of a strangely sexless passion for Mark Jordan, a city visitor playing at farming on the doctor's orders, seems at first oddly misplaced in this violently sexualized and naturalistic landscape. Her role, however, is crucial for an understanding of the structure of the heroine's generational conflict and quest for selfhood. As a representative from civilization, a self-made woman, and, significantly, as a schoolteacher, Lind acts as a catalyst for Judith's escape. Beyond lending Judith soap and perfume, she senses that her mere presence is important in the Gare home:

> She felt vaguely that her coming had incited Jude to greater rebellion. Lind wondered . . . if there were any means in her power by which she might bring a little happiness into the lives of the Gares. And then in a moment, she was overwhelmed by the hopelessness against the intangible thing that held them there, slaves to the land. (24)

Judith, too, fears that "Perhaps with the going of Lind the dream would go—and there would be nothing but another winter of frozen manure and hungry cattle" (236).

Although Judith is too overly determined to escape into other than an erotic destiny—it's obvious that she will marry, as opposed to, for instance, becoming a schoolteacher herself—it is sig-

nificant that the schoolteacher's mere presence can trigger such
emotion. *Wild Geese* presents a dramatization of the role of education in the ethnic woman's novel: as a schoolteacher, Lind
awakens desire, sets into motion the yearning of the heroine to,
in Yezierska's terms, "make herself a person." Learning—often,
literature—evokes in the ethnic heroine an awareness of the possibilities of overcoming the weight of generations and the naturalistic forces exerted by either the midwestern farmland or New
York's Lower East Side. Moreover, in a context in which education was set forth as the primary agent of the Americanization
process, education promised an American identity, success, and
autonomy to the ethnic novelist's heroine.

Blanche Gelfant, in a recent article, notes that the "hungry
heroine" is a critical figure in many novels by American women,
and that often the hungry heroine is an ethnic woman. Heroines
like Francie Nolan in Irish-American writer Betty Smith's *A Tree
Grows in Brooklyn* (1943) and Selina Boyce in black writer Paule
Marshall's *Brown Girl, Brownstones* (1959) have a yearning for
education and books that is often explicitly expressed, argues Gelfant, as voracious hunger.[8] The heroine in Yezierska's "How I
Found America" in her suitably titled 1920 collection *Hungry
Hearts* is most drawn, among the "golden legend[s] of the golden
country," to the axiom "Learning flows free like milk and honey":
"The words painted pictures in my mind. I saw before me free
schools, free colleges, free libraries, where I could learn and learn
and keep on learning."[9] For Russian-American writer Mary Antin,
who spread the gospel of education and Americanization reli-
giously, her school dress hanging on the wall for the first day of
school is a "consecration robe awaiting the beatific day."[10] In the
black tradition, education was doubly weighted because of its association with the subversive tradition of literacy during slavery.
Black writer Pauli Murray, in her autobiographical *Proud Shoes*
(1956), refers to a desire as primal as hunger, an "almost universal desire for education among the freedmen. . . . It struck deep
chords in human memory, like the first elemental urge of man to
lift himself from all fours and stand face to face with his God."[11]

Education held out to the ethnic woman a possibility for overcoming or bypassing the generational conflict her acculturation
often seemed to entail. Indeed, the ethnic woman who embraced a

self-made rather than an ancestrally determined identity often fantasized that she was reborn, or as Russian-American writer Elizabeth Stern put it, "made over again."[12] In her 1917 *My Mother and I,* an account of her education and Americanization, Stern writes that college "meant not only a new life; it meant to me a new self. Entering college was to me as if I had in truth been born anew."[13] For Mary Antin, whose 1912 *The Promised Land* begins with the remarkable statement, "I was born, I have lived, and I have been made over,"[14] America is a "pleasant nursery," her early years here "a second infancy."[15] As Werner Sollors has pointed out, rhetoric of this kind reflects a familiar American typology of regeneration and rebirth, implicit in the ideological rhetoric first set forth by those "first immigrants," the Puritans. It also implies, on a familial level, a rhetorical answer to the problem of generations raised in the immigrant's acculturation.[16]

The interplay of education and generational conflict is sometimes expressed in the heroine's fantasies of parenting not only herself but also her own parents, fantasies that had some symbolic grounding in reality. *Bread Givers*'s Sara Smolinsky imagines a child's dream of choosing her own parents: "Here, in America, where girls pick out for themselves the men they want for husbands, how grand it would be if the children could pick out their mothers and fathers."[17] Mary Antin argues the point explicitly:

> When I discovered my own friends, and ran home with them to convert my parents to a belief in their excellence, did I not begin to make my father and mother, as truly as they had ever made me? Did I not become the parent and they the children, in those relations of teacher and learner?[18]

In fact, in "those relations of teacher and learner," the immigrant often did act as a kind of parent to her parents in a different kind of generational conflict, and this is reflected in much ethnic women's fiction. It is by now a commonplace that a rift can develop between first-generation parents and their second-generation children brought about by the children's education in the new world values. Elizabeth Stern's *My Mother and I* is a representative text by an ethnic woman that recounts this process. In a recurrent scenario, the heroine brings home to her parents what she has learned in school; she convinces her parents not to allow the neighbors to borrow their tub, to transform a bedroom into a living room, and, in a particularly interesting passage, to celebrate Thanksgiving, the immigrant's typologically favorite holiday. Stern describes the family's turkey,

> which mother compared to ducks and chickens and geese that had been the pièce de résistance at ceremonies and weddings long past. From the head of the table . . . father told us many a tale from the Talmud while mother listened with rapt attention. Duly modest, I then explained the meaning of the day; though mother expressed her approval she advised me seriously that I must not give thanks only on one day and for one bird![19]

The heroine of *My Mother and I* is more successful in educating her mother than she is her father; her mother takes a vicarious pleasure in all her daughter's achievements, and knows the narrative of every book her daughter reads. Yet this mother is an embarrassment, and the narrator throws away the foreign lunches the mother prepares on the way to school each day. Her mother cannot learn English:

> As I grew older I refused to speak anything but English. In the street I would whisper constantly to mother to speak English. Mother would try, but the most she could manage was an occasional "You know" or a "please-ameecho" to introductions.[20]

Stern's emphasis on the vast gulf between her parents and herself is even broader, she feels, between her father and herself because of his rigid Judaism. In fact, Stern introduces a concept familiar to Antin and Yezierska, that her father belongs to the Middle Ages and she to the twentieth century. The father in *My Mother and I* says to the narrator, " 'I belong to the fifteenth century—and you, my daughter, to the twentieth,' "[21] and Stern says of her father, "His creed was that of Judaism, brought to the twentieth century from the fifteenth."[22] Mary Antin, in *The Promised Land,* writes, "I began life in the Middle Ages . . . and here I am still, your contemporary in the twentieth century, thrilling with your latest thought."[23] Yezierska, whose Sara Smolinsky decides her father "could never understand. He was the Old World. I was the New,"[24] in her widely anthologized 1920 story, "The Fat of the Land," creates an immigrant mother who, despite her children's success and her Riverside Drive apartment, is still most comfortable in the kitchen, entertaining old Lower East Side friends behind her servants' backs. Rejecting rich American fare, she still craves herring and onions. Her most understanding son puts the problem succinctly: "The trouble with us is that the ghetto of the Middle Ages and the children of the twentieth century have to live under one roof."[25]

To understand the way in which generational conflict came to be expressed in such a rhetoric, it is necessary to examine the meaning education has held in the ethnic experience. Through education, the ethnic heroine acquired the common language of America, one she could share only incompletely with her parents. Whether education succeeded in the Americanization of the ethnic population or not—and many revisionist historians, reminding us of the example of those blacks still excluded from equal educational opportunity, insist that it has not—it has always been perceived as the single most effective means toward that end.[26] In the first place, as I have argued, second-generation immigrants felt that education could "make them over" into Americans. The narrator of Stern's *My Mother and I,* recruited for high school by a representative from the Board of Education, is convinced not by his promise that education will help her in finding a profession, but by his argument that school provides "effective Americanism." Mary Antin titles the chapters describing her education "Initiation" and "My Country." A Yezierska heroine exhorts herself, "Make a person of yourself. . . . Begin to learn English. Make yourself for an American if you want to live in America.' "[27]

Although ethnic women's fiction often represents immigrant parents as thwarting their daughter's hunger for learning, generally immigrant parents valued the role education played in the Americanization of their children. Such novels as Betty Smith's *A Tree Grows in Brooklyn* (1947) and Louise Meriwether's *Daddy Was a Numbers Runner* (1971) present heroines whose mothers insist that education will save their daughters from the lives of drudgery they have suffered. The immigrant matriarch in Martha Ostenso's *O River, Remember!* (1943) sets as her pioneering colony's first priority in their new western settlement the hiring of a schoolteacher—though she knows the only available teacher will threaten her marriage. Mary Antin describes how her father "brought his children to school as if it were an act of consecration":

If education, culture, the higher life were shining things to be worshipped from afar, he still had a means whereby he could draw one step nearer to them. He could send his children to school, to learn all those things that he knew by fame to be desirable. . . . His children should be students, should fill his house with books and intellectual company; and thus he could walk by proxy in the Elysian fields of liberal learning. As for the children themselves, he knew no surer way to their advancement and happiness.[28]

In Antin's case, her father was eager to learn American ways, but her narrative reveals him as unqualified to become an American in the way that she feels she can. The education of the Antin children leads to a "sad process of disintegration of home life," "that inversion of normal relations which makes for friction," which Antin claims "is the cross that the first and second generations must bear, an involuntary sacrifice for the sake of future generations."[29]

Education played so crucial a part in the generational conflict engendered by acculturation in part because immigration authorities and social reformers believed that education was the principal means by which immigrants were Americanized. While it is problematic to discuss the role of the schools among immigrants without historical specificity, it is possible to work with generalizations that have been made about the schooling of immigrants in the years following the outbreak of World War I, when the Americanization movement was developed. Even if the ultimate goal was not to be realized—though many ethnic groups were Americanized in limited ways—the teleology of Americanization efforts shaped the kind of education immigrant children received. In this respect the rhetoric of reformers like Jane Addams and Jacob Riis (who declared, "The battle against the slums would be fought out, in, and around the public schools") is important, for it suggests the weight given to education in the Americanization experience.[30]

The role of education in Americanization is inextricably bound up with the goals of progressivism in education, so it is difficult to isolate those factors in the schooling of immigrants that are of particular importance in studying ethnicity. In general, school reform in the early twentieth century sought to enlarge the domain of the school's influence to include concern for health and family and community welfare, and to apply the principles of psychology and the social sciences to education. Implicit in the democratization of culture that historian of education Lawrence Cremin suggests accompanied progressive public schooling was the assumption that schools could respond to the needs of immigrants, and the broadened function of the school in American life ensured that education would prove a potent force in the lives of new Americans.[31]

In this context, the school came to be perceived, writes Cremin, "as an instrument par excellence for inducting newcomers into the 'responsibilities of citizenship.' "[32] In part because of fears about foreigners aroused by World War I, the goal of the education of immigrants was not to teach them about America but to teach them to behave as Americans. The implicit assumption of the Americanization movement was that there was *an* American identity which immigrants must assume as quickly as possible, and generally that identity was an Anglo-Saxon ideal.[33] Ellwood Cubberly, a representative figure in the Americanization movement and a leading proponent of Anglicization, wrote that the task at hand was

> to assimilate and amalgamate these people as part of our American race, and to implant in their children as far as can be done, the Anglo-Saxon conception of righteousness, law and order, and popular government, and to awaken in them a reverence for our democratic institutions and for those things in our national life which we as a people hold to be of abiding worth.[34]

Just as the forces of progressivism provided models of progress that were far from value-free in application, so the movement to Americanize the immigrant argued for a value-laden system of education. To teach the immigrants to behave as Americans was to teach a very specific mode of American behavior. Immigrants were to learn to speak the common language of America.[35] This model of education, which stressed the inculcation of patriotic values and civic pride, was to have consequences for a study of ethnic fiction that should become clear.

In his important study, *Assimilation in American Life* (1964), Milton Gordon argues that the Americanization process worked along the lines of a melting pot, but a melting pot refined to encompass the idea of transmutation: "rather than an impartial melting of the divergent cultural patterns from all immigrant sources, what has actually taken place has been more of a transforming of the later immigrant's specific cultural contributions into the Anglo-Saxon mold." He cites Will Herberg's influential argument in his *Protestant-Catholic-Jew* (1955) that, while American culture has partaken of its ethnic elements (as in the case of American cuisine), the ethnic American's self-image is *not* that of a composite of America's ethnic elements:

> It is nothing of the kind: the American's image of himself is still the Anglo-Saxon ideal it was at the beginning of our independent existence. The "national type" as ideal has always been, and remains, pretty well fixed. It is the *Mayflower*, John Smith, Davy Crockett, George Washington, and Abraham Lincoln that define the American's self-image, and that is true whether the American in question is a descendant of the Pilgrims or the grandson of an immigrant from southeastern Europe.[36]

In the Americanization process, the immigrant was confronted with an ideal type of American behavior: a model of patriotism bound up with legends of the founding fathers, flag-saluting, and celebration of national holidays. By adopting a new language, new rituals, new heroes, new founding fathers and thus metaphorical fathers, the immigrant was both to be adopted by and to possess America. These attributes of American identity were to replace the immigrant's old values much like a suit of new clothes, and the new clothes were to make the new man.

In ethnic women's fiction, the writer's emphasis on American education is marked by obsessive concern with these trappings of American identity—and, in particular, with the idea of the founding fathers. If the immigrant daughter understands the Thanksgiving holiday easily, analogizing her experience to the Pilgrims', Washington's Birthday awakens in the ethnic heroine a special reverence. Mary Antin's experience is again representative; the chapter in which she describes learning about George Washington is titled "My Country," for it is through adopting Washington as a metaphorical father that she feels she understands the concept of "my country."

Antin's "conversion" takes place in stages: first, Washington is an awesome religious figure whose name she cannot pronounce "without a pause." "Never had I prayed," Antin writes, "never had I called upon the Most Holy, in such utter reverence and worship as I repeated the simple sentences of my child's story of the patriot." Washington's example is momentarily daunting to Antin; like countless schoolchildren, she is fascinated by the legend of his truthfulness, and "was for the first time truly repentant of [her] sins." Moreover, he was brave and she is not, and of course, as a girl she can never be President: "This wonderful George Washington was as inimitable as he was irreproachable." With this new sense of humility, she also realizes that George Washington, "like a king in greatness," was a "Fellow Citizen."[37] Feeling tremors up and down her spine, she sings "America" and "The Star Spangled Banner" with the intensity of a patriot. From this point, Antin as the heroine of *The Promised Land* undergoes a transformation, and the book documents the experience of a self somehow made public, of one who has entered history. Even Antin's inner life is transformed: "I was no longer the central figure of my dreams; the dry weeds in the lane crackled beneath the tread of Heroes."[38] And, significantly, Washington provides the motivation for Antin's first act of public authorship. On the day of her school's Washington's Birthday celebration, Antin recites a clumsy poem ("Nothing but 'Washington' rhymed with 'Washington' ") dedicated to her new hero. As just over a hundred years ago Phyllis Wheatley, an ex-slave, had duly composed a poem addressed to Washington, so too Antin feels she must pay an act of homage in gratitude for her deliverance.[39] In spite of the poem's awkwardness—Antin's Washington writes the Constitution—she is lionized as an exemplary patriot, and her very public career is launched. She feels pride when her poem is published in a Boston newspaper, "but what gave a divine flavor to my happiness," she writes, "was the idea that I had publicly borne testimony to the goodness of my exalted hero, to the greatness of my adopted country."[40]

The figure of George Washington and the legends of the founding fathers provide for the ethnic woman a means by which she can insert herself into an American history marked by a paradoxically ahistorical rhetoric of national identity. The education of the American schoolchild in civic values and patriotic legends provides an important context for the adoption of a new national self. The poet Sylvia Plath, a daughter of German-Americans, described her public schooling in a 1963 essay, "America! America!," in a familiar rhetoric of ethnicity and Americanization, characterizing the "genuinely public" school she attended as "a great loud cats' bag of Irish Catholics, German Jews, Swedes, Negroes, Italians, and that rare, pure Mayflower dropping, somebody *English*. On to this steerage of infant citizens the doctrines of Liberty and Equality were to be, through the free, communal schools, impressed." Her description of the inculcation of patriotic values is ironically akin to Mary Antin's:

> Every morning, hands on hearts, we pledged allegiance to the Stars and Stripes, a sort of aerial altarcloth over teacher's desk. And sang songs full of powder smoke and patriotics to impossible, wobbly, soprano tunes. One high, fine song, "For purple mountain majesties above the fruited plain," always made the scampi-size poet in me weep. In those days I couldn't have told a fruited plain from a mountain majesty and confused God with George Washington (whose lamblike granny-face shone down at us also from the schoolroom wall between neat blinders of white curls). . . .[41]

The ethnic woman writer inevitably looks to models of American history to describe her own experience. A character in black writer Ann Petry's *The Street* (1946) realizes the problems of extrapolating a black female identity from American historical identity, yet unsuccessfully resists placing herself in a classic American tradition: in this case, that of Ben Franklin. Lutie Johnson, a black woman struggling to keep herself and her child alive on New York's 116th Street, counts out pennies for some hard rolls and is reminded of Ben Franklin's carefully bought loaf of bread:

> [She] grinned thinking, you and Ben Franklin. You ought to take one out and start eating it as you walk along 116th Street. Only you ought to remember while you eat that you're in Harlem and he was in Philadelphia a pretty long number of years ago. Yet she couldn't get rid of that feeling of self-confidence and she went on thinking that if Ben Franklin could live on a little bit of money and could prosper, then so could she.[42]

Of course, Washington and the founding fathers have awakened reverence and the sense of mission in American writers fairly consistently throughout the nation's history. Historian George Forgie, for instance, provides a compelling analysis of the familial quality of political rhetoric in America in *Patricide in the House Divided: A Psychological Interpretation of Lincoln and His Age* (1979). Forgie's premise is that the postheroic generation, the followers of Washington and the founding fathers, felt and acted upon the Oedipus situation, by which the sons play out an inevitable drama of filiopietism and patricide, which was to culminate in the fratricide of the Civil War. Though Forgie recognizes that a nation cannot have an Oedipal complex, he posits the "resolution" of this conflict in national identity with the end of the Civil War, and though he concentrates on "the sons," many of his observations are applicable in considering gender and ethnicity in American fiction. Forgie reminds us of the persuasive imaginative and associative resonance of a figure like Washington, and the way in which all Americans, within historical limitations to be sure, forge their national identities out of the necessarily familial context our "founding fathers" provided. Although Forgie's claim is for historical specificity, his persuasive insistence on Freudian principle belies such historicism, and allows us to extrapolate from familial rhetoric a relatively ahistorical national identity. Just as Washington was "only" metaphorically a father to the postheroic generation, in that metaphor in the Freudian scheme of things implies a remarkable closing of the gap between metaphor and referent, so Washington can retain metaphoric power for generations of (post-) postheroic sons—or daughters.[43]

This is particularly true in light of the rhetoric of rebirth that surrounds the immigrant's Americanization or the slave's emancipation. If one's own father is renounced, indeed, erased, the bastardized immigrant is free to adopt the founding fathers as her own. Moreover, by this act, she adopts an American identity and the sense of mission that Sacvan Bercovitch has located as the predominant feature of that identity. When one's "true fathers" are identified "not by their English background but by their exodus from Europe," as Bercovitch writes, one begins to participate in the "ritual of errand" by which Americans seek to fulfill the mission of those fathers. This is reflected in much of the rhetoric of immigrant writing, in which the immigrant virtually adopts the rhetoric of the Puritan jeremiad.[44]

This process can be seen clearly in another text by Mary Antin, a 1912 essay called "A Woman to Her Fellow-Citizens," which is a vehement defense of Theodore Roosevelt and the Progressive party. Antin again insists on the relevance of Washingtonian principle to contemporary affairs. She confides that as a schoolgirl she was envious of the Revolutionary patriots, feeling that "the Republic was finished, perfect from the hand of Washington." Now, however, she sees that even she, or especially she, has a role to play along with the founding fathers. Chiding her non-Progressive fellow-citizens, Antin writes: "They talk as if American history ended with our last war, whereas the most superficial survey of the life of the Nation shows that the Republic is still in the making." In fact, "the Progressive movement fits easily into a general outline of American history. The war of the Revolution was a fight for political standing-room; the Civil War was a fight for order within our domain; the Progressive movement is a fight for righteousness that shall hallow our heritage of independence and unity."[45]

It is to this aspect of American rhetoric that Margaret Mead addresses herself in her essay, "We Are All Third Generation," in her national character study, *And Keep Your Powder Dry* (1942). She makes the important point that American reverence for the founding fathers is often misunderstood as ancestor worship. On the contrary, argues Mead, "Washington does not represent the past to which one belongs by birth, but the past to which one tries to belong by effort. . . . Washington is not that to which Americans passionately cling but that to which they want to belong, and fear, in the bottom of their hearts, that they cannot and do not."[46] The future orientation of the American reverence for the past is reflected in the last lines of Mead's essay, "It is onward and upward, *towards* the world of Washington and Lincoln; a world in which we don't fully belong, but which we feel, if we work at it, we some time may achieve."[47]

The persuasiveness of this rhetoric is reflected in the heroine's inability to go beyond it even as she critiques it. Bercovitch's argument regarding dissident movements like feminism in the 19th century seems relevant here; critiques of America's mission were enlisted in the cause of the continuing revolution. It is implicitly difficult to challenge ideological rhetoric from within.[48] To continue with the case of George Washington, this problem emerges when ethnic heroines challenge the language of founding fathers as inappropriate and exclusionary. The mulatto heroine of Pauli Murray's autobiographical *Proud Shoes* claims that as a child she rejected the rhetorical allegiance American identity required:

> It is little wonder, then, perhaps, that I was strongly anti-American at six, that I hated George Washington, mumbled the oath of allegiance to the American flag which we children were taught in the second grade and was reluctant to stand up when we sang "The Star-Spangled Banner." I was unmoved by the story of Washington's crossing the Delaware, nor was I inspired by his truthfulness and valor. My thin knowledge of history told me that the George Washingtons and their kind had stolen the country from the American Indians, and I could lodge all my protests against this unforgivable piece of thievery.[49]

Murray uses the examples of the founding fathers to draw attention to the hypocrisy of patriotism in public schools that fail to educate black children. While she never reclaims George Washington, she does, nonetheless, describe her conversion to a chastened patriotism. At her grandfather's death, she proudly plants at his grave a Union flag in the midst of other graves decorated with Confederate flags. This act brings her eventually to pride in her American identity:

> Upon this lone flag I hung my nativity and the right to claim my heritage. It bore mute testimony to the irrefutable fact that I was an American and it helped to negate in my mind the signs and symbols of inferiority and apartness. In those early years there was little identity in my mind between the Union flag which waved over my grandfather's grave and the United States flag upon which I looked with so much skepticism at West End School. It would be a while yet before I realized that the two were the same.[50]

Inevitably, then, the heroine moves back within ideological formulations as she attempts to critique them. Language itself insists that she do so. Perhaps this is why the ethnic heroine seeks language, literacy, and the act of writing so insistently; she wants to reinvigorate American language to include women and outsiders. Only by learning the language can she begin. Those ethnic heroines who do not understand this process are often thwarted in their attempts at self-expression. The heroine of an uncollected Yezierska story, "Wild Winter Wind" (1927), is driven to despair by her inability to write. In another Washingtonian passage, the heroine explains her frustration with the rhetoric of the dominant culture. Ruth is trying to learn to write in her night-school classes:

> Every evening this week they were reading in my class how Washington crossed the Delaware. Here I'm burning with the crossing of my own Delaware. And I have to choke down my living story for a George Washington, dead a hundred years. All that waste, only to get the teacher's help for a few minutes after class.

Ruth analogizes rightly; she is crossing her own Delaware, but she does not recognize the authority this gives to her experience. She inserts herself within American rhetoric but fails to expand its limits.[51]

The use of the language of the founding fathers not only places the ethnic woman back into an ideology that has excluded her, but provides her with the opportunity to expand that rhetoric to include her, in effect by subverting it. It is possible to trace this process by examining the use by women writers of characters named after the founding fathers. When black writer Pauline Hopkins names a black boy who sells chitlins in the Washington market General Washington, she is not simply responding to the preponderance of Washingtons in the black population. The hero of her 1900 "General Washington: A Christmas Story," a black orphan redeemed from a moral underground by discovering the meaning of Christ in Christmas, is named Washington because Hopkins wishes to extend the rhetoric of American experience—in this case, the sentimental conversion tale—to include him. He also takes his name from the Washington Market of which he is a *general;* he commands the marketplace that has exploited him. Significantly, a portrait of Washington hangs over the mantelpiece of Uncle Tom's cabin; he smiles on us all, Stowe reminds us.[52]

I would like to turn at this point to the issue of naming, not only because the notion of an ideological rhetoric is challenged and expanded in ethnic traditions in which children are named after the founding fathers, but because the self-conscious use of names in women's fiction suggests connections between women and language that shed light on the ethnic woman's relationship to American rhetoric and to America, as well as to the act of authorship. The very act of naming a child ties language to action in a way that is fundamental to the woman writer who seeks to reinvigorate the American language.

Moreover, in certain ethnic traditions, and particularly the black and Indian traditions, one's name is inextricable from identity. Eugene Genovese, in *Roll, Jordan, Roll,* traces the importance of naming in black culture from slavery to freedom, when blacks began to choose their own names. Rather than selecting new names randomly or contenting themselves with given names, ex-slaves attributed special importance to their names, considering them historical determinants. Explaining why many blacks kept their slaveholders' family names, Genovese writes, "The important thing was to establish a real history, preferably well back in time but in any event a family experience. . . . One way or another, the name had to be 'real'; it had to embody a living history without which genuine identity could not have become possible."[53] Citing the popular spiritual lines, "O nobody knows who I am, who I am/ Till the Judgment morning," Genovese suggests blacks' awareness of the complex relationship between naming and social identity: "Slave practice in its many variations [in naming] represented a striving toward personal identity and self-respect, which the names marked."[54]

Ralph (Waldo) Ellison, in "Hidden Name and Complex Fate," states the problem succinctly: "Our names, being the gift of others, must be made our own." In a complex argument, he suggests that blacks, many of whom he feels can be characterized as "manipulators of words," realize that language is not action and names are not qualities because they are in fact so aware of the suggestiveness of language and of context. Because of this, however, they can reinvigorate language, reclaim their names, and, in a seeming paradox, make language action. Moreover, they can inherit the legacies their borrowed names both efface and reinscribe:

And when we are reminded so constantly that we bear, as Negroes, names originally possessed by those who owned our enslaved grandparents, we are apt, especially if we are potential writers, to be more than ordinarily concerned with the veiled and mysterious events, the fusions of blood, the furtive couplings, the business transactions, the violations of faith and loyalty, the assaults; yes, and the unrecognized and unrecognizable loves through which our names were handed down to us.[55]

Given this tradition, it is not surprising that ethnic women writers use the concept of naming to draw together issues like the relationship of language to action, the meaning of generations and inheritance in ethnic identity, and the viability of American rhetoric. The following passage from Ann Petry's *The Narrows* (1953) suggests the complex way in which these issues are related. The novel's hero, Link (for Lincoln) Williams, reflects on Abraham Lincoln and the meaning of his name:

> The Emancipator with the big toobig bony hands, the sad deep-set eyes, the big bony hands almost always resting on the outsize knees, an outsize man with outsize ideas. Man of the people. . . . All men free and equal pursuit of happiness—words on paper and he believed them. Emancipation Proclamation Williams. Named after him. Why? The women name the children, reward for services rendered, award for valor, for the act of birth, the act of creation. So the creator names the child. What did my mother mean? What was it? Act of gratitude? A way of saying thankyou?[56]

The Emancipation Proclamation, "words on paper" that Lincoln believed, is brought to life in Link Williams. Link's mother, in naming her child after Lincoln, not only performs an "act of gratitude" but reanimates history. Link Williams, in investigating his name, is acting analogously to the writer, reconnecting language to action.

The connection between names—or language—and identity emerges in all of its complexity in a very recent novel by an important black woman writer, Toni Morrison's *Song of Solomon* (1977). This novel represents a culmination of an ethnic female tradition that seeks to question the meaning not only of the common language of America but of language itself. *Song of Solomon,* the story of Macon Dead, his son Milkman Dead, his sister Pilate, and the Dead ancestors, is a novel obsessed with the meaning of names. In black history, Morrison acknowledges, names have often been conferred as meaningless entities. Macon Dead's father got his awful name from a clerk registering him at the Freedmen's Bureau after emancipation, got it, Macon says, " 'messed up because he couldn't read.' " Macon's mother liked the name; she believed that the Dead name could make the past dead—an assumption Milkman will challenge: " 'Said it was new and would wipe out the past. Wipe it all out.' "[57]

Morrison herself likes to play with the invocative nature of names, describing how the Dead family had named their horse, her foal, their cow, and their hog President Lincoln, Mary Todd, Ulysses S. Grant, and General Lee respectively. The boy Macon extrapolates the personalities of America's heroes from the personalities of these farm animals: "Macon had always thought of Lincoln with fondness since he had loved him first as a strong, sturdy, gentle, and obedient horse. He even liked General Lee, for one spring they slaughtered him and ate the best pork outside Virginia." Macon reflects to his son, " 'General Lee was all right by me. . . . Finest general I ever knew. Even his balls was tasty.' "[58] Morrison not only manages to call Robert E. Lee a pig, she insists that even names chosen playfully have meaning.

Milkman, the novel's hero, has a name that derives from an act associated ambivalently with the maternal: a passerby coined the nickname, having seen Ruth Dead nursing her son standing up in knee pants. Milkman's quest, which culminates in his deciphering a childrens' song—the song of Solomon, is to rediscover the invocative power of names. In a world in which men and women are possessed of "names they got from yearnings, gestures, flaws, events, mistakes, weaknesses," names, Morrison asserts, bear witness. "Under the recorded names were other names, just as 'Macon Dead,' recorded for all time in some dusty file, hid from view the real names of people, places, and things. Names that had meaning. No wonder Pilate put hers [in a box on an earring] in her ear. When you know your name, you should hang onto it, for unless it is noted down and remembered, it will die when you do."[59] The riddle of Milkman's ancestry and of his proper name is as difficult to unravel as the mystery of the sack of bones his aunt Pilate carries with her as her "inheritance," bones that Milkman discovers are her father's, and the burying of which will bring death and finally a kind of transcendence for both Pilate and Milkman. Not a simple reclaiming of ancestry and right names, Milkman's quest and Pilate's obsession represent the complicated relationship between legacy and selfhood in the American ethnic tradition. Names for Morrison signal an identity derived from a re-created past. The individual must decipher and reanimate language and history, and learn the derivation of his name.

In a larger sense, Morrison argues that the writer must constantly examine the ramifications and connotations of American rhetoric. The name "President Lincoln," invoking as it does attributes of strength and steadiness, is perhaps more usefully applied to a horse than chanted with the reverence with which Mary Antin pronounces the name of Washington. Again, it is possible to trace a growing self-consciousness in the woman writer's use of language, much as it is possible to see the tradition of ethnic female authorship as one that moves toward authorial and linguistic authority. For accomplished writers like Hurston, Morrison, and Stein, the trappings of American identity, the mechanical rotes of the rhetoric of nationality, lose their fetishistic qualities and begin to acquire new meaning. Exclusionary language is expanded, national heroes reclaimed in personal and individualistic terms.

To return to the idea of generational conflict, with which this chapter began, it is possible to trace in this tradition a corresponding development of a more complex and less mechanistic view of generations. Writers like Yezierska and Antin struggle to cast off their own literal fathers to become children of America. A writer like Morrison does not so much "reclaim her roots" as discover the meaning of ancestry. Generations—or history—are defined less narrowly, in a sense, less privately. On the other hand, what the ethnic woman moves toward is a sense of history and generations that is personalized rather than private. She need no longer struggle against her own literal father but is free to examine her place in history.

CHAPTER 5

"America is a lover's land": The Pocahontas Marriage, Part I

Ethnic women's fiction, as I have argued in my introduction, constitutes a questioning and reexploration of what is perhaps the single most important received metaphor of female ethnic identity—the story of Pocahontas. The legend is about love and marriage between an ethnic woman and a white man; it is also about sexuality. The dominant features of the Pocahontas story are those that every schoolchild remembers: she saved one white man, and she married another one. Pocahontas, who seems to have offered herself rather buoyantly to the man she saved from death and to whom she passed on the secrets of the wilderness, was rejected by John Smith and eventually married John Rolfe—for legend, a distinctly asymmetrical choice. The persistence of the legend despite this aesthetic flaw suggests that Americans have conflated the features of the Pocahontas story into one hugely rich and contradictory image. Philip Young, an early student of what a recent scholar has termed the "Pocahontas perplex," conflates Pocahontas's rescue of Smith and her marriage to Rolfe by insisting that her ritualistic act of laying her head over Smith's implied marriage. He insists that precisely what moves us in the Pocahontas story

is that her candor was that of a bride. . . . The ritual we feel in her action is itself an unorthodox and dramatic ceremony of marriage, and we are touched. We see Pocahontas at the moment of womanhood, coming voluntarily from the assembly to the altar, where she pledges the sacrifice of her own integrity for the giving of life. . . . It is an act which bespeaks total renunciation, the giving up of home, land, faith, self, and perhaps even life, that life may go on.

Young suggests that this element—the sacrificial aspect of her marriage—explains the interest women writers have taken in the Pocahontas legend. He continues, "Perhaps this helps to explain why it
is that what, in its flattery of him, is at first glance so much a man's
story should be greatly promoted by women. Apparently it is a
very pleasant vicarious experience for us all."[1]

At first glance, Young would "apparently" seem right. Certainly there is little to distinguish female-authored Pocahontas
treatments from the sentimental male-authored norm. The sacrifice
entailed in the "marriage" that Young rightly equates with Pocahontas's act may have appealed to the arguably martyred and
sentimental 19th-century sensibility—as, for instance, in the verses
of Pocahontas eulogizer Lydia Huntley Sigourney[2]—but it must be
remembered that that sensibility was in its turn a culturally patriarchal requirement of Victorian womanhood. Young is right, I
think, when he characterizes the American obsession with Pocahontas as "vicarious"—especially in the case of American women.
Among the complex of identifications provided by the Pocahontas
story *is* "the giving up of home, land, faith, self, and perhaps even
life, that life may go on" that Young speaks of. But it seems unlikely, given the ramifications of such a renunciation, that the
American woman's vicarious experience of the Pocahontas story
has been, as Young suggests, "very pleasant."

The metaphorical dimensions of the Pocahontas story have been
substantially different for women from that which they have obtained for men. Rayna Green, in her article on the image of Indian
women in American culture, flatly concludes that Pocahontas is an
"intolerable metaphor."[3] The Pocahontas legend, in its symbolic
capacity, insists that the Indian woman fill an impossible variety of
functions. Green writes about the Indian woman, but her remarks
have application to American women of all ethnicities:

> Both her nobility as a Princess and her savagery as a Squaw are
> defined in terms of her relationships with male figures. If she
> wishes to be called a Princess, she must save or give aid to white
> men. The only good Indian . . . rescues and helps white men.
> But the Indian woman is even more burdened by this narrow
> definition of a "good Indian," for it is she, not the males, whom
> white men desire sexually. Because her image is so tied up with
> abstract virtue—indeed, with America, she must remain Mother

Goddess-Queen. But acting as a real female, she must be partner
and lover of Indian men, a mother to Indian children, and an
object of lust to white men. To be Mother, Queen and lover is,
as Oedipus' mother, Jocasta, discovered, difficult and perhaps
impossible.[4]

Following Leslie Fiedler's example, Green suggests that the image
of the Indian woman in American culture has been split into that
of the noble Princess and that of the randy and fertile squaw (or
Fiedler's "anti-Pocahontas"), and that the image of the Indian
woman has suffered from what is in effect a cultural whore/ma-
donna complex.[5] But it is precisely because the Pocahontas figure
is expected to embody *both* aspects of this image that hers is so
convenient, compelling, and ultimately intolerable a legend. Here
it is helpful to recall Philip Young's suggestion that Pocahontas's
ritual of salvation and sacrifice is arresting because it implies "the
candor of a bride." Pocahontas's imaginative power lies in her
sexuality, or, more precisely, in the promise she holds out of sexual
union between a white male representative of the dominant culture
and an exotic, or ethnic, woman. Her story functions as a compelling locus for American feeling toward what W. E. B. DuBois
has called the "stark, ugly, painful, beautiful" fact of American
life: miscegenation, or sexual relations between white men and
ethnic women.[6]

Miscegenation—or intermarriage—is, implicitly or explicitly, a
predominant theme of American ethnic women's fiction. For reasons that I will detail, the notion of sexual relations between an
ethnic woman and a white—or "non-ethnic" man—allowed the
ethnic woman to explore concurrently problems of female ethnicity
and female sexuality and to suggest conclusions about the role of
sexuality in ethnic female identity. As I will argue, the ethnic
woman writer's realization of the centrality of miscegenation to
the ethnic identity varies widely both in terms of extent and expression. It is in the nature of the human imagination to metaphor-
ize sexuality—or, in these writers, miscegenation—often in terms
of a classically American rhetoric of love and marriage. On the
other hand, when the sexual content of the metaphor emerges most
starkly—as in relations between black women and white men—the
idea itself becomes the indicator of a disruption, and the fiction of
those writers who consider this aspect of miscegenation in some

senses moves beyond metaphor. In this chapter, I will examine the ways in which ethnic women writers themselves in effect metaphorized sexuality, and in turn questioned its metaphorization and the effects such metaphorization had on their own lives. Just as in the last chapter, my subject is the use to which women have put American myths, metaphors, and symbols.

It is not my argument that all intermarriage, or miscegenation, occurred only between white men and ethnic women, although in the case of black and Indian women, historical evidence suggests that has overwhelmingly been the case. Indeed, in the jumble of ethnicities that America has become, it is difficult to say who is the "ethnic" partner. Nevertheless, the union of a white male and an ethnic woman continues to possess substantial metaphorical weight in the American imagination. If the concept of intermarriage or miscegenation is central to American ethnicity, the particular contours it assumes in the female ethnic experience need to be clarified. The ethnic woman writer sees in the Pocahontas metaphor both her sexual and her ethnic oppression. Precisely because this oppression cuts across ethnic lines, the ethnic woman writer is especially prone to feminist representation of the metaphor in her fiction, which in turn is especially accessible to feminist interpretation. The Pocahontas metaphor represents sexuality seen through a prism of ethnicity, and as such suggests ways in which the American female identity can better be understood.

Furthermore, intermarriage seems to yoke in a rather neat fashion the concepts of ethnicity and American identity. As I will argue, intermarriage is not only a metaphor but, in a theoretical sense, a necessary condition for, or at least a shortcut to, Americanization. Werner Sollors, explaining the complicated and often conflicted relationship between ethnic and American identity, suggests that American identity might profitably be understood as a relationship "in law" and ethnicity as a relationship "by blood." Citing Horace Kallen's well-known statement, "Men change their clothes, their politics, their wives, their religions, their philosophies, to a greater or lesser extent: they cannot change their grandfathers," Sollors explains:

> Grandfathers are imagined as "blood," "wives" are viewed as "law." In America, we feel "filiopietism," but we pledge "alle-

giance" to the country. To say it as bluntly as possible: American identity is like marriage, ethnicity is like ancestry.[7]

In this sense, intermarriage, whether legally solemnized or sexually consummated, is a solemnization or consummation of American ethnic identity. This formulation is, of course, related to the paradox of Americanization: it both worked absolutely ("We are all Americans, in spite of our ethnicity") or failed utterly ("We are all Americans because of our ethnicity"). By marrying into the American "family," the ethnic woman combines filiopietism and allegiance. The conflicts that this might theoretically entail (marrying within the family is incest) mirror the literal conflicts that intermarriage sometimes psychically entails (in exogamous relations, when parentage is unknown, incest is a real possibility). The ethnic woman writer seldom approaches the idea of intermarriage without some awareness of these difficulties.

In another sense, intermarriage has been a compelling and difficult idea because it questions our notions of difference and sameness, the boundaries of the self. The ethnic lover is attractive to the white man as the other, but the intimacy involved in sexual union, the "mingling" of two "bloods," calls into question individuation or identity itself. Winthrop D. Jordan, in his *White Over Black,* explains the ambivalence historically attached to sexual relationships between black women and white men:

> [In interracial union] desire and aversion rested on the bedrock fact that white men perceived Negroes as being *both alike and different* from themselves. Without perception of similarity, no desire and no widespread gratification was possible. Without perception of difference, on the other hand, no aversion to miscegenation nor tension concerning it could have arisen. Without perception of difference, of course, the term *miscegenation* had no meaning.[8] (Jordan's emphasis)

The paradox inherent in Jordan's explanation had, of course, paradoxical expression in historical reality: the *partus sequitur ventrem* designation of slave status to those with "one drop" of black blood, the attribution of race to a child on the basis of the mother's race, the ambiguous status of the mulatto, the phenomenon of the passing black, and so on. Fiction about miscegenation is often shaped by these paradoxes. The attraction of the mulatto as a subject for

ethnic fiction can best be explained by the fact that as a product
of an interracial union he represents a testing of the boundaries of
the self, or, in Simone Vauthier's terms, a *"cas limite,* the smallest
difference that marks the point where the Other turns into the
Same, when the either/or disjunction is no longer possible."[9] Because the mulatto is usually illegitimate, denied his father's name,
denied his inheritance, he becomes a locus for cultural anxiety
over ancestry, the meaning of the past, and—because parentage is
undefined—incest, and, for the ethnic woman writer, a locus for
protest against the disruption of inheritance interracial union can
represent.

At this point it might be useful to attempt a definition of terms.
Unfortunately, and perhaps significantly, the term has not been
invented for what I wish to define. "Intermarriage" refers, of
course, to a marital relationship, which in many cases was not an
option for the ethnic woman. It would be an insult to the experience of black women, for instance, to term sexual relations between black women and white men "intermarriage." Before emancipation, intercourse with white planters, son of planters, overseers,
or slave traders was by and large not a voluntary arrangement;
in many cases it amounted to rape, and marriage was never
possible under the law. Although historians have argued significant
exceptions to the concept of forced miscegenation, and although
conditions probably changed to some extent during Reconstruction and beyond, the sexual and economic oppression historically
and psychically implicit in sexual relationships between black
women and white men makes it impossible to apply the term
"intermarriage" to such unions, and in these cases I have usually
used the term "miscegenation." "Miscegenation," however, implies
sexual intercourse between "non-white" and "white" races, and
cannot accurately be applied to all unions between white men and
ethnic women. Interestingly, such relationships, when they do not
involve black, Indian, or Asian women, are discussed in the socio-
logical literature as "intermarriages." David Heer, in his essay on
intermarriage in the *Harvard Encyclopedia of American Ethnic
Groups*, divides his subject under the headings of "Intermarriage
between National-Origin Groups," "Interfaith Marriage," and
"Interracial Marriage." As I have suggested, "interracial marriage"
is, as valid as it may be today, a misleading term to apply histori-

cally.[10] On the other hand, no term exists for nonmarital unions between white men and ethnic women who are not black, Indian, or Asian; the term "intermarriage" suggests that such unions were legally sanctioned—and many of those that I wish to discuss were not—and implies rather serious racist and class-based assumptions about marriage as an exclusively "white" institution.[11]

Out of this muddle of definition—which raises in turn troubling questions of defining "race" and "ethnicity"—one thing becomes clear: "intermarriage" or "miscegenation" has not been considered along lines of gender, which I will try to do here. I have been forced to use the terms arbitrarily and often inaccurately, but the reader should keep in mind the dimensions of the Pocahontas legend: that of a white male, representative of the dominant culture, in sexual union with an alien or "ethnic" woman.

The concept of "difference and sameness" embedded in the concept of intermarriage operates on two different levels, neither of which excludes the other. On the one hand, it expresses some of the anxieties about taboo, incest, and inheritance that I have outlined above, and that I will explore more fully in my next chapter. On another level, the concept suggests the initial reason for the attraction that impels the union, and invests the metaphor with a not inconsiderable charm. On this level, intermarriage between white men and ethnic women becomes a symbolic literalization of the American dream, both in terms of success and of love: variously, it suggests an assertion of melting-pot idealism, of the forging of a "new man," of Cinderella success, of love "regardless of race, creed, or color," of the promise of America itself.

Most of the fiction discussed in this chapter, which embraces the benign or romantic dimensions of the Pocahontas marriage, is predominantly either by or about immigrants rather than blacks: I do not think this is entirely accidental. Black women have been much more aware of the racial and sexual oppression historically endemic to interracial sex. Writers like Gayl Jones, whose subject in her 1975 *Corregidora* is the horrifyingly violent ramifications of interracial rape, are not likely to see the Pocahontas story as symbolic of American promise. Furthermore, it is possible that non-black writers are incapable of recognizing the psychological "underside" of intermarriage. The possibility exists, but I do not think it is borne out. The two dimensions of the intermarriage metaphor are not mutually exclusive; in fact, each dimension contains, of course, aspects of the other. The woman writer who embraces the metaphor of intermarriage as one of promise just as surely interlards her fiction with expressions of protest, anxieties about taboo and inheritance, subversions of the metaphor; the woman writer who explores the "underside" of the metaphor often asserts, if not the *value* of the metaphor, at least its aptness, its factuality. The subject of *Corregidora,* in this sense, is the identity of the heroine as defined by a violently racist, but horribly apt, metaphor. The potentiality of the metaphor is, in those writers who reject it, expressed in terms of their disillusionment with it. Because of its very richness and complexity, the metaphor is seldom used without ambivalence and ambiguity.

For those ethnic women, and particularly immigrant women, who considered the Pocahontas story symbolic of promise, marriage with a native-born white male could entail, in one fell swoop, love, success, Americanization, freedom from her family, modernity, and participation in the American way. Melting-pot ideology reinforced the ethnic woman's attempt to actualize the promise: though few purveyors of this ideology made the point explicitly, something sexual had to happen if a Crèvecoeurian new man was to emerge from the pot. It is perhaps typical of our cultural sexual uncertainty that the sexual nature of the melting-pot image is vague, contradictory, and prone to racist interpretation. In many of its guises, the melting-pot itself is female, both sexual and maternal. Werner Sollors, in his defense of the much-maligned melting-pot image, draws on Crèvecoeur's reference to the broad lap of the Alma Mater on which immigrants are received to be reborn, in order to trace a persistent tradition of a rejuvenating and fruitful mother figure in whose lap or womb immigrants are reborn. Pocahontas herself figures in this maternal/sexual complex, equated as she is with an Indian Ceres, or the American land itself, "like a woman, ripe, waiting to be taken," in Hart Crane's words. This female pot, womb, or lap is conceived, significantly, both maternally and sexually. Sollors points out that only men seem to partake of the melting-pot experience in melting-pot iconography; he suggests that "sexual polarization . . . is absent from the portraiture of reborn immigrants; and what takes its place is the polarization between men and land."[12] In light of the persistent cultural equation of the land with woman, however, such polarization is profoundly sexual. If the melting-pot is female, to be both impregnated and life-giving, it is not surprising that the image has historically provoked profound psychosexual ambivalence, and that such adjectives as "seething," "simmering," "devouring," "curdling," and complexes of female imagery relating to cooking and weaving attach to it.[13]

Not only does the melting-pot function culturally as a complex sexual/maternal image and a locus for sexual ambivalence, but also in a more literal way as a brothel or marriage-bed, in which intercourse between ethnicities can occur freely. The language of "fusing," "blending," "weaving," and "amalgamation" makes explicit the necessity of sexual union if a "new man" is to be "born"; in effect, it reminds melting-pot romanticists that ethnic women are not their mothers but their mates. The resultant ambivalence must have been profound, and perhaps lies at the heart of the vigorous renunciations of the melting-pot made by racial supremacists like Henry Fairchild, who criticized the melting-pot concept because it, in Philip Gleason's words, "focussed on the process of interaction rather than the result."[14]

The ethnic woman writer, confronted with the complex image of the melting-pot, tended to take it as a symbol of promise, a sanction for and encouragement of sexual union with a native-born American. In fact, she often literalized the erotic dimensions of the image. Anzia Yezierska, a Jewish-American writer obsessed with the possibilities and implications of a Pocahontas union, draws heavily on the mandate of the melting-pot in her romances of intermarriage. " 'Are we not the mingling of the races? The oriental mystery and the Anglo-Saxon clarity that will produce a new race of men?' " wistfully hopes one of Yezierska's fictional lovers.[15]

If such union was sanctioned by melting-pot ideology, it had implicit and profound attraction for the ethnic woman. America held out to the immigrant woman freedom from arranged matches and the right to choose her own husband. " 'America is a lover's land' " writes Hannah Hayyeh to her Old World neighbors in Yezierska's 1920 story, "The Miracle."[16] In their countries of origin, immigrant women often would have been married according to their parents' wishes. In European Judaism, for instance, the language of love did not exist. Abraham Cahan wrote, "If a Jewish bridegroom loved his bride, one said 'He wants her,' or 'She pleases him,' or 'He faints for her.' But love—love was for gentiles, primarily the wealthy gentry."[17] In America, however, immigrant women discovered the language of love, and dismayed their parents by choosing as husbands men they loved. In 1916 Isaac Goldberg commented,

> The modern Jewish girl is feminist enough to see the degrading commercialism inherent in the *shadchen's* trade and to recognize the insult to her individualism which is thus implied.[18]

But love often implied a new commercialism; the rhetoric of love is, after all, the rhetoric of persuasion, and in fact love was advertised in the New World as a desirable commodity. The Americanization of the immigrant population was to a considerable extent based on principles of advertising; just as surely as they had been lured to America by promises, so immigrants were "sold" on the American way of life, Americanized by advertisements for it, through various forms of mass culture. Movies of the century's early decades, for instance, as Stuart and Elizabeth Ewen suggest, provided "a visual textbook to American culture, a blend of romantic ideology and practical tips for the presentation of self in the new marriage market of urban life."[19] The commodification of romantic love was a powerfully influential factor in the Americanization of the immigrant woman, who was herself commodified on the marriage "market."

Raoul de Roussy de Sales, writing for the *Atlantic Monthly* in 1938 on the difference between European and American conceptualizations of love, commented on the American "national problem" of love:

> In America the idea seems to be that love, like so much else, should be sold to the public, because it is a good thing. The very word, when heard indefinitely, becomes an obsession. It penetrates one's subconscious like the name of some unguent to cure heartaches or athlete's foot. It fits in with the other advertisements, and one feels tempted to write to the broadcasting station for a free sample of this thing called "Love."[20]

Love has always been woven into the rhetoric of America, a rhetoric that immigrants, willingly or not, inevitably moved within.

To varying degrees, ethnic women writers accepted the terms of the discourse. In a 1935 story by Tess Slesinger, a Jewish-American writer often drawn to immigrant themes, America explicitly represents the promise of love. Although Mariedel, the heroine of "The Times So Unsettled Are," does not emigrate from Vienna to marry an American, she equates America with successful love and marriage. In Vienna Mariedel and Heinrich, lovers who cannot marry because "the times so unsettled are," are befriended by Molly and Richard, two American newlyweds honeymooning in Vienna. Mariedel perceives a difference in the quality of the two couples' love, a national difference:

> Mariedel knew that theirs was a different sort of love; they had been brought up, Mariedel and Heinrich, in too much poverty and change, and their love was more of a refuge than a source of gayety to them, it was a necessity as bitter as their need for bread.[21]

Urged by Richard and Molly (whom Mariedel calls Mähli) to come to America, where conditions are better for lovers, Heinrich and Mariedel choose instead to continue their socialist activity in Europe. After Heinrich is killed on the parapets of the Karl Marx Workers' Home (love *is* doomed in the Old World), Mariedel resolves to travel to the "lovers' land": "And perhaps it was this that she was really going to America for, to find [her love] again in the lives of Richard and Mähli and keep it somehow vicariously lighted in herself through them."[22] In a pattern that becomes familiar to the reader of ethnic women's fiction, Slesinger deflates the American promise of love: Mariedel, arriving in New York, finds Richard and Molly divorced. Slesinger's political message is clear. Mariedel thinks, " 'Here in America too—the times unsettled are.' "[23]

Implicit in the notion of America as lovers' land, where a woman was free to choose her husband, was the notion that her choice could also bring her wealth and success. The connection between love and success was a complicated one, and can perhaps best be understood in the "selling" of Cinderella marriage stories to the American public. The pauperess-marries-millionaire stories of Anna Walling and especially Rose Pastor Stokes received extensive coverage in the popular press, capturing the imaginations of immigrant women. Rose Pastor, a Polish immigrant who came to America after ten years in London, interviewed millionaire Graham Stokes in 1903 as a reporter for *Tageblatt,* an orthodox Jewish weekly. In her enthusiastic but oddly contradictory write-up, she expressed her admiration for Stokes's "Americanness":

> Mr. Stokes is very tall and I believe, six feet of thorough democracy. A thorough-bred gentleman, a scholar and a son of a millionaire, he is a man of the people, even as Lincoln was.[24]

Stokes, perhaps intrigued by this description of himself as a democratic Republican millionaire populist gentleman scholar, arranged to meet Pastor, and the two became engaged. After the announcement of their marriage in 1905, Sunday supplements enthusiastically heralded the "ghetto romance," emphasizing Pastor's humble origins and her Judaism. The couple insisted that the difference in their backgrounds and religions presented no obstacle (although Stokes was quoted as saying, "We both consider ourselves Christians. She is of Jewish ancestry; I am not.") and seemed willing to act as endorsements for the romantic ideal they represented.[25]

This is Pocahontas converted, renamed Lady Rebecca, bedecked in European finery, the toast of the British court. This dimension of the legend had immense attraction for ethnic women writers; references to the Pastor/Stokes story appear in much immigrant fiction, and Yezierska based her 1923 *Salome of the Tenements* on Pastor's "conquest." It is, of course, the story of Cinderella—or *Pamela*—rewritten, with an ethnic twist. Black writer Ann Petry, in her 1953 novel *The Narrows,* describes how a butler entrances the Scottish housekeeper and maids with the story of his previous employer's son, who married a Polish coal-miner's daughter:

> Then Powther, sure of his audience, would tell all over again the world's favorite fairy story, how Cinderella (twentieth century so she was the daughter of a coal miner) and the prince (youngest son of the richest man in the United States) were married. The housekeeper and the maids, all the female help, would lean forward, listening, listening.[26]

What seems to have captured the ethnic female imagination in the ethnic Cinderella story was the fact that love and material gain seemed to mesh so felicitously. Sociologist Robert Merton has pointed out a paradox of interclass marriages that seems to apply in this case: such marriages seem to make such good sense for the lower-class (or immigrant) partner and at the same time they are supported by the illogic of "the romantic complex, which emphasizes the dominant importance of 'love' rather than utilitarian calculations in choosing a marriage partner."[27] The ethnic woman, attracted by this paradox, was as often as not undone by it. In fact, the ultimate failure of the Pocahontas marriage is the dominant theme of those writers who make it their subject. In most cases, love is confused with the attraction of opposites, and the native-born male rejects the ethnic woman for the very qualities he once sought in her. John Smith may have learned the secrets of the wilderness from Pocahontas, but the latter-day native-born male had little to gain from a union with a foreign-born exotic—beyond the alleviation of his anxieties about immigrants and a little titillation: essentially, he already possessed America.

In the fiction of Anzia Yezierska, this problem is played out analogically and obsessively. In a recurrent Yezierska scenario, America is embodied in a cold, rational, successful American male, who is initially as eager for union as his warm, emotional, distinctly foreign counterpart. In fact, the heroine's foreignness is the basis for the initial attraction. When "The Miracle" 's heroine Sara Reisel tells her lover, " 'I'm burning to get calm and sensible like the born Americans. . . . How can I learn to keep myself on earth like the born Americans?' " he replies,

> But I don't want you to get down on earth like the Americans. That is just the beauty and wonder of you. . . . If you would only know how much you could teach us Americans. You are the promise of centuries to come. You are the heart, the creative pulse of America to be.[28]

For the immigrant woman, marriage with an American represents the goal she strives for—assimilation and Americanization. "Wings" and "Hunger" in Yezierska's 1920 collection, *Hungry Hearts,* relate the relentless striving of Shenah Pessah for John Barnes, who is sociologically slumming on New York's Lower East Side. Even after Barnes rejects her, marriage with him retains its metaphorical value: " 'Him I want—he ain't just a man. . . . He is the golden hills on the sky.' "[29] The possibility of regaining him shapes her intense efforts at Americanization:

"By day and night you got to push yourself up till you get to him and can look him in his face eye to eye," she exhorts herself.[30] Disdaining the herring and onions offered her by her worthy immigrant suitor, Shenah explains her continued determination to become American: " 'There's something in me—I can't help—that so quickly takes on to the American taste. It's as if my outside skin only was Russian; the heart in me is for everything of the New World—even the eating.' "[31]

The sense of a relationship based on a similar tension seems to have characterized Yezierska's brief but intense friendship with educator John Dewey, as Dewey scholar Jo Ann Boydston has recently argued.[32] In 1904 Yezierska received a degree from Teacher's College of Columbia University in domestic science. After years of frustrated boredom in her teaching efforts, she seems to have presented herself dramatically at Dewey's office in 1917; he enrolled her in his seminar on social and practical philosophy. During their one- or two-year friendship, Yezierska studied a Polish community in Philadelphia under Dewey's direction, and later described this experience in her 1932 novel, *All I Could Never Be*. Evidence from this novel and from Yezierska's semi-autobiographical 1950 *Red Ribbon on a White Horse* suggests that Dewey saw in Yezierska the possibility her fictional lovers initially see in the women they court. *Red Ribbon*'s John Morrow writes to the Yezierska figure, " 'Without you I'm the dry dust of hopes unrealized. You are fire, water, sunshine, and desire.' "[33] Dewey's poems to Yezierska, lines from which appear with modification in both novels, suggest his awareness of the contrast between the two. In "Two Weeks" he writes,

> I am overcome as by thunder
> Of my blood that surges
> From my cold heart to my clear head—
> So at least she said—[34]

In *Red Ribbon,* John Morrow, Dewey's fictional counterpart, eventually withdraws his attention, rejecting her, as Yezierska critic Babette Inglehart has pointed out, for the very qualities he once celebrated—her intensity and vitality.[35] " 'You're an emotional, hysterical girl, and you have exaggerated my friendly interest,' " says Morrow/Dewey.[36] This unstintingly awful pattern, obsessively recurrent in Yezierska's fiction, reflects a compelling problem in the Pocahontas metaphor, and in this sense the Yezierska/Dewey relationship seems paradigmatic.

Dewey himself embraced, as Philip Gleason has pointed out, a "rather baffling prescription for [American] nationality," a strange variant of the melting-pot theory. Dewey asserted that the true American is "not American plus Pole or German. But the American is himself Pole-German-English-French-Spanish-Italian-Greek-Irish-Scandanavian-Bohemian-Jew and so on."[37] Yezierska's Manning/Dewey, in *Salome of the Tenements,* calls for a new race of men pioneered by her "oriental mystery" and his "Anglo-Saxon clarity." It is difficult to gauge the extent to which Dewey's theories of ethnic identity influenced his interest in Yezierska, and, in fact, the extent to which he was interested in her at all. It is probably unfair to accept Yezierska's "version" without qualification. On one level, Dewey seems simply to have encouraged Yezierska's writing—perhaps seeing in her sometimes overblown and always passionate prose a counterpart to his own. Quentin Anderson's description of Dewey's valuation of communication suggests how directly antithetical to Yezierska's it was: "[His] notion of communication as a literal making common of the information possessed by two or more people can only be realized within a system as impersonal as that of a computer."[38] One of Dewey's poems about Yezierska, in which he refers to "generations within you, crying for a voice," suggests not only that Dewey admired Yezierska's powers of articulation,[39] but that he saw in her confirmation of his notion of the potentialities of the individual within a democratic society as well as a challenge to his ideas about human uniqueness and history. On the whole, however, Yezierska's impression of the relationship is compelling, and is supported by the discovery of Dewey's poems, most of which were rescued from his wastebasket and the cubbyholes of his desk.[40] The image of Dewey at his great desk writing rather mediocre poems to Yezierska, most of which he never showed her, is a difficult one to relinquish.

To Yezierska, whose life consisted of a constant struggle between accepting and denying her ethnicity, her "otherness," remained fixated on her relationship with Dewey, perhaps because it represented a possible union of opposites, a resolving of the split between other and self—a split that was finally and irrevocably dissolved. When interethnic union is perceived in such a way, as I will argue in my next chapter, the resultant emotional ambivalence is profound. Yezierska's daughter reports that her mother never would have consummated her relationship with Dewey because to do so would have been an act of sacrilege (because she saw Dewey as God), incest (because she saw Dewey as her father), and just plain adultery (because Dewey was married).[41] The combination of horror and desire with which Yezierska viewed Dewey in part explains her lifelong obsession with metaphorizing their relationship. In a 1920 review of Dewey's *Democracy and Education,* Yezierska makes explicit the emotional ambivalence implicit in her fictional treatments of their relationship. While she begins the review by calling Dewey "the American Tolstoy" and his book "the new Bible of America," somewhat disingenuously describing herself as reading the book on her lunch hour at the factory, Yezierska then complains that his style "lacks flesh and blood." In a passage that speaks in a remarkably personal way to the nature of their relationship, Yezierska emphasizes the dichotomization of the relationship between the native-born man and the ethnic woman:

> One wonders why a man so imbued with the spirit of democracy must use such undemocratic language, and wonders if the reason lies in the man himself. . . . Can it be that this giant of the intellect—this pioneer in the realms of philosophy—has so suppressed the personal life in himself that his book is devoid of the intimate, self-revealing touches that make writing human? Can it be that Professor Dewey, for all his large, social vision, has so choked the feelings in his own heart that he has killed in himself the power to reach the masses of people who think with the heart rather than with the head?[42]

The difficulty in interpreting the relationship between Dewey and Yezierska lies, of course, in puzzling out the perpetrator of the terms of the dichotomy. Which of the two first attributed warmth, sexuality, "thinking with the heart" to the ethnic woman, and coldness, impassivity, and "thinking with the head" to the male partner? On the other hand, our knowledge of the personalities of the two seems to support the terms of the dichotomy, albeit in subtler form. Perhaps what is most important is that Yezierska and Dewey problematized and privileged the dichotomy, and, in fact, elevated it to the metaphorical. In this sense, Yezierska and Dewey, at first consideration the unlikeliest couple of the twentieth century, may well have been the likeliest.

The pattern that characterizes Yezierska's relationship with Dewey and her treatment of it in her fiction accentuates another aspect of the Pocahontas legend that was problematic for ethnic women and necessitates a brief review at this point of the erotic dimensions of the Pocahontas story. Its complex erotic weight provides an explanation for the enormous hold it has had on the American imagination. The Pocahontas tradition has been passed down with more than its share of authorial winks and leers. John Smith, who seems to have seen himself as something of a swash-buckler, presents in his romantic and conflicting accounts of his Jamestown experience the first erotic version of Pocahontas. He reminds us that he could have "done what he listed" with Poca-hontas, and complains of his sexual harassment at the hands of this 12-year-old and her friends: "All these Nymphes more tor-mented him that ever, with crowding, pressing, and hanging about him, most tediously crying, Love you not me?" William Strachey, the colony's secretary, in his *Historie of Travaile into Virginia Britannia,* describes how this "well-featured but wanton young girle" would "get the boyes forth with her into the markett place, and make them wheele, falling on their hands, turning their heeles upwards, whome she would followe and wheele so herself, naked as she was, all the fort over."[43] Historical accounts such as John Davis's *Travels of Four Years and a Half in the United States* continued to emphasize Pocahontas's seductiveness, and the titles of plays like Philip Moeller's 1918 *Pokey; or the Beautiful Legend of the Amorous Indian* and Boyce Loving's 1932 *The Origin of Necking, a Travesty on the Pocahontas-John Smith Episode* speak for themselves. In one of the most recent fictional treatments of Pocahontas, John Barth's 1960 *The Sot-Weed Factor,* all the men in the Jamestown neighborhood compete to penetrate the hymen of a lustful Pocahontas.[44] These accounts, it may be argued, border either on the burlesque or the pornographic and as such constitute a kind of lewd lunatic fringe in the Pocahontas tradition. Certainly they do not take into account other important features of the legend: Pocahontas's sacrifice, her conversion, her true metaphoric function. Hart Crane, in his 1930 epic poem *The Bridge,* provides the fullest exploration of Pocahontas's sexuality as an American symbol. In a poem titled "The Dance" in the "Powhatan's Daughter" section, Crane recreates Pocahontas's love for Maquokeeta, an Indian chief; the lines of the facing page indicate what Crane sees as Pocahontas's place in the American imagination: "Then you shall see her truly—your blood remembering its first invasion of her secrecy, its first encounters with her kin, her chieftain lover . . . his shade that haunts the lakes and hills." As the poem progresses, Pocahontas becomes equated with the fertility of the American land; in his notes Crane described her as "the continent" and "the natural body of American fertility." The complex nature of her sexuality—"virgin to the last of men," she appears in the poem as a bride, a pioneer mother, "our native clay"—suggests not so much Crane's sexual confusion as what Annette Kolodny points out is the cultural and sexual confusion that results from equating the American land with a woman. Kolodny's brilliant analysis of this equation in *The Lay of the Land* is instructive in that it reminds us that the erotic symbol is seldom used without confusion, ambivalence, and, in fact, hostility.[45]

The eroticization of Pocahontas suggests much about the contours of female ethnicity in American culture. In the case of the black woman, for instance, white male ambivalence toward the equation of the ethnic and the erotic takes on its most hostile and racist dimensions. Of course, racist assumptions about black sexuality implicated black men as well as black women, but a complete discussion of white attitudes toward black sexuality is beyond the scope of my study. While some historians of the relationship between masters and slaves have documented prevailing assumptions about black female sexuality, most have studied white notions of black male sexuality, especially the interesting complex of anxiety and guilt that continues to shape such attitudes today.[46] The relevance of this work to twentieth-century race relations notwithstanding, it seems curious that most historians of slavery and Reconstruction have focused on relations between black men and white women, of relatively scant statistical relevance, as a locus for white attitudes toward black sexuality. Moreover, significant historical debate persists over who really bore the responsibility for sexual relations between masters and slave women. James Johnston, an historian of miscegenation, asks, "Was the white man or the black woman the aggressor? The answer is a matter of speculation, but in every case a problem of human relations and not a problem of white or black character."[47] Could he mean "a problem of *gender* relations"? Eugene Genovese says mildly, "Slave women, like their men, brought a healthy attitude to sex and did not deserve the reputation for lewdness that white propaganda hung on them."[48] Winthrop Jordan writes, with some credibility, "There may well have been, of course, objective basis in fact for this assessment of Negro women [as especially passionate], for just as the white woman's experience tended to inhibit sexual expression, so the Negro woman's different situation may have encouraged it."

In fact, a thorough study of white male attitudes toward black female sexuality has yet to be written. Its outlines, however, are not difficult to trace. Jordan, in his important study of American attitudes toward blacks, provides the fullest discussion available, though he too is more interested in perceptions of black male sexuality. He cites a 1777 poem that presents the black woman as "the sunkissed embodiment of ardency":

> Next comes a warmer race, from sable sprung,
> To love each thought, to lust each nerve is strung;
> The Samboe dark, and the Mullattoe brown.
> The Mestize fair, the well-limbed Quaderoon,
> And jetty Afric, from no spurious sire,
> Warm as her soil, and as her sun—on fire.
> These sooty dames, well vers'd in Venus' school,
> Make love an art, and boast they kiss by rule.

Jordan suggests some possible sources of prejudicial reinforcement for these perceptions: the association of hot climates with increased sexuality, the "natural" ease with which black women were thought to give birth, and what Jordan calls "the old equation of barbarism with sexual abandonment." Furthermore, he points out that white men justified their actions by what was in essence victim-blaming, not uncommon in cases of rape today. But Jordan inadvertently makes his most relevant point for my purposes when he explains the reasons for his inability to gather white female attitudes toward miscegenation:

> Since the English and colonial American cultures were dominated
> by males, . . . sexually-oriented beliefs about the Negro in
> America derived principally from the psychological needs of men
> and were to a considerable extent shaped by specifically mas-
> culine modes of thought and behavior.[49]

The point is not that female attitudes toward miscegenation or
intermarriage were difficult to gather—I have attempted to do so
in these chapters—but that they have been overpoweringly shaped
by white male attitudes, guilts, and anxieties, or, to put it another
way, that women writers' responses to the Pocahontas legend con-
stituted questionings and explorations of that received story.

A controversial 1944 novel by a white civil-rights activist,
Lillian Smith, explores the curious sexual dynamics of the white
male/black female relationship. *Strange Fruit* is the story of Tracy
Deen's tragic affair with a local black woman in a small town in
the South. The novel is a confusion of theoretical Freudian explanations for the emotionally loaded nexus of race and sexuality,
concerns Smith was to return to with more coherence in her non-
fiction writings. At one point in the novel, Brother Dunwoodie, a
hypocritical evangelist preacher, sanctions Tracy Deen's affair at
the same time as he urges him to settle down with a white woman:

> Lot of men, when they're young, sneak off to Colored Town.
> Let their passions run clean away with them. And they get to
> thinking . . . they'd rather have that kind of thing than mar-
> riage. A lot rather! Scared of white girls. Scared nice white girls
> can't satisfy them. And they're right! Of course no decent fine
> white woman can satisfy you when you let your mind out like
> you let out a team of wild horses.[50]

Smith's attempt to explain black women's sexual attraction as an
antidote to the repressed sexuality of white Southern womanhood
is, if limited and problematic, at least a beginning.[51] The tragedy of
the novel concerns Tracy Deen's ultimate racism and his inability
to comprehend his own sexual impulses. When Nonnie gets pregnant and wants to keep her child, Deen reflects, "Now damn it,
isn't it the strangest thing how nigger will out! Here's Nonnie, col-
lege-educated, smooth as any Atlanta debutante could hope to
be. . . . Yet when it comes to a thing like this, she doesn't mind
any more than a turpentine nigger gal."[52] Smith's real achievement

is in removing the blame for the sexual relationship and its consequences from the black woman. She raises the possibility that the white male's rejection of the ethnic lover is based on his own ambivalence toward black—and white—female sexuality.[53]

The "old equation of barbarism with sexual abandonment" that Jordan speaks of is a recurrent theme in American ethnic women's fiction. In those women writers who were attracted to the Pocahontas story as an apt or positive metaphor for the ethnic female experience, the eroticism or exoticism of the alien woman was recognized as a powerful attraction that could lead to a desirable union with a native-born white male. Generally, ethnic writers who acknowledged this attraction not only wrote out of a descriptive impulse, i.e. to describe their perception of how they appeared to white men, but also out of an impulse to integrate their own sexual identity with the image associated with it in the minds of white men. Much of this fiction is marked by a poignant privileging of ethnic sexuality; it was, so to speak, their trump card in a society that objectified them sexually. Elizabeth Stern, in her autobiographical 1926 *I Am A Woman—And A Jew* recounts a confiding remark made by Nellie Frost to the narrator:

> "I think I'll become a converted Jew. A poor little Methodist hasn't a chance here in New York! If you aren't an interesting Jewess, not a person wants to notice you!" She spoke, with mischief, of Rose Pastor Stokes, of Mrs. Rose Walling, of all the Jewesses who were then holding the imagination of New York in a strange captivity.[54]

But Nellie speaks "with mischief"; Stokes and Walling's successes captivated the female, not the male, imagination; and Stern's account of her marriage to a gentile is marked by extreme ambivalence,[55] suggesting that her description of the desirability of Jewish women in New York City is either ironic or bitter. Rose Pastor's marriage to a millionaire had, I suggested earlier, a great hold on the female ethnic imagination, but only out of irony or wish-fulfilling fantasy could the ethnic woman extrapolate her desirability from that of Rose Pastor.

In Yezierska's fiction, as we have seen, the heroine is rejected and ultimately blamed for the sexuality (euphemistically, her "fiery blood," "warmth," "passion," "oriental mystery") her suitor once celebrated. Although Yezierska was to come to terms with the paradoxical implications of the ethnic woman's sexual attractiveness by undermining the Pocahontas marriage in her fiction, other ethnic writers responded by presenting heroines who accept or internalize the dominant culture's ambivalence toward their eroticism. Harlem Renaissance writer Nella Larsen creates in her 1928 *Quicksand* a complex psychological study of a mulatto woman's struggle to accommodate her sexuality and identity to the demands of both black and white society.[56] The heroine, Helga Crane, flees to her white relatives in Copenhagen to escape her feelings of isolation in Harlem, only to find herself treated as a piece of erotic exotica. Her aunt, seeing Helga as a potential social advantage, insists that Helga wear brighter colors, lower neck- and back-lines, more rouge and jewelry in her appearances in Danish society. Although Helga gives herself over to "the fascinating business of being seen, gaped at, desired,"[57] she senses the humiliation in society's objectification of her: "Helga . . . felt like nothing so much as some new and strange species of pet dog being proudly exhibited" (153). Society painter Axel Olsen, succumbing to "delight in her exotic appearance" begins painting her portrait and courting her (170).[58] When Helga shys away, Olsen reveals the true nature of his attraction to her: " 'You have the warm impulsive nature of the women of Africa, but, my lovely, you have, I fear, the soul of a prostitute. You sell yourself to the highest bidder' " (194). After she rejects him, he indicates, "I think that my picture of you is, after all, the true Helga Crane.' " The portrait he has painted reveals Helga's eroticism, and as such it upsets her. Despite the acclaim the portrait receives—it, like Helga, "attracted much flattering attention and many tempting offers"— Helga remains troubled: "It wasn't, she contended, herself at all, but some disgusting sensual creature with her features" (198–99). Throughout the novel, Helga remains haunted by the fear that she really is "some disgusting sensual creature"; her internalization of Olsen's ambivalent attraction to and rejection of her prevents her from coming to terms with her own sexuality and ultimately her own identity.

In a different vein, Mourning Dove, probably the first female Indian novelist, treats the exotic attraction of the ethnic woman and the white male's disillusionment with her charms in high melodramatic fashion. Mourning Dove's 1927 *Co-ge-we-a,* discussed in detail in Chapter 1, describes Alfred Densmore, a villainous

Easterner ignorant of the ways of the Wild West, in lustful pursuit of Cogewea, a high-spirited half-blood Indian woman who, swayed by Densmore's blandishments, temporarily abandons her worthy half-blood cowboy suitor, Jim LaGrinder. Cogewea herself is a wonderful comment on Mourning Dove's views on the results of intermarriage: an educated cowgirl, she can in one sentence tell Densmore to "skiddo" and in the next bewail her half-breed fate in highly educated cadence: "Regarded with suspicion by the Indian, despised by the Caucasian; where was there any place for the despised breed?"[59] Faithful Jim comments on her linguistic schizophrenia:

> By gollies! . . . You'r 'bout the queerest I ever saw. Sometimes you talk nice and fine, then next time you go ramblin' just like some preacher-woman or schoolmarm. Can't always savey you. (33)

Alfred Densmore, the naive Easterner who finds to his dismay, after he takes a bet to ride one, that a bronc is not "a western word for donkey" (49), is disappointed in the Wild West, expressing "vexation and disgust for the writers who had beguiled him to the 'wild and woolly' " (44). But he is not disappointed in Cogewea; indeed, "the cold, calculating business man out from the East for adventure and money, was half in love with this wild, tawny girl of the range, the romantic 'Chipmunk of the Okanogans.' " But Densmore, rebuking himself, does not entirely lose his objectivity regarding his romantic chipmunk: " 'A bepistoled woman who can swear a little on occasions may be picturesque, but she is no mate for a gentleman of the upper society' " (81). In one remarkable internal soliloquy, Densmore catalogues almost all the contradictory and stereotypical images of the ethnic woman as potential lover:

> Perhaps he had been too harsh in his deductions. . . . What could be expected of the best with such environments? Her forward ways were but those of innocence. A wild flower unscathed by sun-blight or frost—a ruby unflawed—a jewel worthy of any setting. But after all, she was a *squaw,* while he was of an altogether higher cast. Densmore brushed aside all his feelings kindred to love, but he gazed at her with a fascination ill becoming one of his superior breeding. (82) (Mourning Dove's emphasis)

When Densmore tries to persuade Cogewea to marry him according to distinctly extralegal tribal rites, Cogewea balks, and turns
to her grandmother, the Stemteemä, for advice. The Stemteemä,
after relating many admonitory tales, each of which has the moral,
" 'All that the pale face desire of Indian women, is pleasure and
riches' " (103), attempts to banish Densmore. He slinks off, cursing her as a " 'root-eating old squaw' " and " 'accursed she-
savage' " (249), but he is soon joined by a stubbornly misled Cogewea. After the story reaches its melodramatic climax—Densmore
steals Cogewea's money and pistols and leaves her tied to a tree,
wishing her " 'a merry time and pleasant dreams as you hear the
coyotes squalling tonight' " (265)—Cogewea returns docilely to
her old life and eventually agrees to marry Jim. However melodramatic and overtly didactic Mourning Dove's treatment of the
theme of intermarriage might be, she endorses the metaphor of
intermarriage even as she undercuts it, endowing her half-blood
heroine and hero with superior intelligence and sensitivity, and
marrying off—in the novel's last lines—Cogewea's sister, curiously
named Mary MacDonald, to "Eugene LaFleur, a polished and
worthy Parisian scholar" (285). *Co-ge-we-a* is, finally, less remarkable for Mourning Dove's treatment of her thematic concern
than for the remarkable texture of its discourse and the *fact* of its
thematic concern. That the first novel by an Indian woman should
have as its subject the seduction of an Indian woman by a white
representative from "civilization" attests to the centrality of the
Pocahontas metaphor in the ethnic female imagination.

Novels of passing or novels about mulattoes in white society, an
important literary sub-genre that will be discussed more fully in
my next chapter, often seem to carry the same overt message as
does Mourning Dove's *Co-ge-we-a:* the mulatto woman, after a
sojourn in white society and a possible marriage with a white man,
returns to the black community to find her true identity and her
"proper" mate. As I will try to show in that chapter, the trajectory
is usually more complicated than this. In Nella Larsen's *Quicksand,* for instance, Helga Crane so internalizes the erotic image
bestowed on her culturally that happiness is inaccessible to her.
She mentally carries with her Axel Olsen's portrait of her as "some
disgusting sensual creature with her features," wondering if the
portrait represents the true Helga. Wavering between repulsion

and desire, she rejects an old and faithful lover, offers herself to an older man she admires, and finally has a breakdown that drives her, on the streets in a storm, into a Harlem revival meeting. Seeing her red dress, the congregation confirms Helga's fears: " 'A scarlet 'oman. Come to Jesus, you pore los' Jezebel!' " (251). Exhausted, Helga submits to religious ecstasy and is taken up by the Reverend Mr. Pleasant Green, a "rattish yellow man" who marries her and brings her to his Alabama parish. After the spiritual and mental exhaustion of her life, Helga becomes a different person: "With him she willingly, even eagerly, left the sins and temptations of New York behind her to, as he put it, 'labor in the fields of the Lord . . .' " (263). Here, Helga's sexuality finally gains expression:

> And night came at the end of every day. Emotional, palpitating, amorous, all that was living in her sprang like rank weeds at the tingling thought of night, with a vitality so strong that it devoured all shoots of reason. (273)

But the result of Helga's reclaimed sexuality is as joyless and squalid as her partner; she submits to pregnancy after pregnancy, loss of faith and disillusionment, and the novel closes with her pregnant with her fifth child in four years.

Helga Crane's dilemma testifies to the special problem of female erotic identity in a culture that endows ethnic female sexuality with a bewildering variety of accusatory and admiring contradictory images. Jessie Fauset's 1929 *Plum Bun,* another novel of the Harlem Renaissance, follows a similar trajectory as do *Co-ge-we-a* and *Quicksand,* and treats the heroine's narrowly averted marriage to a white man in similarly ambivalent fashion. A novel of passing, *Plum Bun* follows the experience of Angela Murphy, a black woman who successfully passes, nearly marries a white man, and returns to the black community at the close of the novel: it is a familiar pattern of descent and rejuvenation. Fauset is a less complicated novelist than Larsen, who problematizes the notions of "descent" and "rejuvenation" so effectively in *Quicksand* and her 1929 *Passing,* but *Plum Bun* is nevertheless an important novel for its treatment of the difficulties engendered by the ethnic woman's search for her place in an ambivalent white society.

Angela's relationship with white millionaire Roger Fielding has, at the outset, all the characteristics of the ethnic Cinderella story. Though Fielding does not know she is black, he is attracted by her exoticism and unmindful of the class difference between them: "she had for him the quality of a foreigner" and he believes her to be of " 'poor but proud' " parents.[60] Angela, determined to win him both out of love and social ambition, resolves, "Well, she was sick of tragedy, she belonged to a tragic race. 'God knows it's time for one member of it to have a little fun.' "[61] Unlike the heroines of Yezierska, Mourning Dove, and Larsen, whose lovers reject them for the qualities that initially attract them—their ethnicity and eroticism—Angela, because she passes successfully, is spared Fielding's overt rejection while she suffers it covertly. Like Clare Kendry in Larsen's *Passing,* who is married to a white man unaware of her blackness, Angela must bear the rejection implicit in her white lover's blatant racism.[62] Though Angela's relationship with Fielding fails because he tires of her, Fauset makes an important point about the dynamics of the interracial union. Angela, as Fielding's mistress, suffers from a familiar internalization of the dominant culture's stereotypes of ethnic eroticism. Angela triumphs, and Fauset's message is, if obliquely rendered, more didactic than other female novelists whose subject is the complex attraction of the Pocahontas metaphor.

As I suggested earlier, the extraordinary contradictions implicit in the concept of intermarriage as a symbol for the ethnic woman's experience find their fullest and most tireless expression in the life and fiction of Anzia Yezierska. In Yezierska's more interesting plots, the heroine rejects the threats to her selfhood and power embedded in the Pocahontas legend. For the ethnic woman, the mythic paradigm of a Pocahontas marriage almost invariably fails. Either the man recoils from the very qualities he once sought in her, or the woman rejects the idea of marriage as misdirected, misconceived, and potentially dangerous. Such a marriage symbolically represents, on the one hand, a sense of selfhood unavailable to women, and on the other, relations of power in which women participate only as victims.

Salome of the Tenements, Yezierska's 1923 novel based on the Rose Pastor Stokes story and emotionally informed by Yezierska's relationship with Dewey,[63] documents the failure of marital assimilation in the ethnic woman's experience. Determined Sonya Vrunsky, the novel's heroine, stalks her native-born prey in a series of adventures that has ironic parallels to a medieval fulfillment-of-the-tasks scheme. Against all odds, Sonya secures a stunning outfit to win John Manning, engineers a renovation of her apartment and her tenement hallway, wheedles new furniture from reluctant creditors, and finally secures a dozen roses. Manning, a philanthropist whose high ideals Sonya will come to find hypocritical, comments on the ease and simplicity with which Sonya surrounds herself with beauty. Sonya's worthy suitor, Fifth Avenue dressmaker Jacques Hollins (a.k.a. Jaky Solomon from Division Street), watches her maneuverings first with pained amusement and later with growing alarm: Manning to him is a "pale-blooded Puritan" (68).

Under the terms of the familiar white man/ethnic woman dichotomy, Manning is inevitably drawn to Sonya. Sonya explains:

> "I am a Russian Jewess, a flame—a longing. A soul consumed with hunger for heights beyond reach. I am the ache of unvoiced dreams, the clamor of suppressed desires. I am the unlived lives of generations stifled in Siberian prisons. I am the urges of ages for the free, the beautiful, that never yet was on land or sea."
>
> "And I," [Manning] breathed, impelled by her sublime candor to apologize for himself, "I am a puritan whose fathers were afraid to trust experience. We are bound by our possessions of property, knowledge, and tradition." (65)[64]

Sonya is one of Yezierska's more complex heroines, although *Salome of the Tenements* is an overly schematized and melodramatic novel. Through Sonya, Yezierska attempts to define the motivations and meanings behind love itself. Sonya's desire for Manning grows out of an extraordinary complex of sexual desire, greed, love of beauty, ambition, sexual revulsion, and, ultimately, love. Sonya asks herself, in a moment of doubt, "Was her love for Manning merely a delirium of the senses. . . . was it only the drunkenness of desire? Did other women who loved go through the blood and fire of such disillusion? Or did she suffer so merely because she loved . . . a man without blood in his veins?" (154–55). Yezierska's question seems to be whether love spawned the metaphorical construct, or vice versa. The rhetoric itself acts as impetus for the love affair. After the affair is consummated, Yezierska embroiders on the metaphor, likening their love itself

to a melting-pot: " 'Races and classes and creeds, the religion of
your people and my people melt like mist in our togetherness,' "
says Sonya. With the legalization of their union, all ethnic difference seems to fall away:

> Sonya walked like a joyous pagan up the red-carpeted aisle of
> the church of Manning's fathers. So enraptured with romance, so
> drunk with the wine of love was she, that her wedding seemed no
> mere ceremony or religious rite, but a triumphant entry into hap-
> piness—a union that would last forever after. Revelling in the
> rich, blending colors that streamed through the stained glass
> windows. . . . she cared little whether the man who officiated
> was rabbi or priest. Her only god was love. (174)

Disillusionment, in the Yezierska plot, inevitably follows. After
Sonya's victory, she finds herself unhappily ensconced in an up-
town mansion with a husband she does not understand or love.
Yezierska writes,

> Sonya and Manning, tricked into matrimony, were the oriental
> and the Anglo-Saxon trying to find a common language. The
> over-emotional Ghetto struggling for its breath in the thin air of
> puritan restraint. An East Side Savage forced suddenly into the
> strait-jacket of American civilization. Sonya was like the dyna-
> mite bomb and Manning the walls of tradition constantly men-
> aced by threatening explosion. (209)

Because a Pocahontas marriage insists, on one level, that a woman's ethnic selfhood "struggle for its breath," and on another, that
her power be "forced into a strait-jacket," the immigrant woman
must reject it.

Sonya finds her life in the uptown mansion strangely unreal, as
unreal, she thinks, as it must seem to "one of the million girl readers of society columns" (190). Her disenchantment with her husband's philanthropic ideals, her difficulty with his relatives, her inability to choose the right fork for oysters—all are expressions of
Yezierska's insistence that the Pocahontas marriage cannot work,
that it constitutes, in fact, false advertising. What is really at issue
is Sonya's sexuality, and in this, Yezierska's most sexually explicit
novel, the marriage founders finally when Manning rejects Sonya's
advances one night in bed. Yezierska's description of this scene is
a clear indictment of what she sees to be the repressed and hypo-

critical nature of white male sexuality. Manning, perusing Kant's *Critique of Pure Reason* before turning in, is moved by the sight of his wife's body under the bedclothes, but then recoils: "The puritan in him stiffened in alarm. What madness had come over him, what carnal indelicacy possessed him? he questioned, bewildered" (228). After much guilty mental struggle, Manning does approach his wife, only to turn away again: "There was nothing at the moment in his puritan heart but an apology for his lust. . . . Turning away from her he lay on his back, staring baffled into the dark. What was this sharp sense of guilt that so quickly blotted out his passion?" (231). Sonya, frustrated and angry, decides that night the marriage is over. "[S]he knew that just as fire and water cannot fuse, neither could her Russian Jewish soul fuse with the stolid, the unimaginative, the invulnerable thickness of this New England puritan" (232). In the scenes that follow, Sonya's disillusionment is complete; Manning's "hidden hate of the Jew" emerges, hate that is, of course, tied to his sexual ambivalence. The plot, at this point, begins to follow a distinctly feminist trajectory. Sonya leaves Manning for Jacques Hollins, and finds a vocation in their dressmaking and fashion-design business. Marriage to a fellow-immigrant, and one with whom she can work, does not represent the same serious compromise of selfhood and power.

The renunciation implicit in Sonya's seduction to the Pocahontas marriage recalls Philip Young's suggestion that the attraction of the Pocahontas legend lies in the image of the sacrificial bride. When Pocahontas laid her head over John Smith's to prevent her father's men from clubbing him to death, she simultaneously defied Powhatan and rejected her own Indian and familial identity. After her marriage to John Rolfe, Pocahontas converted, was renamed Lady Rebecca, and led to England in triumph, her Indian selfhood renounced. As I pointed out in my last chapter, the generational and racial conflict engendered by the immigrant's Americanization—or Pocahontas's Europeanization—have had considerable resonance in American female ethnicity as it is represented in the fiction of ethnic women. For the immigrant woman, the conflicts inherent in the assimilation process simultaneously shaped identity and threatened to destroy it. Americanization seemed to demand the rejection of her family and her culture. The parental bond was to be sundered and the immigrant, in effect, born anew.

The imagery of rebirth that attaches to the melting-pot concept and to the Americanization process seems relevant here, as does Pocahontas's "born-again" conversion and her rechristening as Lady Rebecca. The rhetoric of Americanization demanded a complete severance of all ties to the past. John Quincy Adams recognized this as early as 1818, when he wrote,

> To one thing [immigrants] must make up their minds, or they will be disappointed in every expectation of happiness as Americans. They must look forward to their posterity rather than backward to their ancestors; they must be sure that whatever their own feelings may be, those of their children will cling to the prejudices of this country.[65]

The significance of severance of generations, of inheritance, of ancestry, in ethnic women's fiction has already been discussed: what I wish to emphasize here is the nature of the rhetoric. One is reminded of Henry Fairchild's objection to the melting-pot concept on the grounds that it "focussed on the process of interaction rather than the result." The rhetoric of American ethnicity is indefatigably forward-looking. Of course in one sense, national rhetoric always possesses this quality; the present is only an index for the possibilities of the future, which will in turn fulfill the prophecies of the past.[66] But the rhetoric of Americanization denies the actuality of the present, or, specifically, of the process of intermarriage that will result in Americanized children. One is reminded of the paradox of melting-pot rhetoric: de-eroticized by its proponents, re-eroticized by racial purists. Intermarriage is privileged in American rhetoric only insofar as it produces American children. The fictional response to this massive cultural denial has been, among first-generation immigrant writers, an obsessive concern with rejection of the past and quasi-religious rebirth, and, among later ethnic writers, an obsessive concern with ancestry and the meaning of descendancy or, in fact, childhood.[67] These themes run throughout the fiction I have discussed in this chapter. Mourning Dove, for instance, tries in *Co-ge-we-a* to imagine a thoroughly modern cowgirl who can still partake in ritual sweats with her grandmother. Elizabeth Stern describes how, after her marriage, she is "dead to [her] family"[68] but insists that immigrant parents, "they who recede into the shadow, they are old, and they do not understand America. But they have made their important contribution—their sons and daughters."[69] Yezierska, in important stories like "The Fat of the Land" and in her novel *Bread Givers* obsessively writes and rewrites her own painful generational conflicts. The black writers discussed here, in their concern with mulattoes and light-skinned blacks, reiterate ancestry as they delineate the struggle of descendants to find their place in America. What is remarkable about these writers is their refusal to deny the present, the actuality of intermarriage in American life. It is useful here to recall DuBois's insistence regarding the "stark, ugly, painful, beautiful" fact of American life: "The colored slave woman became the medium through which two great races were united."[70] Ethnic women writers denied the immaculate conception of the Crèvecoeurian new man. Those ethnic women who saw the Pocahontas story as—for good or ill—an apt metaphor for their American experience, were fully aware of the erotic coloration of the melting-pot and of Pocahontas herself. That the Pocahontas marriage ultimately compromised them attests to an insistence on realism that can only be characterized as brave.

The writers discussed in this chapter found in the concept of intermarriage confirmation of the centrality of ethnic female sexuality in American culture. They were, by and large, seduced by the metaphor, by the persuasive language of love. In spite of, or perhaps because of, their awareness of and insistence on the sexual content of the symbolic content of the Pocahontas story, they remained unable or unwilling to forgo it, or to explore its darker and more profound manifestations. Unlike the writers I will consider in the next chapter, who found in the concept of intermarriage a psychic sore spot of American culture, to be poked at and worried like a wound, writers like Yezierska and Mourning Dove insisted on the factuality of intermarriage to such an extent that it became a barrier beyond which they could not travel in their fiction. In some cases, the results were delightful, and it is in this sense that the Pocahontas marriage expressed fictionally is not without its charm. Certainly one valid response to a contradictory or emotionally troublesome concept is to revel in it, or at least to revel in its basis in fact. This response characterizes the works, for

instance, of Jewish-American writer Edna Ferber, whose voluminous oeuvre could be said to have as its subject the voluminous
multiethnic and multiregional character of American life. Although she is not above exploiting its dramatic possibilities,[71] intermarriage in her novels loses some of the contradictory emotional connotations it carries in most ethnic fiction. Ferber's 1929
Cimarron, a novel that I would like to consider in some detail, perhaps best typifies Ferber's response to the fascinating nexus of
American and ethnic identity.

A novel about the settlement of oil-rich Oklahoma, *Cimarron*
is filled with absurd happenings and exaggerations, satirical stereotypical portraits of every American ethnic group imaginable except perhaps Eskimos (to whom Ferber was to turn her attention
in her 1958 *Ice Palace*). The oil that erupts beneath the Oklahoma
plains is a great equalizer in the way it allots unheard-of millions
arbitrarily, perversely, and gleefully. Ferber's descriptions of over-
fed oil-rich Indians, grotesque with wealth and mesmerized by re-
frigerators, Pierce Arrows, and "clear and blue-white and costly"
diamonds,[72] are characterized by a gross exuberance that is ob-
jectionable only if the reader overlooks the evenhandedness with
which Ferber metes out such overblown observations. Wealth
comes to Jewish Sol Levy, the Osage Indians, the Irish Learys,
and the socially connected Anglo-Saxon Wyatts, working its grotesque wonders on their lives as surely—or as randomly—as it
passes over the novel's heroes, the black characters, and other Indian tribes. Yancey Cravat, who functions as a locus for Ferber's
Indianist views just as his wife does for her feminist beliefs, positively revels in the ethnic blindness of the American way:

> The joke gets better and better. We took their land away from
> them and exterminated the buffalo, then expected them to squat
> on the Reservations weaving baskets and molding pottery that no
> one wanted to buy. Well, at least the Osages never did that.
> They're spending their money just as the white people do when
> they get a handful of it—chicken and plush and automobiles and
> phonographs and silk shirts and jewelry.

When his wife objects that the Osages might share their wealth
with other, poorer Indian tribes, Yancey replies, " 'Maybe they
will—when Bixby gives away his millions to down-and-out hotel-

keepers who are as poor as he was when he ran the Bixby House, back in the old days.'" Muting the cynical implications of this, Yancey adds, "'The wonder to me is that they don't die laughing and spoil their own good time.'"[73]

In this novel, intermarriage is as American as oil wells. The novel's titular hero, captivated from childhood by his father's representations of the heroic and tragic lives of nineteenth-century Indians, grows into an adolescent who distresses his mother with his peyote use and inevitably and naturally marries Ruby Big Elk, the daughter of an oil-rich Osage chieftain. Sabra Cravat, who throughout the novel has been less than sympathetic to her Indian neighbors, is initially shocked by her son's marriage. But in a masterfully ironic stroke, Ferber transforms Sabra's narrow-mindedness into the natural bias of a middle-class American mother against her son's bride. Ferber playfully presents the incident of the marriage as a parody of twentieth-century marriage rituals. The Cravats return home one day to find "Chief and Mrs." Big Elk ensconced in their gimcracked and jerry-built drawing room, paying a call as parents of the prospective bride. The wedding feast that follows is marked by the same distrust, uneasiness, and grudging alliance that characterizes most weddings in a multiethnic and exogamous society. Sabra Cravat, too nervous to eat, at her husband's urging ("'They consider it an insult,'" he whispers), nibbles at a meat-filled pastry, and inquires of her Indian neighbour whether the meat is "chopped or ground through a grinder." The polite answer, at which Sabra faints away, is "'Naw. Chawed.'"[74] Yancey Cravat[75] immediately composes an ironically conceived item for the local paper:

> Ex-chief Big Elk, of the Osage Nation, and Mrs. Big Elk, living at Wazhazhe, announce the marriage of their daughter Ruby Big Elk to Cimarron Cravat, son of . . . Mr. and Mrs. Yancey Cravat, of this city. The wedding was solemnized at the home of the bride's parents and was followed by an elaborate dinner made up of many Indian and American dishes, partaken by the parents of the bride and groom, many relatives and numerous friends of the young.[76]

Intermarriage, for Ferber, is smoothly translated into a classically middle-class American rhetoric, absorbed as an inevitable feature of the American way. Sabra, making her political debut on the

Washington scene, anticipates criticism of her son's Indian bride, but nips it in the bud by staging a "coup so brilliant it routed the enemy forever."[77] She holds an enormous reception featuring Ruby Big Elk, tactiturn and overweight (no Indian princess this) in full native regalia. Rather than romanticize the significance of Ruby's Washington success, Ferber deflates its romanticism in a way that reinflates its realistic significance. Pocahontas, we remember, became the rage in London, appearing at court, inspiring a rash of pub-naming in her honor, sitting for portraits in English dress. Not so Ruby Big Elk:

> For the benefit of those who had not quite been able to encompass the Indian woman in her native dress Ruby's next appearance was made in a Paris gown of white. She became the rage, was considered picturesque, and left Washington in disgust, her work done.[78]

In *Cimarron,* intermarriage is woven seamlessly into the multiethnic fabric of American life, and becomes one of a multitude of unforced, natural, benevolent metaphors for the multiethnic American way.

CHAPTER 6

Miscegenation and the Mulatto, Inheritance and Incest: The Pocahontas Marriage, Part II

In Gayl Jones's powerful 1975 novel *Corregidora*, Ursa Corregidora, the blues-singer heroine, a descendant of a slaveowner named Corregidora who fathered and prostituted Ursa's grandmother and her mother, learns to accept her identity as one of "Corregidora's women." The paradox implicit in Ursa's "plot" is two-fold: first, Ursa, in aligning herself with the women owned and fathered by a brutally cruel white slaveowner, aligns herself with a tradition of sexual violence and oppression; second, the definition of selfhood based on ownership or descendancy seems at first consideration contradictory. This paradox, however, seems to lie at the heart of American female ethnic identity. It raises questions of incest, sexual violence, inheritance, selfhood—all of which are central concerns in ethnic women's fiction.

The action of *Corregidora* is straightforward: Ursa, a singer at Happy's Café, has had a hysterectomy to correct injuries caused by her husband's violence; she moves in with the café owner and tries to make sense of the changes in her life. Much of the novel follows Ursa's lyrical dream thoughts and memories of her childhood. Ursa, raised by her great-grandmother, grandmother, and mother, a trio of Corregidora's women, is told and retold the horrible story of Corregidora's sexual cruelty. Ursa tells Tadpole, the café owner,

> My great-grandmama told my grandmama the part she lived through that my grandmama didn't live through and my grandmama told me what they all lived through and my mama told me what they all lived through and we were suppose to pass it

down like that from generation to generation so we'd never forget.
Even though they'd burned everything to play like it didn't
never happen.[1]

The insistent moral to a heritage of violence and disruption of all
human values is, the women tell her, that one must "make generations." Because Ursa cannot bear children, the paradox of this
moral is literalized. Her husband's sexual violence has foreclosed
the only available female response to a heritage of such violence:
Ursa cannot make generations. How then to come to terms with
the past? What does inheritance mean? Ursa says at one point in
the novel, "I am Ursa Corregidora. I have tears for eyes. I was
made to touch my past at an early age."[2] Corregidora's women refuse to forget the past, not only because they refuse to forgive, but
because the past, as one's inheritance, defines selfhood. Corregidora, in making her mother and grandmother half-sisters, and in
owning and trading in human beings, had so disrupted all notions
of individuality and inheritance that the women's only response is
to reaffirm them. The novel's meanings are extraordinarily complex; Jones lets no one off easily, including the reader. Ursa, in
affirming her identity as one of Corregidora's women, is doomed
to repeat the pattern of his women: to be prostituted, mistreated,
owned. But her husband Mutt, who denies the significance of
"generations" in his own life, also suffers from—and perpetu-
ates—his inheritance as a man and a descendant of slaves; he too
is doomed to participate in the continuing pattern of sexual violence. Ursa's identification of herself as a descendant works both
to damn her and to redeem her, but it is, Jones asserts, inevitable.
Corregidora speaks in an extremely complex way to the meanings
of miscegenation, ancestry, and descendancy in ethnic female
identity.

Miscegenation, or intermarriage, functions in the American cultural imagination and in ethnic fiction as a locus for the ambivalence of author and readers to questions of gender, ethnicity, inheritance, and identity. In fiction by and about ethnic women, the
concept becomes central to definitions of ethnic female identity.
As I argued in my last chapter, the concept has had considerable
attraction for the ethnic writer in terms of its aptness and its promise. It also allows the ethnic writer to explore her own ambivalence and that of her culture to female sexuality and ethnicity,

to protest against the ways in which intermarriage has assumed oppressive meanings and has expressed an oppressive actuality, and to displace into fiction complex social and economic problems. Intermarriage is seldom the *subject* of the fiction I discuss here, but it informs this fiction imaginatively. I am not looking to literature for social evidence of, for instance, the mulatto. In this sense it is necessary to draw important if basic distinctions between the novel and life. I have argued that some ethnic women assert the factuality of the Pocahontas story, reclaiming its often oppressive actuality by, in fact, representing "life" in their "novel." But all fiction moves beyond representation, and representation of miscegenation in ethnic fiction is not only important *per se,* but because through it the writer moves to larger conclusions about ethnic female identity. In fact, I would argue that miscegenation's more complex functions as an indicator of a disruption, a freakish window into the unconscious mind, a contradiction, are the features that attract the ethnic woman writer to it. Simone Vauthier, a critic who has written extensively on plantation fiction, says that the bastard appears obsessively in American fiction not because a lot of Americans are illegitimate but because he is an indicator of a disruption. More generally, she writes, "The novel concerns itself by definition with the accidental, the unusual, from which comes a rupture in continuity, in order. The novel speaks; it implies the extraordinary." Tony Tanner, making a similar point, argues in *Adultery and the Novel* that the bourgeois novel as a form was characterized by the extraordinary disruption and transgression adultery represents. In a similar way, ethnic women writers find in the Pocahontas story an intensification of extraordinary cultural ambivalence, a subversion of the bourgeois reality they purport to represent.[3]

To understand more fully why the concept of intermarriage touches a nerve in the ethnic female imagination so directly, it is necessary to reconsider sexual relations under slavery, because the meanings of miscegenation in post-Civil War ethnic fiction are the legacy of slavery. If sexual relations between black women and white men became less common after slavery, and those between black men and white women less of a rarity; if, in other words, miscegenation's historical reality was compromised for the writers I consider, its psychic reality remained profound. Slavery, a far

greater transgression than adultery in human history, informs all
fiction that follows it. The most literal manifestation of this is the
formidable mulatto tradition in literature, in which the legacy of
miscegenation is embodied in fictional characters who are the children of interracial unions.

The profound contradictions embedded in the Pocahontas marriage resonate in the profoundly contradictory conditions of female
slave life. The most basic of these is the paradox that allowed one
human being to own another. The objectification of black women
implicit in sexual relations between slaveowners and slaves is
a central theme of all black female fiction, which seeks first of
all to reclaim the human status of black women by, in effect, telling their stories. Black novels about slavery, from Frances Harper's
1892 *Iola Leroy* to Margaret Walker's 1966 *Jubilee,* by presenting
the stories of black women who historically existed only as chattel,
protest against this simple but enormous paradox. From this paradox follow a number of others. Among these is the confusion of
standards that allowed Christian slaveowners to have sexual relations outside of marriage with their slaves. The attraction of the
black woman to the white slaveowner was, I have argued, based
on deep-seated ambivalence toward female sexuality and ethnicity.
Intercourse with a black woman raised troubling but intriguing
questions of difference and sameness, of the boundaries of the self.
John Irwin, in his study of Faulkner, *Doubling and Incest/Repeti-
tion and Revenge,* examines the ways in which the black functions
as a psychic double for the white mind—a double with a difference—and a testing of the boundaries of the self. He writes, "The
double evokes the ego's fear and love because it is a copy of the
ego, but it evokes the ego's fear and hatred because it is a copy
with a difference."[4] The black woman, as I have argued, evokes
the white man's love as well as his fear and hatred in precisely this
way; furthermore, sexual relations between the white slaveowner
and the black woman were generated by and confirmed a common
humanity even as the attraction was based on the woman's otherness, and the relationship forbidden because of it.[5] This relationship was further confused by male ambivalence to white female
sexuality. In their insistence on black female supersexuality, white
men displaced—or perhaps exacerbated—their anxieties about the
sexuality of their wives and daughters. Sexual relations with black

women, in short, presented almost intolerable contradictions for the white male, which found expression in laws forbidding miscegenation and designating the children of interracial unions slaves.[6]

The white woman's response was no less complex. Mary Boykin Chesnut, in her Civil War diary, comments on the blindness of some white mistresses toward their husbands' behavior:

> Like the patriarchs of old our men live all in one house with their wives and their concubines, and the mulattoes one sees in every family exactly resemble the white children—and every lady tells you who is the father of all the mulatto children in everybody's household, but those in her own drop from the clouds, or pretends so to speak.[7]

Many wives of slaveowners, one would imagine, found these conditions as intolerably contradictory—though in far different fashion—as did their husbands. The resultant ambivalence has found expression in white-authored novels about slavery as diverse as Harriet Beecher Stowe's 1852 *Uncle Tom's Cabin* and Willa Cather's 1940 *Sapphira and the Slave Girl*. Eugene Genovese, warning that "no pattern emerges" in white women's attitudes toward black concubines, suggests that strong bonds often existed between black house servants and their mistresses.[8] Somewhat romantically, he sees black and white women acting as confidantes and helpers in intrigues of love. According to his conception of slavery as a paternalistic institution, he sees slave women and their mistresses united in "mutual dependence," which often, he admits, caused "inevitable resentments."[9] Pauli Murray, whose 1956 *Proud Shoes* is a valuable record of the complex inheritance of the mulatto child, describes a white ancestor's reaction to the birth of the narrator's mulatto grandmother:

> Try as she might to avoid the truth, it struck her with shattering clarity that this was Sidney's child, a *Smith!* She couldn't get around it. Slavery had produced its own monstrosity in Miss Mary's home as it had done elsewhere. Smith progeny had been born into slavery. It could be bought and sold like any other property and in time this girl child of Smith blood could be bred to other men no better or worse than her own father. Miss Mary Ruffin realized with horror that this bastard slave child was also her own flesh and blood—in fact, her niece.[10]

Miss Mary Ruffin raises her brother's slave children both as slaves and as Smith children; as one might expect, "her feelings of kinship collided with her sense of propriety as their mistress."[11] Miss Mary Ruffin's "feelings of kinship," her horrified realization that "this bastard child was her own flesh and blood," directly express one of the central contradictions implied by miscegenation—that of kinship and inheritance. What happens to the white woman's notions of family when children of another race become part of it? How are boundaries of the self and other to be preserved if the two mate and bear fruit? "The problem of ancestry," writes Winthrop Jordan, "was the inescapable concomitant of interracial sex."[12]

In Genovese's interpretation of slavery's paternalistic dimensions, he writes that slaveowners saw themselves as "authoritarian fathers who presided over an extended and subservient family, white and black."[13] Under the rules of paternalism the white "father" could mate freely with his black slaves. The product of such unions was, of course, born simultaneously into the father's extended "family" and into his biological family, but not into his legal family.[14] The mulatto child, identified according to his mother's family, deprived of his father's name, born a slave, was denied his inheritance. The disruption of genealogy the mulatto represents lies at the heart of the complex fictional uses of miscegenation and helps to explain why the mulatto figures so centrally in ethnic women's fiction. A primary concern of this fiction is the enormous practical and psychic significance that the denial of the mulatto's inheritance represents.

Although significant numbers of slaveowners may have freed their black mistresses and mulatto children, at least in their wills, most mulatto children were, first, denied the legacy of their fathers' freedom. Even if freed by their masters, black and mulatto women and children could always be reclaimed by the slave system.[15] In Frances Harper's 1892 *Iola Leroy, or Shadows Uplifted,* the heroine, daughter of a slaveowner and a mulatto slave whom he marries and frees, is remanded into slavery after her father's death. Iola's father, in marrying her mother, insists that marriage is necessary to ensure a legacy of freedom, and protests against the banning of such marriages:

> Should not society have a greater ban for those who, consorting with [rather than marrying] an alien race, rob their offspring of a right to their names and to an inheritance of their property, and who fix their social status among an enslaved and outcast race?[16]

Through Marie, Iola's mother, Harper protests the disruption of inheritance that usually characterized relations between white men and black women under slavery. Precisely what bothers her is the fate of the children:

> I can understand how savages, fighting with each other, could doom their vanquished foes to slavery, but it has always been a puzzle to me how a civilized man could drag his own children, bone of his bone, flesh of his flesh, down to the position of social outcasts, abject slaves, and political pariahs.[17]

Denied their inheritance, Iola and her brother are sold back into slavery, and the family disrupted. The plot of *Iola Leroy,* like those of other Reconstruction novels by women writers, concerns the heroine's attempts to gather her scattered family members together. Herbert Gutman, in his important study, *The Black Family in Slavery and Freedom,* argues that the black family in slavery maintained a cohesiveness of which slaveowners were unaware. In Reconstruction, Gutman suggests, blacks reconstructed family ties to compensate for destructions and disruptions of family ties under slavery. An important aspect of Reconstruction was not only socio-economic and political but also familial readjustment.[18] While Reconstruction fiction is usually read as fictional documentation of the social problems of an emergent black middle class, it is equally profitable to read Harper's novel as an expression of protest against inheritance denied and an attempt to reestablish genealogy and reclaim ancestry.

Denied the freedom, material legacy, and name of the father, the mulatto child was also illegitimate. This has had enormous psychic ramifications in the ethnic imagination. Bastardy, a recurrent theme in American literature, has carried with it since Oedipus the threat of incest. If his parentage is unknown, the illegitimate child runs the danger of unwitting incest. Simone Vauthier, in a discussion of the plantation novel *Old Hepsy,* extends Genovese's concept of the slave family to accommodate this element. The plantation system purported to be a family order, but only insofar as it disowned from the biological family certain members. These excluded members could then logically have relations with members of the family from which they were disowned or among themselves. "When refusing to acknowledge his slave son," writes Vauthier, "the father fails to transmit with his surname what Jacques Lacan calls the-Name-of-the-Father, i.e. the universal law that prohibits incest."[19] Slaves and ex-slaves, denied knowledge of their parentage, ran the risk of actualizing Freud's "family romance," of intercourse with family members, particularly siblings. This is not to say that there was historically a high incidence of incest involving slaves and ex-slaves and their white families. In fact, as Gutman points out, strong exogamous beliefs among the slave community dictated certain cultural requirements regarding marriages between cousins and naming practices that made clear the relationships between generations of blood kin. He cites a secular work song that makes clear the acknowledged connection between kinship ties and exogamous marriage practices:

> Herodias go down to de river one day,
> Want to know what John Baptist have to say,
> John spoke de words at de risk of he life
> Not lawful to marry you brudder's wife.

Cultural expressions of injunctions against tabooed practice, of course, arise from and may parallel the possibility of actualized taboo behavior. Two children of slave parents interviewed by Gutman acknowledged that sales of slaves often led to violations of incest taboos. A Mississippi woman recollected for Gutman the story of a man who married his mother after emancipation; his mother eventually recognized him from a scar on his thigh. Gutman writes, "Taboos rooted in exogamous beliefs had traveled with slaves in the forced migration that carried hundreds of blacks from the Lower to the Upper South."[20]

Conditions of sale, then, may have threatened kinship ties; so too may have conditions of miscegenation. The mulatto child in the slave family, even if aware of his white father's identity, may not have been aware of half-brothers and sisters fathered by his white father. In cases in which he was unaware of his father's identity, the mulatto child risked violating the incest taboo, in effect, every time he had sexual relations with whites. It is not surprising that the mulatto who passed for white raised such profound anxiety in the white—and black—mind. The underlying threat of incest may help to explain black novelists' insistence that their mulatto characters marry within the black community where, as Gutman has shown, strong kinship ties were asserted in the face of the fluidity of boundaries threatened by slavery. Freud has shown us that the psychic weight of the possibility of incest is at least as significant as its actuality. Miscegenation disrupted the *idea* of family, which is after all the stuff of fiction.

In the Reconstruction novels of Frances Harper and Pauline Hopkins, incest, usually between brother and sister, is often threatened and sometimes occurs. The anxiety surrounding the taboo of incest informs the plot structure of this fiction, in which families are reunited against impossible odds. These writers sought to restore order to the familial chaos threatened by slavery and found in melodrama the form that allowed them to do so. Robert Bone suggests the early black novelists were attracted to melodrama because, among other reasons, "its moral extremes make it a natural vehicle for racial protest. . . . The moral absolutism of melodrama served the strategic needs of the period, which called for colored heroes and heroines of exaggerated virtue and white villains of bottomless perfidy."[21] When we think of melodrama, I would argue, we *do* think of supposedly opposing absolutes—good and evil, or, in fact, black and white. Though the analogy is a crude one, one could argue that early black novelists chose the genre of black and white distinctions in order to protest the absolutism of race distinctions that they recognized in Reconstruction society. The concept of a black hero and a white villain is a subversion of such absolutism. The mulatto becomes a central figure in this fiction because he or she represents the effacement of absolute "black and white" distinction, a "grey" area in which limits are tested and boundaries of selfhood in flux, a locus of protest against oppressive conditions that resulted from racial distinction.

The multiplicity of the mulatto "tradition" derives from the mulatto's psychic function in the literary imagination.[22] For racial supremacists like Thomas Dixon, the mulatto is a vicious and lustful brute who represents the worst qualities in both races. At the other extreme, best exemplified in Jean Toomer's 1923 *Cane* and

Gertrude Stein's 1909 *Melanctha,* is a tradition in which the mulatto is elevated both spiritually and sensually and endowed with an air of mystery. In between is the formidable tradition of the tragic mulatto, usually a woman, who is divided between her white and black blood. The tragic mulatto trajectory demands that the mulatto woman desire a white lover and either die (often in white-authored versions) or return to the black community. As Judith Berzon points out in her study of the mulatto in fiction, *Neither White Nor Black,* this tradition "is usually the product of the white man's imagination and often expresses his deepest (usually unspoken) fantasies about the largest marginal group in our society: specifically, his assumption that the mixed blood yearns to be white and is doomed to unhappiness and despair because of this impossible dream."[23] Sterling Brown argues, in fact, that white use of the mulatto character is an expression of white narcissism. He writes, "The tragic mulatto stereotype stemmed from an anti-slavery crusade, whose authors used it, partly to show miscegenation as an evil of slavery, partly as an attempt to win readers' sympathies by presenting central characters who were physically very like their readers."[24]

Regardless of race, the American author found in the mulatto problems central to the idea of American identity. In this respect the concept of a mulatto "tradition" is unnecessarily limited. In the white literary tradition, the mulatto is often tragic not only because the white author thinks she wants to be white, but precisely because she is physically like the white author; so like, in fact, that she might be kin. In black-authored fiction, the mulatto functions in much the same way. The "tragic" mulatto—the adjective might well be salvaged, if only to remind us of the mulatto's profound importance—is the American hero. Faulkner's *Light in August* and *Absalom, Absalom!* confound critics of the mulatto "tradition," for Faulkner's concerns with classic American subjects—the significance of the past for the future, the role of the individual in society, the meanings of ethnicity and ancestry in American identity—all suggest that Faulkner saw in the mulatto a metaphor for the American experience. It is equally misleading to isolate mulatto "types," to differentiate unduly between Thomas Dixon's lustful brute and James Fenimore Cooper's passionate brunette, or indeed Nella Larsen's existential heroine. The tragic mulatto *is,* as Sterling Brown suggests, "a lost, unhappy, woebegone abstraction," but only insofar as is the American hero.[25] Like the miscegenation relation that spawned him, the mulatto is a locus for fictional ambivalence about problems that cannot be approached without ambivalence.

At the center of the melodramatic plot of the Reconstruction novel, the mulatto searches to find family connections that will verify her mixed blood and her parentage. As I have pointed out, this is in part a stay against incest. In Harper's *Iola Leroy,* Iola cannot marry until she locates her family. When Dr. Gresham, a white Union doctor, urges Iola to marry him and pass for white, Iola rejects him on the basis of her unknown parentage, reminding him of the ultimate punishment for transgression, the possibility of a coal-black baby. In Harper's novel, the mulatto characters staunchly ally themselves with blacks, joining black regiments in the Union Army and marrying black partners. This racial identification represents not only Harper's awareness of a white audience that might have been made uneasy by successful passing, but a stay against the chaos that Harper seems to have felt might result if boundaries were to remain fluid.

Reconstruction novelists, in accord with a certain genteel tradition, often asserted their seriousness of purpose by inserting into their novels long-winded and high-minded discussions of the "race question," with all the novel's characters, character motivation aside, joining in.[26] Such interjected scenes allowed the author to air and answer prevailing assumptions about such subjects as the mulatto and "race mixture." In *Iola Leroy,* Harper argues the point that motivates her plot: the parody of inheritance that the mulatto has suffered. One Dr. Latimer accuses a Dr. Latrobe of consorting with black women while refusing to associate with them socially:

> "I think," said Dr. Latrobe, "that feeling grows out of our Anglo-Saxon regard for the marriage relation. These white negroes are of illegitimate origin, and we would scorn to share our social life with them. Their blood is tainted."
>
> "Who tainted it?" asked Dr. Latimer, bitterly. "You give absolution to the fathers, and visit the misfortune of the mothers upon the children."[27]

Harper's protest is against a patriarchal society that breaks the rules of patrilinear inheritance only when it suits white men. Her insistence on the sexual hypocrisy implicit in the disruption of inheritance is shared by all women writers who make miscegenation their subject.

Pauline Hopkins, another writer of what DuBois called the Talented Tenth, addresses the meaning of interracial romance in her 1901 novel *Contending Forces* and in two short novels serialized in 1902 and 1903 in *Colored American Magazine,* of which she was literary editor. *Contending Forces,* perhaps because it was her only novel published in toto, has been the only Hopkins work to receive critical attention. It is basically a straightforward if melodramatic tale of the reunion of families separated by slavery and the restoration of rightful inheritance. (Ma Smith, in the classically titled case, *"Smith vs. U.S.,"* wins her right to the legacy of Jesse Montfort, her long-lost mulatto father.) *Winona: A Tale of Negro Life in the South and Southwest* and *Of One Blood: Or the Hidden Self* have the same concerns, but Hopkins's melodramatic flair in these novels is carried to extremes that reveal some of the remarkable contradictions to which interracial romance is prone. In *Winona,* for instance, the titular heroine is the daughter of a mulatto fugitive slave woman and a white man who has been adopted by an Indian tribe as their chief. Raised from infancy with a white orphan named Judah, Winona is forced to choose between Warren Maxwell, an Englishman who is visiting America to find a client's missing heir, and Judah, who "[knows] the worth of a white man's love for a woman of mixed blood; how it swept its scorching heat over a white young life, leaving it nothing but charred embers and burnt-out ashes."[28] After many plot twists, it is revealed that Winona's father, the white Indian, is the heir Maxwell has sought, and Winona and Maxwell are free to marry after her inheritance (and, by extension, her parentage) has been set aright.

Of One Blood: Or the Hidden Self, an occult tale of remarkably ornate complexity, as a Gothic text suggests the close proximity of disruption of inheritance with the quality of the uncanny. The Gothic genre, argues Nancy Goulder, expresses Freud's notion of the uncanny, in terms of which, Goulder suggests, the boundaries of the conscious and unconscious mind, between self and other, are effaced; the uncanny experience is generated by a repetition-compulsion principle that repeatedly forces repressed anxieties to the surface. In the text of the uncanny, distinctions and boundaries are repeatedly effaced and redrawn. The connection between the uncanny and the experience of miscegenation is clear: the mulatto herself is a kind of uncanny text about the coherence and limits of the self.[29] Hopkins's attraction to the Gothic genre, the genre of the uncanny, is inevitable, given the anxiety over boundaries that the mulatto represents. *Of One Blood: Or the Hidden Self*—a title of ominous significance—is almost a survey of Gothic tropes: incest, the return of the repressed in the reanimation of the dead, suicide in the fact of knowledge, hauntings. All are the result of the disruption of inheritance engendered by the white father's refusal to pass down his name. Reuel Briggs, a mulatto scientist with a mystical bent, is literally haunted by the vision of Dianthe Lusk, a beautiful mulatto singer. Dianthe dies, but Reuel, who has "stumbled upon the solution of one of life's problems: *the reanimation of the body after seeming death"* (Hopkins's emphasis),[30] brings her back to life, at which point she develops total amnesia and does not remember she is black. Reuel, in Gothic fashion, has a white double, Aubrey, with whom he must vie for Dianthe's love. Throughout the novel, a ghost named Mira appears and prophesies that "there is nothing covered that shall not be revealed." After elaborate plot developments and much perfidy on Aubrey's part— Dianthe again dies and is again reborn, and Aubrey tries to kill Reuel a few times—Reuel marries Dianthe, and leaves her behind as he undertakes a scientific trip to Egypt. In Egypt Reuel has heroic and occult adventures that rival those of Indiana Jones in Steven Spielberg's 1981 *Raiders of the Lost Ark:* he is adopted by the inhabitants of the hidden city of Telassar, who recognize him as their long-awaited king by a birthmark on his chest in the shape of a lotus lily. Meanwhile, Aubrey has convinced Dianthe that Reuel is dead and has married her, and Reuel's slave, bought off by Aubrey, has convinced Reuel that Dianthe is his sister. Reuel returns to America to undo the horror he has committed in marrying his sister, but he is too late: Dianthe has visited an old ex-slave woman, who reveals herself as Dianthe's grandmother and tells Dianthe that she and Aubrey are brother and sister. Dianthe, in horror at her incestuous marriage, tries to poison Aubrey, who murders her and then kills himself. The impossible entanglement of genealogy—Reuel is also, I think, Aubrey's half-brother—leads inevitably to the experience of the uncanny.

When a white woman wrote to *Colored American Magazine* asking why Hopkins always wrote about interracial love, Hopkins responded:

> My stories are definitely planned to show the obstacles persistently placed in our paths by a dominant race to subjugate us spiritually. Marriage is made illegal between the races and the mulattoes increase. Thus the shadow of corruption falls on the black and on the whites, without whose aid the mulattoes would not exist.[31]

Hopkins protests the refusal of white males to acknowledge their mulatto children, and the fluidity of boundaries that results from this disruption of inheritance; it is not surprising that she turned to the Gothic genre to explore these concerns.

The connection between miscegenation, the disruption of inheritance, and the unconscious appears again in an overwrought but oddly moving short story by a white woman, local colorist Grace King. Although King's "The Little Convent Girl," from her 1893 *Balcony Stories,* is characterized by racialist assumptions about the horror of discovery of black blood that characterize many white responses to miscegenation, my argument is that black and white women wrote out of their common perception of a common complex of problems. In King's story, for instance, the little convent girl is ignorant of her black blood because she has been denied knowledge of her parentage; although in this case her white father has forbade her knowledge of her black mother. The language of King's story is a powerful testament to the effacement of distinctions—in this case, between the conscious and unconscious mind—that is the inevitable result of a sundered inheritance. The little convent girl, traveling down the Mississippi to find her mother after her father's death, experiences the river as a kind of great unconscious, which occasionally erupts into consciousness in moments that prefigure the uncanny. Every time the boat lands, for instance, "she thought it was shipwreck, death, judgement, purgatory; and her sins! her sins!"[32] The Mississippi itself is described in terms that suggest the nature of the unconscious:

> It was [the pilot's] opinion that there was as great a river as the Mississippi flowing directly under it—an underself of a river, as much a counterpart of the other as the second story of the house

is of the first; in fact, he said they were navigating through the upper story. Whirlpools were holes in the floor of the upper river, so to speak; eddies were rifts and cracks. And deep under the earth, hurrying toward the subterranean stream, were other streams, hurrying to and from that great mother-stream underneath, just as the small and great overground streams hurry to and from their mother Mississippi.[33]

When the girl learns her mother is black, she drowns herself; she cannot bear the threat to the boundaries of the self that the mulatto condition represents. Her body is never found, and King's language suggests that the little convent girl has retreated into the unconscious, beyond the limits of boundaries: "Perhaps, as the pilot had told her whirlpools always did, it may have carried her through to the underground river, to that vast, hidden, dark Mississippi that flows beneath the one we see; for her body was never found."[34] The little mulatto girl is, in King's story, a "hole in the floor of the upper river," a chink into the vast underworld that threatens the conscious mind, a window into the uncanny.

The novels of Jessie Fauset, an important Harlem Renaissance writer, can at first consideration in no way be classified as texts of the uncanny, or Gothics, at least in Goulder's sense. Critics agree that Fauset's fiction belongs to the category of "the Rear Guard" to which Bone relegates it. Like that of Walter White, DuBois, and to some extent Nella Larsen, her work is very much in the spirit of the novels of the Talented Tenth. In response to the black realism of other Harlem Renaissance fiction, these novelists "still wished to orient Negro art toward white opinion," explains Bone. "They wished to apprise educated whites of the existence of respectable Negroes and to call their attention—now politely, now indignantly—to the facts of racial injustice."[35] Fauset's concerns, however, place her very much in the female ethnic literary tradition. The characters in her novels are motivated by the search for familial identification and lost inheritance, and her treatment of the passing black and the mulatto is informed by the same ambivalence and confusion that characterizes other female-authored mulatto novels.

Fauset's 1924 *There is Confusion*, for instance, has as its subject the routinely thwarted but ultimately triumphant course of love between the heroine, Joanna Marshall, and Peter Bye, but it is imaginatively informed by the complex Bye family genealogy, which traces Peter's ancestry back to two Bye families in Revolutionary Philadelphia—one black and one white. The resolution of the novel lies not only in Joanna and Peter's marriage but in Peter's unraveling of his ancestry, and his ultimate refusal to allow his white ancestor to make Peter's son his heir. Peter's true inheritance, which he cherishes, is a Bible given to his mulatto grandfather by that grandfather's white father.[36] Similar concerns about inheritance inform Fauset's 1933 *Comedy: American Style,* which basically rehearses the different roles available to black women in America. In that novel, however, parentage is denied when one black daughter passes, a dark-skinned son is disowned by his light-skinned mother and kills himself, and a black son embraces his birthright when he takes in his aging father. Fauset's 1928 *Plum Bun* explores the meaning of familial identification for the passing black. Although Angela eventually returns to the black community, the confusion endemic to her condition causes her to sever her ties to her sister in order to maintain her relationship with a white man. Her sister is reminded of the conditions of miscegenation under slavery when she sees Angela with her white lover: "Suddenly she remembered that it had been possible for white men and women to mistreat their mulatto relations, their own flesh and blood, selling them into deeper slavery in the far South or standing by watching them beaten, almost, if not completely, to death."[37]

In Fauset's 1931 *The Chinaberry Tree,* these themes achieve their fullest expression. In *The Chinaberry Tree,* the parallel stories of Laurentine Strange and her cousin Melissa both reiterate the confusion of the mulatto's inheritance. Laurentine is the daughter of Sal Strange, the beloved black mistress of white Colonel Holloway, a couple whose lifelong love affair (he fetches up the titular tree from Alabama to New Jersey for Sal) provides the town's "one and great scandal."[38] Holloway's material legacy to Sal and Laurentine is a percentage of the income from his factories—which his legal widow deliberately mismanages so as to deny the Stranges material comfort.[39] But Laurentine's psychic legacy is, as her last name suggests, ostracism from the town and rejection by men on the grounds of her mother's reputation. One character explains:

Well their mothers wan't no good wuz they? And what does the Bible say about the sins of the fathers,—and mothers too that means. . . . Everybody knows about Laurentine's mother [.] Ain't that very house they're living in the wages of sin?⁴⁰

Laurentine feels she is "nobody, not only illegitimate . . . but the child of a connection that all America frowns upon. I'm literally fatherless."⁴¹ But Laurentine is rewarded with a black doctor who rejects these misapplications of the concept of inheritance. He says, significantly, " 'I'm not interested in fathers and mothers. . . . I'm interested in sons and daughters.' "⁴²

Similar concerns inform *The Chinaberry Tree*'s parallel plot, but in a more ominous way. Laurentine's rebellious cousin Melissa takes up with Malory Forten, much to the growing consternation of the townspeople, who know what Melissa and Malory do not: that her father was also Malory's, and that Malory is her half-brother. Significantly, Melissa and Malory misunderstand the town's disapproval, thinking that its response is to the Strange legacy of interracial adultery. Their marriage is narrowly averted; and at Malory's revelation of the truth to Melissa, Fauset does indeed venture into the uncanny, as Malory's face assumes to Melissa the grotesque and leering dimensions of a comic mask that Melissa recognizes from recurrent dreams.⁴³ *The Chinaberry Tree* is a novel that acknowledges the connection between the mulatto, inheritance, and the uncanny even as it attempts to repress it.

In a twentieth-century novel by a white woman, Edith Pope's *Colcorton,* a similar complex of concerns emerges and is identified as a particularly American subject. The novel, a Faulknerian Gothic with literary merit in its own right, is about Abby Clanghearne, a white woman whose hidden black blood functions as a symbol of repression in the text. Abby, an admirable if indomitably cranky heroine, takes in her brother's white wife, Beth, and their child, Jad, when Abby's brother dies following discovery of his black ancestry. Their life at Colcorton is disrupted by a visiting writer, Clement Johnson, who wants to buy the farm and, incidentally, make Abby the subject of his next novel. In the inexorably Gothic logic that characterizes the novel, it is Johnson, the writer and outsider, who discovers the fact of Abby's black ancestry; it is as if Pope were commenting on her own special relationship to the ethnicity of her text.⁴⁴

More to the point, however, is the way in which blackness functions in the text as a secret, a symbol of repression. Johnson, in piecing together the slave-trading past of Abby's aristocratic grand-father, is beginning to puzzle out the secret of her ancestry when he suffers a fall and wakes with this knowledge repressed, to re-surface classically in his dreams, in which "a coal black witch with the face of Abby Clanghearne pursued him through a jungle growth of a Colcorton gone to ruin."[45] Johnson's gradual remembrance of the secret is based on a trope that light-skinned blacks grow darker as they age, a trope that, however inaccurate, is essential to the plot: Abby must give up Beth and Jad because in order to allow Jad a white child's advantages her "increasingly" black presence must be removed. As the drama of Abby's story unfolds in John-son's mind, he begins to shape the material into a novel, a text whose plot he recognizes as intrinsically American: "It's like an Orson Welles scenario, he thought. Only of course they would never film it. It's American but it's taboo."[46] What Johnson—and Pope—realize, of course, is that the taboo of ethnicity and the paradox of ethnic oppression are what make Abby's story Ameri-can:

> The pivotal point of any story about the Clanghearnes was that Abby was a mulatto. She knew it, too. It explained Abby as no other single fact could explain her.
>
> America, Johnson thought, what have you done, what have you done to your children? That was the angle he'd play up; he'd make it implicit on every page. . . . We grant you, Abby, a right to your happiness, we guarantee you freedom in which to sit shud-dering in your house, to hide in your woods, fearfully to wonder when the other citizens will hold you to a lifelong strict account of a crime you never committed.[47]

Juxtaposed to Johnson's conception of the drama of American ethnic inheritance and oppression, however, is Abby's anticipation of the tangible oppression in store for Jad if her family's black ancestry is revealed in Johnson's novel. Abby's discovery of his plans rouses her feminist indignation about being objectified, written about; and in Abby's reaction Pope acknowledges her own ambivalence about attempting to understand and write Abby's story, the ambivalence of a white writing about blacks. "Every-thing was a story to Mr. Johnson, nothing real," muses Abby/Pope.[48]

Pope's heroine reacts to the parody of inheritance that has characterized black life by refusing to acknowledge the law of inheritance, by effacing it altogether. If the law deems that a child with one drop of black blood has as its inheritance that one drop, and none of the rights or property willed to him through his white ancestry, the notion of inheritance becomes perverse. Abby burns the will that attests to her family's black ancestry, and painfully and courageously refuses to join Beth and Jad to pass in the North. The loss is considerable. Abby loses Jad and Beth, but also her own inheritance—namely, the love and respect her grandfather accorded his black wife, which is inscribed in the will she burns: " 'Namely has [Abby Magdilaine Iah] always been respected as my Wife and as such I do here acknowledge her; Nor do I think that her truth, honor, integrity, moral conduct or good sense will lose by comparison with anyone.' "[49] In looking toward the future and effacing her own past, Abby is, of course, participating in a drama as American as an Orson Welles scenario. Hers is, as I will argue, a classic American response to the complex interplay of ethnicity and ancestry, at the same time as it is a protest against the mockery made of inheritance by the paradoxes embedded in miscegenation, against a society that makes the past itself taboo. Amanda Crane, the heroine of white author Barbara Anderson's 1949 *Southbound*, reacts in a similarly ambivalent way to her discovery of her white father's name: she writes it out obsessively, feels "new pride in sharing the heritage" of her white father, and yet feels a "grudge against inheritance."[50] Like Ursa Corregidora, these heroines are faced with a paradoxical definition of selfhood based on the denial of an undeniable past.

The mulatto, or "white Negro," is, as Simone Vauthier argues, "a paradigm of the dark sexual secret of generation and a symbol of the rejected child."[51] As such, the mulatto represents a repression. The rejected child that the mulatto symbolizes calls up, as I have argued, the threat of taboo, specifically, of incest. The connection Freud draws in *Totem and Taboo* between taboo and obsessive behavior helps to explain ethnic literature's obsessive concern with disruption of inheritance and, in fact, incest. Similarly, Freud's suggestion that emotional ambivalence is built into the concept of tabooed behavior helps to account for the vast variety of ambivalent fictional uses of the mulatto. Taboo, Freud writes, "has a connotation which includes 'sacred' and 'above the ordinary,' as well as 'dangerous,' 'unclean,' and 'uncanny.' "[52] Freud's remarks can well be applied to the mulatto figure, who represents taboo repressed. The mulatto in fiction is nothing if not *special*, whether "above the ordinary" or "unclean." The mulatto reminds us of something we do not want to remember. This goes a long way toward explaining the extreme anxiety that characterizes racial supremacists' thinking on the subject, an anxiety expressed on any number of different levels. For instance, the notion that intermingling of the races is somehow unnatural is an extreme emotional reaction to the repression the mulatto represents. Residual polygenist theories, which insisted on the distinction of the black race as a separate species, Darwin notwithstanding, seem to have fed on these anxieties.[53] Emotional insistence on the unnaturalness of the interracial union makes explicit the connection between taboo and ambivalence. White supremacist Henry Hughes wrote in 1860:

> Hybridism is heinous. Impurity of races is against the law of nature. Mulattoes are monsters. The law of nature is the law of God. The same law which forbids consanguinous amalgamation forbids ethnical amalgamation. Both are incestuous. Amalgamation is incest.[54]

The contradictory nature of this logic—if blacks are the brothers and sisters of whites, then they share a common humanity that I doubt Hughes would have acknowledged—reflects the contradictions implicit in reaction to miscegenation.

The mulatto, then, as an unsuccessful repression, represents a naming of the taboo, and as such constitutes an implicit threat to cultural equilibrium. Women writers, insistent on the factuality of miscegenation, turned again and again to the mulatto figure, and, in doing so, in effect named the taboo. Frances Gaither, a white writer whose 1949 *Double Muscadine* is in what might be called the *Colcorton* genre, makes this point explicitly. Kirk McLean's wife, attempting to discuss with a family friend her husband's relationship with a black slave, falters, sensing his disapproval: "His eyes were compassionate. No, they said. You can't. Not to me, a man. You would have to break too many taboos of ancient tribal hallowing."[55] McLean's concubine, a slave named Lethe, has been deprived of her rightful inheritance. Lethe's name, which means forgetfulness, implies its opposite: that the fact of the taboo, of sex between the races, can never be forgotten, that lines of inheritance must be preserved. McLean's sister-in-law, Harriet, attempts to restore Lethe to her inheritance, reminding McLean of the clause in her father's will stipulating that Lethe be freed after his death. She realizes that she has transgressed:

> She knew that she had shocked him. To him and to practically every other redblooded man of his acquaintance, the question she had raised was one scarcely so much of morals as of taste. Such things should be kept out of sight. . . . He felt as outraged as if she had cast to earth ancient tablets of stone.[56]

For a woman to acknowledge this question "scarcely so much of morals as of taste"—to use Gaither's remarkably suggestive phrase—is analogous to a literal breaking of the commandments, a casting to earth of the very "ancient tablets of stone" on which God had inscribed them. In attempting to assert the law of inheritance against the transgression the relationship represents, the woman is forced to name the taboo. In this sense the fiction of the ethnic woman writer, in which miscegenation figures centrally as a metaphor, is a representation of her own authorial identity: Lillian Smith's 1944 *Strange Fruit,* a novel about an interracial affair, was, in one of our culture's more literal manifestations of unsuccessful repression, banned in Boston.[57]

Repression is never entirely successful, the return of the repressed always a threat. If, as I have argued, miscegenation represents the testing of the boundaries between self and other, the conscious and unconscious, and calls up social forms of the uncanny that, as Goulder suggests, include incest, and if the mulatto represents the repression of what miscegenation implies, it is not surprising that black and white writers sometimes chose to see the mulatto as irrevocably sterile and at other times to perpetrate the image of a "coal-black baby" born to light-skinned parents. The coal-black baby represents, to black and white minds, the return of what has been repressed. Similarly, the attraction of the idea of atavism to white supremacists and the embrace of African primitivism by Harlem Renaissance writers and contemporary black nationalists are essentially expressions of an interesting connection between roots and repression, and of the meaning of ancestry in the ethnic experience. In the minds of white racists, according to Judith Berzon, "atavism is the notion that the mixed blood who has attained a veneer of white civilization can, at any time, 'revert' to the savage, primitivistic behavior of the jungle from which his ancestors came and to which he is inextricably tied." Berzon adds, "This view of course assumes that all tribal behavior was primitivistic in the first place."[58] The idea of uncontrollable reversion to "type"—whether through the birth of a coal-black baby or sudden "jungle" behavior—appears in both black- and white-authored fiction. For eugenicists and white supremacists, atavism has functioned as a powerful reminder of what has been repressed; for black writers and black nationalists, the same notion has functioned as a powerful celebration of what has been repressed.

In the works of white "romantic racialist" authors—to use a term commonly applied to Harriet Beecher Stowe—atavistic assumptions about mulattoes are exploited for dramatic effect.[59] Black blood, these writers assert, always tells. In Anna Dickinson's 1868 *What Answer,* Francesca Ercildoune, the mulatto heroine, at one point clenches her fist so violently that she frightens herself. She thinks bitterly, " 'So—the drop of savage blood is telling at last!' "[60] Peola, a passing black in Fannie Hurst's 1933 *Imitation of Life,* who from girlhood denies her black mother and attempts to pass, actually has herself sterilized in order to marry a white man and forestall the inevitable black baby, thereby making a connection between reproduction and ancestry that in some ways prefigures Gayl Jones's *Corregidora.* Peola denies both ancestry and descendants, eerily consenting to the stereotype of the sterile mulatto.[61]

Gertrude Atherton's 1900 *Senator North* contains a fascinating subplot whose climax hinges on the idea of atavism. The white heroine, Betty, after some consternation at learning she has a mulatto half-sister, brings Harriet to Washington, where she will help her pass in white society. Betty attempts to stifle Harriet's proclivity for hymn-singing, and to teach Harriet that she must never laugh, lest she reveal "the fatuous grin of the Negro."[62] In ghoulishly racist scenes, Harriet reminds Betty repeatedly of her blackness. She points out her bluish fingernails to Betty (who "dropped her hand with an uncontrollable shudder and covered her face with her muff."[63]) and constantly insists on her innately lazy and deceitful nature, traits Atherton clearly associates with blackness. After Harriet reveals to a horrified Betty her secret marriage to Betty's Southern and racist cousin, Betty's fear that Harriet's black blood will tell increases. Inevitably, Harriet is drawn (by something in her black blood, Atherton suggests) to a black camp-meeting, becomes "drunk with religion," and confesses all to her husband; double suicide follows.[64]

Indefensibly racist, Atherton's novel is also a satire. Betty's racist hypocrisy is one of her favorite targets. Betty, a bored little rich girl looking for a cause, visits a black church, is moved by the mulatto "plight," "went home and for twenty-four hours fought with the desire to champion the cause of the Negro and make him her lifework."[65] Atherton's treatment of Betty's response to the knowledge of her father's illegitimate mulatto daughter suggests a more serious concern, and places Atherton in the female ethnic tradition as I have described it. On first hearing of her mulatto half-sister, Betty feels intense sympathy: "Could duty be more plain? and was she a chosen instrument to right at least one of the wrongs perpetrated by the brilliant, warm-hearted, reckless men of her race?" But Betty was "Southern to her finger-tips. . . . The repulsion was physical, inherited from generations of proud women, and she could not control it."[66] Betty does, finally, take Harriet in, with a certain cynical sense of duty. (Atherton writes that Betty "remarked philosophically, 'I suppose I may consider myself lucky that I have not had one of his brats thrust on me before.' "[67]) Significantly, she restores Harriet's rightful inheritance by giving over to her the money left to Betty by their father. Atherton's retreat to a racist use of atavism constitutes a representation of the complex attitude of a white woman to her father's "sins." Harriet is a constant reminder of an unsuccessful repression: she can "revert"; she can produce, as Senator North warns Betty, a coal-black baby. Atherton's racist humor becomes a defensively hostile response to the return of the repressed, to the threat of the mulatto.

In a similar way, Kate Chopin's use of the black baby born to "white" parents as the tragic impetus for her short story "Desireé's Baby," collected in her 1894 *Bayou Folk,* suggests Chopin's troubled apprehension of the complex interplay of inheritance and racial identity. Her subtly racist assumptions about the "tragedy" implicit in the discovery of black ancestry suggest affinities between "Desireé's Baby" and the contemporary Grace King story discussed above, "The Little Convent Girl." Desireé, because she is an orphan and does not know her parentage, accepts the "blame" for her baby's black blood and allows her husband to drive her from their home and to suicide. Chopin withholds until the story's last lines the fact that Desireé's husband, the son of a mulatto woman and a white man, has kept from Desireé his knowledge of his parentage. Chopin's story carries a feminist protest—muted, as is usual in Chopin—against the notion of the patrilinear inheritance of blood and the matrilinear inheritance of blame.

As I have suggested, black-authored novels also play on notions of atavism and "reversion," on the theme of the coal-black baby. Related to these notions is another common feature in mulatto novels or novels of passing: the heroine returns after a sojourn in the white world to the black community (or "her own people," as it is commonly and not entirely accurately described). Helga Crane, in Nella Larsen's *Quicksand,* does so with a vengeance: she marries a black preacher and moves with him to the deep South. Jessie Fauset's heroines pass only for fun or convenience or find such misery in passing that they return to the black world. Harper's Iola Leroy marries another light-skinned black who refuses to pass. In fact, the more light-skinned her heroine, the more insistent is the novelist that she realign herself with the black race. The black novelist's awareness of the danger of alienating white audiences who might have been made anxious by the phenomenon of successful passing explains this insistence only in part. In fact, the idea of successful passing seems to have worried the black novelist as well. As I have suggested above, this is largely in response to the threat of tabooed behavior—specifically, of incest. The light-skinned black who passes successfully may marry her white half-brother. In returning her to the black community, the novelist ensures that she will not. Within the black community, as Gutman has shown, strong kinship ties act as injunctions against the familial chaos threatened by slavery—and, in addition, by miscegenation. The black novelist's protest against the disruption of inheritance implicit in miscegenation expresses itself in a reaffirmation of kinship ties, of the inheritance of black "blood."

The heroine's black blood is, of course, usually the legacy of the mother: this helps to explain the strongly matrilinear bias of the black woman's novel. Vyry, the mulatto heroine of Margaret Walker's 1966 *Jubilee,* denies her patrilinear inheritance when she protests her husband's reminding her of her white ancestry: " 'You done called me a white folks' nigger and throwed my color in my face cause my daddy was a white man. He wasn't no father to me, he was just my master.' "[68]

In the sense that black blood is also a legacy, an inherited quality, it is not surprising to see in novels by black women a similar insistence to that which shapes white women's fiction about blacks—that "blood will tell." Repression in the black-authored novel in this sense functions more positively; the black woman wants to remind white society of what has been repressed, or to celebrate it. Fictional uses of "reversion," the coal-black baby, and even atavism are positive affirmations of true inheritance. On the other hand, they present a real threat to a passsing or mulatto woman in a racist society, and the black writer in general presents the mulatto or passing black with some ambivalence.

In Nella Larsen's 1929 *Passing,* Irene Redfield, a mulatto heroine who has chosen to marry a black man and live in Harlem, explains to her husband, " 'It's funny about 'passing.' We disapprove of it and at the same time we condone it. It excites our contempt and at the same time we condone it. We shy away from it with an odd kind of revulsion, but we protect it.' "[69] This is, I think, largely Larsen's point of view. *Passing* has been generally misunderstood because critics have assumed that Larsen aligns herself with prim Irene Redfield in condemning her passing friend, Clare Kendry. This assessment places Larsen squarely in the ranks of Bone's "Rear Guard" of black bourgeois novelists intent on black social mobility and acceptance in the white world, when actually *Passing* is a strongly feminist novel that attempts to explicate the meanings of ethnic female identity in American culture.[70] The novel addresses directly the meaning of passing and the denial of heritage it seems to represent; it confronts the problem of ancestry in black identity, as Larsen indicates in the novel's epigraph, a quotation from Harlem Renaissance poet Countee Cullen:

> One three centuries removed
> From the scenes his fathers loved,

> Spicy grove, cinnamon tree,
> What is Africa to me?[71]

Irene Redfield, a member of the black middle class who lives in comfort with her doctor husband on Harlem's Sugar Hill, finds her whole life shaken by her renewed acquaintance with a childhood friend, Clare Kendry, who is married to a white man and passes for white. The novel's subject is Irene's struggle to maintain her respectable and secure self-image in the face of the threat Clare's appearance represents to it. Larsen writes, "Above everything else [Irene] had worked, had striven, to keep undisturbed the pleasant routine of her life. And now Clare Kendry had come into her life, and with her the menace of impermanence."[72] Irene Redfield, a woman who does not weep because "weeping did not become her,"[73] refuses to let her husband discuss lynching at the dinner table. Larsen cirtic Mary Mabel Youman points out that it is not Clare but Irene who passes, that Irene "has more truly lost her heritage than Clare who literally removes herself from Black life and lives a white among whites."[74]

Clare is a threat to Irene not simply because she passes but because she is undermining the success of her own passing by visiting Harlem, associating with blacks, and, in effect, retaining her black birthright. Irene has a clear horror that the repressed will return. She herself cannot pass for convenience without terrible anxiety, and Clare's ability to do so calmly alarms and upsets her. She protests that Clare's visits to Harlem are not "safe," and Clare's response is contemptuous dismissal:

> "Safe!"
> It seemed to Irene that Clare had snapped her teeth down and flung it from her. And for another flying second she had that suspicion of Clare's ability for a quality of feeling that was to her strange, and even repugnant. She was aware, too, of a dim premonition of some impending disaster. It was as if Clare Kendry had said to her, for whom safety, security were all-important: Safe! Damn being safe! and meant it.

Clare, whom Irene suspects is "capable of heights and depths of feelings that she, Irene Redfield, had never known,"[75] represents an unrepressed sexuality that threatens Irene's "security." Irene's anxiety is so great, and her horror at Clare's white husband's discovery of Clare's blackness so intense, that Clare herself must be removed. She falls from a sixth-story window, and the text implies that Irene pushes her.

Passing's subject is repression and its consequences. Larsen subscribes to notions of black identity that dictate that her passing heroine hunger for black companions and the streets of Harlem, but in making Clare and not Irene her heroine she suggests that the concept of "blood will tell" be reconsidered as a refusal to deny one's birthright and a reaffirmation of that which has been repressed. The novel asks, what is Africa—or ancestry—to the descendant of Africans, to "one three centuries removed"?

Clare Kendry's coherent black identity is based not so much on a reclamation of her "roots" as on a recognition of the complex interplay of ethnicity and inheritance, of the conflict between "consent" and "descent" that Werner Sollors suggests has characterized American life.[76] Clare Kendry, the passing black who is drawn to Harlem, has it both ways: she is both entirely self-made, denying her inheritance in order to live comfortably in the world, and definitely rooted, embracing her black heritage. Her fictional relative, Helga Crane in Larsen's 1933 *Quicksand,* is an orphan psychologically fettered by the same options that liberate Clare Kendry. Helga Crane belongs, according to Judith Berzon, to the tradition of the mulatto as existential man, alienated, fragmented, unable to identify with either the dominant group or the one that is excluded. The mulatto is an existential heroine, I would argue, only insofar as she represents the paradox of the orphan, who is both free from the past and at the same time firmly grounded in it. Winthrop Jordan, in explaining the historical rationale for laws that defined mulattoes, writes that this question "arose . . . in the cultural matrix of purpose, accomplishment, self-conception, and social circumstances in the New World. The social-identification of children requires self-identification in the fathers."[77] Of course, self-identification for the mulatto was not, as I have argued in this chapter, in the fathers but in the mothers, and that in some senses is the subject of ethnic women's fiction. But Jordan's point is important, for it reminds us of the fragile but meaningful relationship between social- and self-identification, and of the meanings of ancestry for the individual living within a society. America was founded by sons and daughters of the Old World who essen-

tially refused their inheritance to start anew, and then, in the New
World, became positively obessed with their parentage. The fasci-
nation in the American imagination for the bastard, the hero without a father, reflects a national preoccupation with the irrevocably
linked concepts of patricide and filiopietism. American literature
seems to play out obsessively the drama of the search for the father
and the rejection of him. American identity has been shaped by
the conflict between self-made individualism and the concept of
family. Because this conflict is, I would argue, essentially ethnic—
in the sense that it is most tangibly felt in the ethnic experience—
it is not surprising that ethnic literature should return to it over
and over, particularly in the guise of the concept of miscegenation.
In the literature of the mulatto, the conflict receives fullest expression. The mulatto, the product of interracial union, is a literalization of this fundamental conflict between inheritance and
individualism. This helps to explain the persistence of a mulatto
"tradition" in literature, which is, if one has to sum it up, the tradition of the divided self. Neither white nor black, as the title of
Berzon's study of mulatto fiction suggests, the mulatto is also
neither self-made nor ancestrally defined. But division implies
union, and the mulatto, both white and black, is, as all Americans
are, *both* self-made and ancestrally defined. A living embodiment
of the paradox of the individual within society, the fictional mulatto is the imaginative conjunction of a cultural disjunction. One
such character vividly experiences her legacy of division and
union when she learns that her father was white and her mother
black:

> She had always thought of her body as solid, one piece. Now
> she knew it was otherwise. She was black outside, but inside was
> her father's blood.
> She thought about this carefully. And her body seemed to ex-
> pand, to swell, growing like a balloon. She thought of all the dis-
> tance between the two parts of her, the white and the black. And
> it seemed to her that those two halves would pull away and
> separate and leave her there in the open, popped out like a kernel
> from its husk. . . . She wrapped her arms tight around her
> middle to keep herself together, and her ribs quivered and shook
> under her fingers.[78]

CHAPTER 7

Gertrude Stein's
The Making of Americans
as an Ethnic Text

In the 1970s and 1980s, a new phenomenon emerged in the book trade: that of the generational saga, which follows the progress of a family over a period of generations. Subtly different from its sister genres, the historical romance and the contemporary love story, the generational saga is written according to a formula characterized by a triadic generational economy of three generations with a fourth implied in the love plots of the grandchildren. A representative novel of the genre, Belva Plain's 1978 *Evergreen,* has as its epigraph a quotation from *Ecclesiastes,* "One generation passeth away, and another generation cometh: but the earth abideth forever." The jacket of the paperback edition describes the novel's contents and mood fairly accurately:

> From shtetl to mansion—the wonderfully rich epic of a woman's loves, a family's fortunes, and a century's hopes and tragedies. The intensely moving story of Anna Friedman, who came to the golden shores of America in search of a better life. . . . The triumphant epic that spans three generations of an unforgettable family.

Novels like *Evergreen,* spanning the progress of three generations, "from shtetl to mansion," have become a huge business in the book trade as they have climbed hardback and paperback bestseller lists.

At first, the dimensions of this "new" genre seem at best unclear. The "generational saga" has been, in some form, represented in the literary tradition by such works as *Oedipus Rex, The Aeneid, King Lear,* and *War and Peace.* In the twentieth century, writers as diverse as Galsworthy and Faulkner have used "generations" as the subjects of their "sagas." In recent decades, however, the genre has taken on a specific meaning within the publishing business which might be useful for literary criticism. As a new genre, the generational saga emerged from the tradition of Galsworthy and Delderfield, and later from that of Alex Haley's 1976 *Roots;* in the last decade the genre has become far more particularized, defining those works, usually written by women and read by women, that span not only generations but continents, following the immigration of foreign grandparents to the "golden shores" of America and the subsequent careers, loves, and struggles of their children and grandchildren. Concerned with the meaning of ancestry and inheritance in the making of the American self, these novels rehearse a favorite theme in the ethnic female literary imagination, exploring the ethnic woman's "place" in American culture. The generational saga represents a coming together of these concerns, within the context of a heavily plotted—indeed, formulaic—genre that allows the woman writer to tell her story with what often seems the smallest effort possible. Of slight literary merit, novels like *Evergreen* represent a new generation in the ethnic female tradition, one that will, like generations, soon pass away.[1]

On the other hand, these novels remind us of the centrality of concerns about ancestry, inheritance, and generations in American women's fiction. In fact, Belva Plain's precursor in the generational saga is one of America's foremost women writers, and one of the great stylistic innovators of the twentieth century, Gertrude Stein, who in her 1925 *The Making of Americans* wrote what is in some sense the first "generational saga." *The Making of Americans,* like *Evergreen* a "triumphant epic that spans three generations of an unforgettable family," follows the progress of the Hersland family "from shtetl to mansion"; it is, as its subtitle indicates, "the history of a family's progress." Marianne Moore, in one of the few sympathetic reviews of the novel, described *The Making of Americans* as "a kind of living genealogy, which is in its branching, unified and vivid."[2] In the novel, Stein explores the concerns of the ethnic American woman about the meanings of ancestry in female identity. She does so, moreover, in a way that questions not only the concepts of generations and genre but of the

writer's relationship to language itself. Like John Dos Passos and
Jean Toomer, Henry Roth and Maxine Hong Kingston, Stein in-
terrogates the ethnic American's relationship to her acquired—
and, because the writer is the *offspring* of immigrants, inherited—
language. *The Making of Americans,* an ethnic text both in terms
of content and of form, questions literary tradition itself, in that
Stein writes both within and against inherited stylistic convention.
Jewish-American writer Gertrude Stein reminds us that ethnicity
is a concern not only for members of the "realistic" school—as
we might call Mary Antin, Anzia Yezierska, and Martha Ostenso
for instance—but that it is also a fundamental element of twentieth-century modernism.

In fact, Stein's relationship to the English language is one of
the factors that contributed to the remarkable innovation of her
work. A daughter of immigrants who spent her early years not in
America but in Europe, Stein wrote very much with a sense as if
English were her second language. In doing so, she maintained
what she felt was a singularly rarefied relationship to it, one that
she consciously develops and comments on in her work. Her fasci-
nation with English grammar is in part traceable to this, as is her
sometimes stilted, always extremely conscious use of the language.
Similarly, Stein valued her expatriate status in that it allowed her
to perceive herself as more truly American. Just as she could develop a closer relationship to the English language by maintaining
her sense of it as a second language, so too could she value America as her true home by virtue of leaving it. She explained in a
1940 essay, *What Are Masterpieces,* that "one needs two civili-
zations":

> And so Americans go to Paris and they are free not to be
> connected with anything happening.
> That is what foreignness is, that it is there but it does not hap-
> pen. England to an American English writing to an American is
> not in this sense a foreign thing. And so we go to Paris.[3]

Because she saw her relationship to the English language and
America in this way, Stein fully understood the essentially bifur-
cated quality of American identity, in terms of which the American is both defined by her membership in American society, self-
made, and the possessor of an inherited self, ancestrally defined.

Because Stein wrote with such a consciousness, her work does indeed achieve a kind of intensified American quality, as does her use of the English language.

In such a context, a certain tension between the writer and her language is inevitable. Because of this tension, *The Making of Americans* is a difficult novel to read. Far from being a bestseller, a "good read" in the sense of Belva Plain's *Evergreen, The Making af Americans* is at first crack a nearly impossible book to get through. Edmund Wilson, in *Axel's Castle,* confessed that he had not been able to finish the novel and defied any reader to do so:

> With sentences so regularly rhythmical, so needlessly prolix, so many times repeated and ending so many times in present participles, the reader is all too soon in a state, not to follow the slow beginning of life, but simply to fall asleep.[4]

The Making of Americans is a difficult novel; it is also an extremely long one, running in its unabridged form close to 1,000 pages in length.[5] Stein referred to the novel during its composition as, simply, "the long book";[6] ten years after its publication she acknowledged that the writing of it was "an enormously long thing to do."[7] In fact, Stein spent close to eight years in the writing of the novel, from 1903 to 1911; it was not published until 1925; she abridged it in 1935 and gave a lecture on it in the same year; she refers to it in her critical work throughout her career.[8] In some senses, then, the novel was with her almost all of her life, and is best considered less as an apprentice work—though the writing of it certainly helped Stein develop ideas and techniques—than as a lifework.[9]

Stein began the writing of *The Making of Americans* around 1903; the novel's subject at its inception was the marriages of two sisters, and a romantic plot that rehearses the plot of *Q.E.D., or Things As They Are,* written in 1903. One of the two sisters was to become Julia Dehning in the final version of the novel, and the triangle plot is represented in the story of Philip and Martha Redfern and Miss Cora Dounor. As Leon Katz has suggested, this early version of the novel represented a thinking through of Stein's personal experiences, including her difficult relationship with May Bookstaver.[10] Stylistically, the novel at this point was located in the nineteenth rather than the twentieth century, a characteristic that the finished novel in some respects shares. In 1902–1905, writes Katz, Stein wrote parts of *The Making of Americans,* "thinking of it in terms of thorough-going realism and as a thoroughly Victorian chronicle which demanded that the author be conversant with all the surface details of her characters, activities, and milieu."[11] This was, however, only part of the novel Stein intended to write. With the composition of *Three Lives,* in 1905–1906, Stein developed the stylistic techniques and philosophical basis for her later work on the novel. In the years between 1906 and 1908, the bulk of the novel was written, and its uniquely American subject began to emerge. It was during this time that Stein developed the idea of writing a "generational saga," or following the fortunes of immigrants traveling to America, their children and grandchildren. During this time Stein was also developing a theory of representation derived from what she saw going on in modern painting and sculpture, and revising the philosophical underpinnings of her complex understanding of human identity.

In 1908–1911, Stein devoted almost all of her time to *The Making of Americans;* in these years, she sought to develop a theory of personality that she had first begun to test out in the writing of her 1909 *Melanctha.* This complicated theory of personality was essentially a theory of classification, under the categories of attack and resistance. Men and women could be either "dependent independent," or "independent dependent"; the first group fight by resisting, the second by attacking.[12] Stein's interest in characterology grew out of her scientific efforts under William James's direction at Radcliffe in 1893–1897. With the hindsight of the critic, it is tempting to read into Stein's psychological experiments and her reports of them the beginnings of the novelist. She studied human behavior *as* a novelist. For instance, studying the reactions of students in normal activity and in exam-related fatigue, Stein concluded not that such reactions do or do not differ, but instead expressed interest in how the reactions might reflect the individual. "In these actions it will be readily observed that habits of attention are reflexes of the complete character of the individual."[13] Interested in how words and actions reveal character, Stein was further influenced in her development of a theory of "complete character" by a psychology treatise by Otto Weininger, *Sex and*

Character, as Leon Katz has pointed out. Weininger's book, which Stein read and discussed in 1908, is essentially a diatribe against women, dividing character traits according to gender. Stein's inter- action with and eventual transformation of a gender-based charac- terology is extremely interesting, but beyond the scope of this dis- cussion.[14] Stein learned from Weininger a methodology of antithesis that was inherently appealing to her. Simply put, she liked opposites; moreover, she realized that each individual contained op- posites within himself. If we consider her system in this light, it is not without value, even if Stein's close adherence to it becomes tedious, and her growing frustration with it increasingly evident.

The writing of *The Making of Americans* during these years was not an easy process for Stein, in spite of Alice Toklas's con- tinued participation. I will argue that many of Stein's ideas if car- ried to their logical conclusions, become absurd; Stein herself came to realize this during the book's composition. The finished novel bears a real feel of process, as Stein works ideas and tech- niques through, struggling to come to terms with the language of the dominant culture. The novel is not only a history of a family's progress but also a history of its own progress. The alert reader can sense Stein's alternating moods and difficulties; it is even pos- sible to notice when Alice catches up in her typing of the manu- script to the point that she is typing the previous day's work, as the novel becomes at times an intimate dialogue, with a disguised erotic subtext of the sort feminist critics have begun to locate in works like *Tender Buttons*.[15] Sometimes Stein announces her fail- ures and successes, with statements like "I am all unhappy in this writing,"[16] or the poignant and important passage in which she ex- plains in what ways she writes for herself and for strangers.[17] Richard Bridgman, who feels that the work as a novel—rather than as "a psychological and stylistic daybook"—is a "disaster," provides a wonderful analogy that points out the sense of *process* and *progress* the novel conveys:

> It gives the impression of someone learning how to drive. Periodi- cally there are smooth stretches, but these are interrupted by bumps, lurches, wild wrenchings of the wheel, and sudden brak- ings. All the while the driver can be heard muttering reminders and encouragements to herself, imprecations, and cries of alarm.[18]

However much *The Making of Americans* represents a process, or, as Bridgman argues, an apprentice work, it is important to remember that Stein, who gave the concept of genre considerable thought, considered it a novel, in fact, considered it the great American novel, that elusive beast pursued by readers, writers, and critics since the last century. In 1934 and 1935, when Stein was abridging and revising *The Making of Americans* for a second edition that she hoped would reach a larger audience than had the first, she visited America on an extended lecture tour. The lectures she gave, including "The Gradual Making of the Making of Americans," were published as *Lectures in America* in 1935. Steinn, who is a remarkable figure in American letters in the extraordinary enthusiasm and exuberance she brought to almost every experience of her life, found the experience of America particularly exhilarating. Her lectures are in large part an exploration of the *idea* of America, and an attempt to reassess the very American quality of her work. Her idea of America was a complicated one, as I shall argue. She was essentially right, however, when she described her novel in "The Gradual Making of The Making of Americans" as "an American book an essentially American book."[19] With uncharacteristic modesty Stein never wrote about the concept of "the great American novel," but if she had, one senses that she would have done a great deal of tortuous thinking about the article within the phrase. In the Steinian concept of America, there would be no single great American novel but many, and perhaps here it is best to let the sleeping beast lie.

It seems absolutely clear, however, that the subject of Stein's great American novel is America. Bernard Faÿ, in his adulatory preface to the 1935 edition, recognized this quality:

> The family she describes is America itself with its migrations, its flights, its settlements, its conquests. She has shown all the generations, all the adventures of America: business, love, sports, studies. She has shown all the American hopes and all the American fears. She has used all the American words, all the American rhythms, and the big American climax. . . . [T]here has never been a book more faithful to the rhythm of America and more inclined to love the American people while laughing at them and with them.[20]

Faÿ's comment, if less illuminating than effusive, does begin to define the particularly American quality of Stein's novel. For in choosing to write about a family over the course of several generations, from its arrival in America, including "its migration, its

flights, its settlements, and its conquests," Stein found a subject
uniquely and centrally American, for the experience of immigration is the central feature of American life.[21] The concept of generations—generations in the sense that we are all first-, third-, or
seventh-generation Americans—is crucial for an understanding of
American identity and her novel, as is the meaning of ancestry
and inheritance in that identity. In this sense, Stein—whose perception of herself as Jewish is very difficult to puzzle out, connected as it was with her perception of herself as an outsider by
virtue of her homosexuality and expatriate status—was writing
very much within the ethnic literary tradition with *The Making of
Americans.*[22]

Stein begins *The Making of Americans* by questioning the
meaning of inheritance by way of a story from Aristotle's *Nichomachean Ethics*:

> Once an angry man dragged his father along the ground
> through his own orchard. "Stop!" cried the groaning old man at
> last, "Stop! I did not drag my father beyond this tree."

Stein concludes from this story that "it is hard living down the
tempers we are born with" (3). Though the moral of the story is
different from what it was for Aristotle—Stein goes on to discuss
our own, and her own, sins and our view of them[23]—the story as
a prologue to a generational saga constitutes a remarkable statement of the meaning of ancestry. It suggests continuity—sons will
always drag fathers through orchards—and threatens discontinuity—sons will always try to drag their fathers *farther*. Because
the dragged father speaks out, he—we suppose—stops the process
of being dragged, asserts continuity; i.e., language pronounces the
difference between generations, just as Stein's novel does. The
anecdote's "gender" is important—the novel will question the
rhetoric of fathers and sons, and the place of mothers and daughters in it. The anecdote is an announcement of the subject of the
novel: ancestry and identity.

In the third paragraph of *The Making of Americans,* Stein states
with sanguine assurance that American identity is not at all difficult to understand, because it has been shaped by a short history.

> It has always seemed to me a rare privilege, this, of being an
> American, a real American, whose tradition it has taken scarcely

sixty years to create. We need only realise our parents, remember our grandparents, and know ourselves and our history is complete. (3)

This remarkable statement demands scrutiny. How, for instance, does Stein arrive at the figure of sixty in determining the number of years it has taken for the American tradition to have been created? In the first place, Stein says that only "an American, "a real American," has a tradition that it has taken sixty years to create. On one level, she is speaking of herself: the Stein family's American "tradition" began in 1841, when Gertrude Stein's grandfather, Meyer Stein, arrived from Germany, a little over sixty years before.[24] Sixty years also seems a fair figure of time to allot to the process of "realising our parents, remembering our grandparents, and knowing our selves."[25] Stein's noteworthy statement, that this process produces one's complete history, recognizes the extent to which the ethnic American's identity relies on a knowledge of generations, remembering grandparents.

The concept of a generation was extremely important to Stein. Generations both mark time and determine self. In her 1935 lecture, "Portraits and Repetition," Stein discusses the way portraits change over generations. A generation, Stein says, marks history. She uses an analogy of movement and perception of movement to explain: "But the strange thing about the realization of existence is that like a train moving there is no real realization of it moving if it does not move against something and so that is what a generation does it shows that moving is existing."[26] Stein argues, in other words, that the individual can have no conception of her existence without seeing herself in the context of movement, history, generations.

Stein was also drawn to the concept of generations because it expressed for her the notion of repetition. The Hersland family in *The Making of Americans* exists in three generations, with a fourth implied in the children of Julia Dehning and Alfred Hersland. In each generation is a David Hersland and a Martha Hersland— three Davids and two Marthas. How are these Davids and Marthas different? Are they different? Do they "repeat" the older generations of Davids and Marthas in any sense other than that their shared name implies? Repetition with a difference is implied even in the anecdote that opens the novel, about a son dragging his father through an orchard. In the anecdote the son's father reveals that he too dragged his father through the orchard, that his son is repeating an action involving not only himself but three generations. The son repeats the father; the novel tries to locate the difference in repetition.

Stein solves the riddle of ancestry in identity by insisting on the difference implicit in the "repetition" of generations. In the same lecture in which Stein discusses the idea that generations supply a sense of movement and history, she explains the connection between generations and repetition. In film, Stein recognized the realization of her concept of repetition with a difference supplying a sense of movement. A film creates movement by a series of frames, each one repeating the action of the one before it, but with a slight difference. Repetition does not exist: "In a cinema picture no two pictures are exactly alike each one is just that much different from the one before, and so in those early portraits there was as I am sure you will realize as I read them to you also as there was in The Making of Americans no repetition."[27] In the experience of the individual, generations provide a series of frames that make up movement into which the individual can insert himself as a "frame" and thereby perceive the movement of history.

In relating the history of three generations of the Hersland family, Stein tried to show the importance of ancestry in identity, and to puzzle out the relationship of the individual's existence to the generations that preceded him. She began with the grandparents, not only because she was attracted to triads almost as much as to dualities, as Bridgman points out—[28] but because she, like other Americans, perceived her history as complete only in the triad of grandparents, parents, and self. Stein as an ethnic writer fully understood Margaret Mead's statement that we are all third-generation Americans.[29] In *The Making of Americans,* a novel she consciously felt was an American novel in subject and method, Stein literalized this central aspect of American identity by making the Hersland grandparents immigrants, as were her own. If one's American history begins only with the grandparents' arrival in America, one really does only need remember one's grandparents to remember the beginning of one's complete history.

The first Martha and David Hersland come to America on Martha's incentive. "[A] great mountain" of a woman, "that good foreign woman who was strong to bear many children" (40–41),

Martha Hersland convinces her husband, a butcher, to follow the
neighbors' example and move to America to make their fortunes.
Martha makes all the arrangements for passage, selling the family's goods and the shop's fittings, while her husband remains
passive:

> But yes, alright, maybe she was right, there was no reason, the
> neighbors had all gotten rich going to America, there was no
> reason why they shouldn't all get rich too there. . . . Alright he
> would go, they would all go and get rich there, Martha could fix
> it if she wanted so badly to fix it, she would be always talking
> to him about it. (42)

As the date set for the family's departure approaches, David becomes more and more reluctant to leave. Stein writes, "Yes it was
hard to start him but it was almost harder to keep him going." In
fact, during the family's long migration in a wagon to the coast
where they will board ship, David Hersland keeps slipping away,
heading back toward his village, only to be retrieved by his wife.
When the Herslands put enough distance between themselves and
their old home, David accepts their leaving: "They went on and
soon it was too far, there was not now any more going back for
him. And then he was content, and he had the new city and the
ship, and then he was content with the new world around him"
(47). About the Herslands' arrival in America with their children,
and their subsequent Americanization, Stein tells little; in fact, she
dismisses the first Martha and David at this point, looking forward
and describing their deaths before turning to the lives of their children. Perhaps, however, she has told enough; all we need do is remember our grandparents, Stein argues. We can do little more because, as Stein explains, "the grandmother we need only to be
remembering," "those four good foreign women the grandmothers,"
are "always old women or as little children to us the generation of
grandchildren" (49). Their individual lives are significant in this
context only insofar as they have contributed to the history of the
family's progress. Stein writes summarily,

> On the whole it was a substantial progress the family had made
> in wealth, in opportunity, in education, in following out the
> mother's leading to come to the new world to find for themselves
> each one a significant fortune. (48)

The Hersland child whose life and descendants Stein chooses to write about is David Hersland; the choice was to prove a rich one. In constructing her idea of the family whose generations she was to describe, Stein worked in a backwards and roundabout fashion. The novel begins not with the Herslands but with the Dehnings, a Bridgepoint family with resemblances to Stein's Baltimore relatives. In the opening section Stein's subject is Julia Dehning's marriage to Alfred Hersland. From there Stein moves to the Hersland family, and at this point begins to work backwards, imagining what Julia Dehning's husband was like, the kind of parents and grandparents he must have had. This is in itself a rather remarkable technique of imaginative construction, especially if contrasted to the apparent methodology of contemporary generational sagas. Chroniclers of generations, it would seem, start with the grandparents, imagining them and their lives, and then their children and their children's children. Stein, on the other hand, subverts the notion of genealogy even as she insists on it, creating the grandparents from her conception of the grandchildren. The grandchild is the father of the man.[30] Stein herself was writing very much from the perspective of a grandchild, not only in the sense that she agreed with Margaret Mead's description of Americans as grandchildren, but in the fact that she was a Stein grandchild, writing the history of the Stein family's progress. This is less to suggest that *The Making of Americans* is autobiographical— though in many senses it is—than that Stein, as an American writer, inevitably extrapolated the past from her own experience.

David Hersland, in fact, bears significant relation to Stein's own father, with whom Stein seems to have had a relationship characterized at best as indifferent. Stein's mother, who died when Stein was fourteen, seems to have been as ineffectual and mild as the second David Hersland's wife. Richard Bridgman argues that Stein reproduced her parents in fictional characterizations of parents. David Hersland, writes Bridgman, is a model of the Steinian father:

> Bluff and irritated by anything that impedes his progress, swollen with self-importance, frustrated by the failure of his plans to come to fruition, indifferent to his family except when it affords him an opportunity to display his largesse or authority, he is, in short, the inevitable mate for a withdrawn and vaguely discontented wife.[31]

Perhaps because of Stein's identification, David Hersland and his relationship to his children provide the imaginative centers for *The Making of Americans*. Although she felt his second son, David Hersland (III) was the book's hero,[32] although much of the young Stein goes into her creation of his daughter Martha, and although his son Alfred shares attributes of both Leo and Gertrude Stein, Stein is most interested in the *childhoods* of the youngest David, Martha, and Alfred, in how they interact with their father (and, to a lesser extent, with their mother). The novel's subject is in some ways the story of the education of the Hersland children, education in the sense of growing up with guidance.

For Stein's Americanized father, David Hersland, education is the provision of plenitude. Less a means toward his children's Americanization than a confirmation of their American status, education for third-generation children is seen by these parents as of crucial importance. Stein writes, "To him, David Hersland, education was almost the whole of living. In it was always the making of a new beginning, having ideas, and often changing" (55). The options Hersland has for educating his children are enormously varied: he can raise them in what might be called Old World fashion—providing them with a governess, music, and foreign language lessons—or in New World fashion—sending them to public schools, encouraging physical activity and civic responsibilty. David Hersland, in Steinian fashion, chooses all of the above. As Stein's own father had, he vacillates between public and private education for his children, periodically withdrawing them from public schools in order to have them tutored in European languages at home.

Early in the course of the Hersland children's education, David Hersland hires a "foreign woman" who is a good musician to act as governess. Stein writes, "Mr. Hersland had a theory of her in the beginning; he wanted to have a real foreign woman, a real governess with concentrated being, with german and french and who was really a musician" (174). But Hersland comes to feel that the education this governess provides is too foreign for his children; Stein feels it is not "American" enough for her American family. Clearly influenced by progressive theories regarding the importance of physical activity in child development and by an increased emphasis on public schooling, Hersland then fires this governess, hiring "a tall blond woman . . . a healthy person" who would

"not teach [the children] french or german, not teach them anything, just be a healthy person with them." Stein explains:

> Now he wanted the children not to have their english spoiled
> by french and german. Now he was certain that music was a
> thing no one could learn when they were children. This was
> something every one should have in their later living, children
> should have freedom, should have an out of doors gymnasium,
> should have swimming and public school living, should have a
> governess who would live with them such a life. . . . And so this
> next governess was very different from the last one. (175–76)

This governess proves satisfactory to David Hersland; in fact, the
text suggests that this second governess brings to the Hersland
household a sexual vitality as well as physical and civic vigor. "She
was pleasanter for him for she had a physical meaning for him,"
writes Stein. This governess, however, in an action that has connotations suggestive of sexuality and fertility, leaves the Herslands
to marry a baker, and is replaced by Madeleine Wyman, who,
Stein states conclusively, "was everything" (183).[33]

Madeleine Wyman, who becomes an important if elusive subject
of this section of the novel, is a curious compromise of the foreign
and the American, and as such functions as an ideal educator to
Mr. Hersland and as a locus for Stein's perception of American
education and, by extension, the making of little Americans. Stein
introduces Madeleine Wyman as an American—

> Anyway in Madeleine Wyman they had everything, she knew
> french and german, she was an american, she had had good
> american schooling, she was a fair musician, she was intelligent
> and could talk as well as listen to Mr. Hersland about education,
> . . . she was good looking, she liked walking and wanted to
> learn swimming. (184)

For Stein, however, Madeleine Wyman is "american" only insofar
as she is foreign: "The Wyman family was foreign american"
(187), the parents immigrants. In the Steinian scheme of things,
Madeleine and her brothers and sisters are both descendants—
part of history, or a continuum—and self-made—defined in their
own terms, not in terms of history. While the Wyman parents are
"disconnected from every one," "one could reconstruct the foreign
father and mother out of the [Wyman] children and so could come

to an understanding of them, a realisation that they had been alive then and human" (188). The Wyman family, like the Hersland family, and, for Stein, any American family, contains within itself the riddle of human history and its perplexing solution. As a governess, Madeleine Wyman provides the Hersland children with a "foreign" and an "american" education—in other words, with an American education in the upper case.

If, for Stein, the education of the Hersland children is ideal, it is also vaguely frivolous and anachronistic. When the desires of second-generation parents are divided between Old and New World values, the simultaneous conjunction of public and private education seems a natural solution. But children in public schools rarely need a governess, and Madeleine Wyman is extraneous in the Hersland household, becoming an emotional fixture in the life of the mother rather than the children. The Hersland children "had then their regular public school education, they had then too every kind of fancy education that their father could think would be good for them, they had out of door living and swimming and shooting and horse back riding and perfect freedom, they had not then any need in living for a governess in the house with them" (203). Because Stein was herself a granddaughter of immigrants, conversant with Old and New World values, she recognizes the aptness of the Hersland educational system but rejects its frivolity. In fact, as the Hersland children mature, their education becomes more practical, "public," reflective of the values of the Americanized immigrant. The college Martha Hersland attends, for instance, writes Stein, was

> the typical coeducational college of the west, a completely democratic institution. Mostly no one there was conscious of a grandfather unless as remembering one as an old man living in the house with them or living in another place and being written to sometimes by them and then having died and that was the end of grandfathers to them. No one among them was held responsible for the father they had unless by some particular notoriety that had come to the father of some one. (259)

The Hersland children's education—"foreign" and "American"—reflects in many ways the contradictions embedded in Stein's sense of her own national and ethnic identity. The ethnic expatriate

Gertrude Stein was a curious kind of patriot. The author of portraits of Matisse and Picasso was to turn later in her career to portraits of a pantheon of American heroes, ranging from Wilbur Wright to Susan B. Anthony. Stein's attempt to define the nature of the writer's relationship to language, human experience, and the American identity by writing about and around American heroes places her squarely in the American ethnic tradition, which seeks to find in American forefathers and foremothers particularizations and substantializations of the American experience. Stein's attraction to history as it is written through heroes is entirely consistent with her argument in *The Making of Americans* that history consists of the history of individual lives. By representing the rhythms of an individual's living rather than the facts of his or her life—as she does in the "David Hersland" section of *The Making of Americans*—Stein asserts that such rhythms are the determinants of history; similarly, by writing about American heroes, Stein can "represent" American history.

In her choices of American heroes and heroines Stein plays with notions of civic pride, patriotism, and heroism itself. Her efforts were to culminate in the last work of her career, the opera *The Mother of Us All,* whose heroine is Susan B. Anthony. The libretto, peopled with such figures as John Adams, Anthony Comstock, and Lillian Russell, is one of her most explicitly feminist works. In turning to Anthony as a representative American heroine Stein was able to reach personal and political conclusions about American womanhood; she even directly takes on the historical problem of the often conflicting goals of the black and female suffrage movements of the nineteenth century. In pitting Susan B. Anthony against Daniel Webster—whose name, Stein tells us, reminds her of her own father, also named Daniel[34]—Stein plays out a drama of female identification that suggests that her death from cancer truncated what might have been an important new direction in Stein's thought. *The Mother of Us All* is a curious work, but in it she seems more comfortable with her choices of heroes and heroines than she had been in her earlier efforts to define American identity through more traditionally identified American heroes.

Stein's *Four in America,* written in 1933 and published in 1947 with an introduction by Thornton Wilder, is an ambitious undertaking that sets out to subvert our notions of American forefathers by assigning them different occupations. She sees Ulysses S. Grant as a religious leader, Wilbur Wright as a painter, Henry James as a general, and George Washington as a novelist. Some of the analogies seem to work—James with his remarkable edifices of prefaces and campaigns of plots exhibits a certain soldierly quality of flexible planning—while the notion of a saintly Grant remains idiosyncratic and elusive, perhaps derived from Stein's feeling of a divided Southern and Northern identification. Stein's conception of Washington as novelist, on the other hand, seems strikingly apt.

George Washington is, as I have argued, an emotional touchstone in the ethnic imagination, particularly in the experience of the immigrant. On one level, he is often the immigrant child's first example of a hero. Gilbert Stuart's famous portrait of Washington has graced countless American classrooms in which countless immigrant children and children of immigrants have composed countless themes about the father of our country. Because he is an American forefather, I have suggested, the ethnic woman's apprehension of him has been complex, and has received interesting treatment in ethnic women's fiction. Gertrude Stein was no exception; Washington for her was a figure to be reckoned with. Indeed, at times she was to identify with him, placing herself in the pantheon of American fathers. *The Geographical History of America, or The Relation of Human Nature to the Human Mind* (1936) begins with the statement that she, George Washington, and Abraham Lincoln were all born in the month of February. She remarks, a little defensively, "Not even now again can any one this deny, not they nor not I," which is all the more remarkable considering the fact that February is, Stein reminds us, "a short month."[35]

Although Washington does not appear explicitly in *The Making of Americans,* a novel about Americanization, David Hersland, as the consummate father, is a kind of stand-in for him. The Hersland children's public schooling, and Stein's insistence on civic education, imply Washingtonian values. Moreover, certain linguistic referents suggest Washington's inevitable presence in the Americanization of the children of immigrants. Stein's famous passage about the importance of washing to Americans takes off from a description of the Dehning son George:

> The boy George bade fair to do credit to his christening.
> George Dehning now about fourteen was strong in sport and

washing. He was not foreign in his washing. Oh no, he was really an american. (14)[36]

It is as if a boy named George, in Stein's mind, inevitably "does credit to his christening," always washing, and calling to the American mind the linguistic association of George Washington. Excellence in sport and washing, qualities imparted by public schooling in civic values, in turn do credit to the values imparted by the image of the nation's greatest civic hero.

Although Stein's novel is in some senses a text of the child's relation to the father and mother, it has, as I will argue, a subtext of the rejection of the father. Writ large, there is a subtext of subversion of the concept of forefathers running through Stein's work. The intertext for Stein's novel of the role of the fathers in the education and Americanization of the ethnic child is her portrait of George Washington in *Four in America*. As much a meditation on the novel form as on George Washington, the portrait is Stein's attempt to place herself in the male literary tradition, an ethnic woman's attempt to come to terms with her forefathers. Stein argues that Washington is a novelist because in fathering America he produced a novel, and "Believe me," she adds, "it was a nice novel that he wrote."[37] The fact of Washington's authorship confers on him considerable power; creating the text of America requires extraordinary novelistic talent. As Stein felt she herself did, her Washington has unique knowledge of the particularly distinctive quality of the American land:

> It is not a country surrounded by a wall or not as well by an ocean. In short the United States of America is not surrounded.
> He knew.
> He knew that.
> The result of his knowing that was that he said this and in saying this he began a novel, the novel the great American novel. Oh yes he did.[38]

But Stein herself, we remember, felt that she too had authored the great American novel in *The Making of Americans*. What distinguishes George's creation from Gertrude's? The long discussions of the identity of George Washington—of the meaning of name, who "George" is—[39] ask whether Gertrude might in fact be another George. What is the identity of the author? asks the text. In

wondering about the nature of the novel form, Stein questions all
notions of authorship, her own and Washington's. "In a novel,"
Stein writes, "in a good novel there is no distress."[40] What makes
a novel? What is fit subject matter for a novel? George Washington knew: "George Washington was not jealous. He knew what a
novel is. He knew that there are characters in a novel."[41] If Washington wasn't jealous, Stein may well have been. She never in fact
knew, for instance, whether or not there are characters in a novel.
In not knowing, however, Stein was perhaps possessed of a wis-
dom greater than certainty, and Stein's portrait ultimately questions the finality of George Washington's authorship and his heroism. Stein questions the woman writer's place in the male literary
tradition and the ethnic woman's place in America. Her portrait
of Washington is an expression of the woman writer's ongoing
argument with American forefathers, fathers, and, for Stein, history.

In *The Making of Americans,* Stein presents the outlines of this
argument. The Steinian father in the text, David Hersland, is more
truly the hero of the text than are any of his children, much as
Stein might have wished otherwise. Stein's feelings about this
father are mixed, to say the least. Possessed of undeniable strength,
David Hersland emerges as more than a little foolish. David Hersland has "big feelings" in him: "He was of the kind of them that
feel themselves to be as big as all the world around them. Every
one who knew him felt it in him." Like George Washington, the
father of our country, David Hersland is particularly "big" on beginnings: "Beginning was all of living with him, in a beginning he
was always as big in his feeling as all the world around him" (901).

If David Hersland is an analogue not only for Daniel Stein but
also for the fathers of American culture, Stein's representation of
him reflects her sense of herself as a female writer in relation to
male culture and male fathers. In Stein's experience, fathers are a
bore, but a bore to be reckoned with. In the 1930s, in response to
the rise to power of European dictators, Stein assessed the dicta-
torial impulse as fatherly. Even FDR's New Deal, in Stein's view,
was paternalistic. She commented on "father Mussolini and father
Roosevelt and father Stalin and father Lewis and father Blum and
father Franco," concluding, "There is too much fathering going on
just now and there is no doubt about it fathers are depressing."[42]

However depressing, fathers are a fact of life for the American daughter. In Stein's work, she approached the American fathers sometimes as a docile, sometimes as a rebellious daughter. In her stylistic innovations, she questioned the fathers' literary traditions. Often, too, she acted as a father, playing with gender, usurping George Washington's role, "fathering" the great work of writers like Sherwood Anderson and Ernest Hemingway.

Stein's interest in the American father as a felt presence in the American daughter's life reflects the viewpoint from which all her writing evolves, which is that of the child. To the child, and particularly the daughter, the father is a monolithic, unarguable presence. This perhaps helps to explain what some readers may feel is the inadequate, disjointed, incomplete sense of the mother in Stein's creative work, and particularly in *The Making of Americans*. Stein assures us, in that novel, that she can "write" women more easily and enjoyably than she can men: "I like to tell it better in women the kind of nature a certain kind of men and women have in living. I like to tell it better in a woman because it is clearer in her and I know it better, a little, not much better" (143–44). But Stein's women do not emerge as complete, felt presences in the way her men do. Sometimes the result is brilliant: Melanctha, for instance, presented by nuance, event, interaction, is one of Stein's most successful heroines, as is Stein herself as the obliquely rendered heroine of *The Autobiography of Alice B. Toklas*. In *The Making of Americans,* however, the Steinian mother, David Hersland's wife Fanny, is presented so vaguely that we get only a fragmented and incomplete sense of her. She is a titular subject of two sections of the novel, "The Hersland Parents" and "Mrs. Hersland and the Hersland Children," but she never receives the direct treatment her husband does. Stein writes around her, describing her relations with servants, friends, and the lives of those servants and friends. In some ways, this technique succeeds, and Fanny Hersland's presence subtly pervades the novel, though it is far less easy to locate than is her husband's.

Stein realized that for the child—from whose point of view she always tried to look at the world—the mother is not a monolithic or easily definable presence; in the infant's consciousness, the mother is often perceived as an extension of the self in a way the father is not. Because the mother is not perceived as "other" in the way that the father is, as a bounded presence she is less easy to locate. Much of this sense creeps into Stein's fiction, and is at the heart of Stein's stylistic consciousness.

In her book-length consideration of Picasso, published in 1938, Stein expresses her admiration for Picasso's ability to see physical reality through the eyes of a child. She explicitly connects Picasso's vision with that of the child vis-à-vis the mother. She writes:

> A child sees the face of its mother, it sees it in a completely different way than other people see it, I am not speaking of the spirit of the mother but of the features and the whole face, the child sees it from very near, it is a large face for the eyes of such a small one, it is certain the child for a little while only sees a part of the face of its mother, it knows one feature and not another, one side and not the other, and in his way Picasso knows faces as a child knows them and the head and the body.[43]

Picasso's "tendency to paint [faces, heads, bodies] as a mass as sculptors do or in profile as children do," Stein suggests, grew out of Picasso's impulse to represent not reality but reality as it is perceived.[44]

Stein's observation about Picasso applies as well to her own work, and particularly to works like *Tender Buttons* and the pieces collected in her 1922 *Geography and Plays*. It informs *The Making of Americans* thematically more than it does stylistically. Written from the point of view of the child—or, because it is an ethnic text, the grandchild—*The Making of Americans* presents the child's perception of reality rather than reality itself. Within this framework, the mother cannot be treated as a definable subject outside the world. The point of view has other consequences: grandparents, as Stein suggests at one point, appear to the child either as very young or very old people; it is hard to imagine them as conscious adults.[45] Furthermore, the child's relation to the world and the world around him becomes the subject of the text. To what extent does the relationship define self? By placing this question in an ethnic context, a broader framework which seeks to determine the role of ancestry in identity, Stein creates a text that describes not only the identity of the child but that of all America's children.

The Making of Americans seems to have been planned as a novel that would show the progress of a family as that family existed in relation to others. Selfhood, Stein seems to have thought, could only be defined as it existed in an intricate network of other selves and events. Indeed, the very premise of the novel—"being the progress of a *family*'s history"—suggests that the individual could only be understood in context, in the context of the family and of history. Stein accordingly promises far more than she can deliver, vowing to describe each of her novel's characters in terms of every person who has ever known them. In a pattern repeated throughout the novel, Stein writes,

> In the history of the young David Hersland there will be written much description of the character and living of every one the Hersland family ever came to know in all the time they were living in the ten acre place in that part of Gossols where no other rich people were living. In the history of Alfred Hersland there will be much description of the things Alfred did with them and to them, all of them whom the Hersland family came to know then. Now in the history of Martha Hersland there will be much description of how everyone knowing the Hersland family then came to feel and know her and them, what every one knowing them and knowing her felt about her, knew about her, felt about them, knew about them. (238)

The ambitious nature of this promise confirms Stein's serious intent. If she were to describe everyone the Hersland family ever knew, which would in turn require a description of everyone those characters ever knew, and so on *ad infinitum,* Stein might well have written "the history of every one who ever was or is or will be living" that she calls for so often in her novel.

As *The Making of Americans* progresses, Stein makes similar promises with increasing embarrassment, and by the time she reaches the section on David Hersland (III), she no longer bothers with them. Announcing that "This is now to be some description of him," she acknowledges that she will have to describe others in order to describe him: "This will be naturally a description, some description, many descriptions of very many men and very many women." But her emphasis has shifted, as she indicates: "This will be then very much description of David Hersland, of being, of living, of dying, of listening, of talking, of going on being living, of going on being in living, of ways of eating" (357). Unlike the other sections of the novel, which are peopled with seamstresses, neighborhood children, dinner partners, hotel dwellers, and governesses who have contact with the Herslands or the Dehnings, David is the sole character in his section, and Stein's subject is in fact less David and more living, going on being living, and dying. However insistent that the individual can only be realized in relations with others, Stein bridled under this idea in the writing of *The Making of Americans.* Although she begins the novel by way of Aristotelian example to assert that "it was difficult to overcome inherited character," Stein moves increasingly throughout the novel toward the paradoxical notion of an unrelated individual, ever attracted to the idea of overcoming all inherited character. In fact, in her writing career, Stein became increasingly interested in this notion, which she expressed in terms of a theory of writing that differentiated what she called "entity" from "identity."

According to this theory, which Stein was to set forth most thoroughly in her 1936 *The Geographical History of America, or the Relation of Human Nature to the Human Mind,* "identity writing" is the writing of relationships, writing whose subject was the relations and resemblances between things and individuals. In identity writing or thinking, the self is perceived in terms of its interactions with other selves and its place in history. Richard Bridgman locates a key identity sentence in *The Geographical History of America,* the famous Stein sentence, "I am I because my little dog knows me." Identity is conferred on the self by external reality—other selves, history, or little dogs. Bridgman argues that another key identity sentence, "What is the use of being a boy if you are going to grow up to be a man," explains Stein's violent disagreement with the concept of identity as she defines it. Memory, which identity entails in that it in part defines oneself, writes Bridgman,

> chained one to time. Boy and man were unrelated except through identity, through birth certificates and aunts (external recognition) and memory (internal recognition). If the adult accepted his connection with the child he had once been, he yielded to human nature, to continuity, and to necessity.[46]

History, an integral factor in identity, implies mortality, a concept that, for Stein, writing *The Geographical History* at the age of sixty-one, was beginning to take on authority. Stein accordingly gave priority to the concept of "entity writing," which, she argues, concentrates on the thing itself, unrelated. In entity writing the object is not defined in terms of other objects or anything other than itself, and the individual not defined in terms of his relations to others and to time. The concept of entity writing is, as Stein herself realized, problematic, positing as it does the existence of a nonreferential language. Even if one were to acknowledge the existence of "entity," it could not be "written," because language always implies associations, relationships, referents; attributes of "identity." The concept is not without practical value, however; it is in fact possible to make a crude division in Stein's own work between identity and entity writing.[47] Under the terms of this division, works like *Tender Buttons* and Stein's poetry and plays, which attempt to divorce language from its referents, are examples of "entity writing," and more autobiographical works like *The Making of Americans* and *The Autobiography of Alice B. Toklas* obviously come into the category of "identity writing." But the places where the two categories overlap—in *Tender Buttons'* amazing portrayal of the associative and referential patterns of the mind and of words themselves, and in the rhythms of language divorced from reality in *The Making of Americans* and works like *Lucy Church Amiably*—are those in which Stein achieves her greatest successes. One of our greatest philosophers of language, Stein attempted in her formulation of "entity" and "identity" writing to express central paradoxes of the human existence in its inextricable relation to language. Is it possible to express in language a self without referents, in effect without language? Some of Stein's admirers, as well as her detractors, would argue that Stein approaches the realization of this paradox.

If the central problem of ethnicity is the relation of the individual to his ancestors, or, in fact, to time, Stein was on the cutting edge of the ethnic "problem." *The Making of Americans* attempts to realize the idea of the individual eternally poised between self-generated and historical versions of self. In choosing immigrants and their children as her subjects, Stein found, I have argued, a topical focus for expressing this tension. In her attempt to express it most truly, in her stylistic innovations, she was inevitably drawn to methods by which she could stretch language to reflect her conceptions of time. In fact, most of Stein's technical advances concern notions of time and history. *The Making of Amer-*

icans is a massive undertaking that sets out to describe the individual within history, and in effect "tries out" new methods for expressing time and history, among them the use of the gerund, repetition as a method and a subject, and the continuous present.

Stein seems to have felt that *The Making of Americans* not only possessed an American subject but represented American writing at its most true. The salient quality of American writing, Stein felt, was its unique relationship to time. In the first lecture of a series of four, collected as *Narration* in 1935, Stein explained her sense that American writing expressed a concept of time that was distinctly nonlinear; "American writing has been an escaping not an escaping but an existing without the necessary feeling of one thing succeeding another thing of having a beginning and a middle and an ending."[48] In acknowledging that American writing "exists" in this way, without the *"necessary* feeling" of the linear nature of time, Stein does not suggest a kind of writing that exists outside of linear time—that is impossible—but one that stretches all notions of linear time, attempting to transcend it while realizing the impossibility of doing so. In this particular lecture, Stein explains her use of the present participle, or the gerund, which she felt was consistent with the American tradition of questioning linear time, or beginnings and endings: "In The Making of Americans I could not free myself from the present participle because dimly I felt that I had to know what I knew and I knew that the beginning and middle and ending was not where I began."[49]

In writing *The Making of Americans,* Stein uses gerunds increasingly as she comes to feel that they express this sense of ongoing time; she is also increasingly attracted to the use of words like *beginning* and *ending* in gerund-filled sentences that describe the limitations inherent in using language to express ongoing time. For instance, in her description of David Hersland, which is in some ways the culmination of her stylistic efforts in the novel, Stein writes, "He was being living from the beginning of being living to the ending of the beginning of middle living" (321), which not only tells us that David Hersland died in early middle age but conveys to us a sense of the movement of his life during his life, which is the subject of the section in which the sentence appears. The sentence simultaneously expresses finality and continuity. The use of the gerund, as Bridgman points out, "at once

represents an entity and a continuous action."[50] The sense such a
sentence carries is that of the famous notion of the continuous
present, a concept that has never been clearly defined by either
Stein or her critics, probably because it is nearly impossible to do
so. Not only difficult to describe, the continuous present is also
implicitly impossible to achieve; Stein acknowledges this when she
calls the feeling of beginnings and endings "necessary," and when
she writes, "A great deal perhaps all of my writing of The Making
of Americans was an effort to escape from this thing to escape
from *inevitably* feeling that anything that everything had meaning
as beginning and middle and ending" (my emphasis).[51] *The Making of Americans* represents in some ways an effort to escape the
inevitable.

A fundamental principle of the continuous present is the notion
of repeating. If there were such a thing as a continuous present,
everything would repeat, endlessly, without variation: it is in this
space that one can repeat, *ad infinitum,* a rose is a rose is a rose.
Because we live in time, however, repetition implies difference. In
order to understand Stein in the most elemental way, one must
look at the concept of repetition in a fresh light. Nothing repeats
itself in the purest sense. The notion of Freud's repetition/compul-
sion principle provides one of the many ways to understand this
concept. As adults we repeat the experiences of childhood, but we
do so with a difference. Paradigms remain, so that others are in-
serted into our repetitions of infantile dramas, but differences proliferate. Freud studied not only the sameness within repetition but
also difference. The most thorough study of an individual's life un-
covers the differences and samenesses of his or her repetitions.
Stein attempts no less than this in *The Making of Americans.* In
writing about parents and children, Stein questions the extent to
which the child is a repetition—with a difference—of the parent.
Moreover, she questions the means whereby we repeat the experiences of childhood endlessly, each time with a difference. Stylistically, she attempts to express—through literal repetitions of difference, as, for instance, when she repeats sentences with subtle
variations over the space of hundreds of pages—the inevitability
of the repetition of difference, its value as an object of inquiry and
its centrality to all notions of the self and history.

Stein's description of Martha Hersland exemplifies this concept and Stein's use of it. After some explanation of the idea of an individual's "bottom nature," and its importance to her work, Stein searches for an incident that will reveal Martha's nature. This bottom nature, Stein argues, repeats itself in the individual's behavior, in effect defining that person. Stein explains:

> In some the nature is clearer when they are very young, in some when they are young, in some when they are not so young, in some when they are old ones. Always in each one it is there repeating, some one knows it in each one, some one will know it in every one that one is ever knowing. (230–31)

This bottom nature, Stein felt, could be revealed by, in effect, slowing down the reel of an individual's life and examining a particular incident.[52] In Martha's case, Stein sees her nature revealed in an incident of childhood, in which Martha Hersland is left behind in a muddy street with an umbrella, her companions having run home ahead of her. Martha announces, with no one to hear her, that she will throw her umbrella in the mud, does so, and announces that she has. Stein seems convinced that this incident explains all; a page later, she writes with some satisfaction, "Knowing a map and then seeing the place and knowing that the roads actually existing are like the map, to some is always astonishing and it is always then very gratifying" (233). Stein seems to have reviewed the linguistic roads of the umbrella incident and her own mental map of Martha and to have found a gratifying correspondence. The reader may be inclined to feel that Stein has not provided much information about Martha through what Stein calls her "little story," but Stein is aiming for a subtle quality of characterization, and the nuances of the story, revealing hints of Martha's angry determination, her will to power, her linguistic assertiveness, do indeed provide a sense of her. The umbrella, too, is to "repeat" at a significant juncture in Martha's life: seeing a man in a street hit a woman across the face with an umbrella, Martha decides to go to college. The umbrella is connected with female independence born out of anger.

More interesting, however, is the way in which Stein uses repetition within the incident, which she repeats three times at approximately three-page intervals. The first description is the most complete; we learn that "bitterness possessed [Martha]" and that "there was desperate anger in her." In this version, Martha announces, " 'I will throw the umbrella in the mud,' " and, in doing so, concludes, " 'I have throwed the umbrella in the mud.' " Stein is interested in the finality that Martha's statement of action gives to that action:

> She had thrown the umbrella in the mud and no one heard her as it burst from her, "I have throwed the umbrella in the mud," it was the end of all that to her. (232)

The passage questions the relationship of language to action, and suggests the inherent power of language in the child's existence. In the second telling, Martha throws down the umbrella "in a moment of triumphing" and repeats over and over, " 'I did throw the umbrella in the mud.' " Stein writes that Martha "went on crying and saying" this (236), giving to Martha's act a sense of the continuous present, so that the sense the reader gets is that Martha all her life is announcing that she has thrown her umbrella in the mud—which is in fact a pretty accurate impression. Why the difference in verb form, however? Why "I have throwed" in the first version and "I did throw" in the second? In the third telling, in fact, Martha *has thrown* her umbrella in the mud correctly:

> . . . and she was saying I will throw the umbrella in the mud and then she was crying, I have thrown the umbrella in the mud, and then later she got home, and the umbrella was not with her. (240)

This time, the throwing of the umbrella is not described, and in fact the reader does not discover its disappearance until Martha arrives home without it. Language—correct language—has in effect replaced action. Martha's journey from the childish "I have throwed" to the correct but stilted "I did throw" to the correct and formal "I have thrown" suggests the process of a child growing to be an adult, an adult who is always announcing that she has thrown her umbrella in the mud, always repeating—with a difference—an experience of childhood.

Stein's use of the repetition of difference in describing Martha Hersland's character helps to explain her attraction to the use of repetition in her style. Simply put, the truest writing repeats repetitions. "[T]he repeating in them," explains Stein, "makes a history of them" (138). Only by repeating repetitions, Stein insists in an important passage, can history be written. The writing of such a history is not easy:

> A history of any one must be a long one, slowly it comes out from them from their beginning to their ending, slowly you can see it in them the nature and the mixtures in them, slowly everything comes out from each one in the kind of repeating each one does in the different parts and kinds of living they have in them, slowly then the history of them comes out from them, slowly then any one who looks well at any one will have the history of the whole of that one. (128)

The technique, however, can be mastered; this proves to Stein that "Some time then there will be a history of every one who ever can or is or was or will be living"—a statement Stein repeats like a litany—even if she must be the one to write it.

In discovering that such a history was possible, Stein was able to abandon it. In her 1935 lecture, "The Gradual Making of The Making of Americans," Stein explained her shift from the writing of *The Making of Americans* and the similar *A Long Gay Book* to *Tender Buttons:*

> When I began The Making of Americans I knew I really did know that a complete description was a possible thing, and certainly a complete description is a possible thing. But as it is a possible thing one can stop continuing to describe this everything. That is where philosophy comes in, it begins when one stops continuing describing everything.[53]

Stein, having seen the logical conclusion to which her ideas could be carried, did not have to take them there. *The Making of Americans* is in this sense a *demonstration* of her ideas; it represented to Stein proof that she was right. It is not surprising that she showed persistent fondness for this great hulking novel throughout her life. The writing of it freed her psychically from doubt concerning her own philosophical capabilities and enabled her, in fact, to turn to other experiments. The ideas behind *The Making of Americans,* however—the notion of a continuous present, the concept of history as the stories of individual lives, the self's relation to the movement of history, the relation of perception to reality, and so on—were to remain Stein's themes throughout her writing. Moreover, if the subject of *The Making of Americans* is America itself, Stein never abandoned this subject for long. America represented for her a place to "put" all questions of the individual's relationship to the world. The most central feature of American life—that of immigration—meant to Stein that Americans, ethnics all, constantly questioned their relation to their grandparents, to ancestry, to each other, to history, and to language, and asked how such relationships defined or did not define the self. *The Making of Americans* represents a culmination of the ethnic female literary tradition, for it brings together all the thematic concerns associated with ethnicity and recasts them in terms of gender. Moreover, form and content are integrated in such a way in the novel that Gertrude Stein in many ways answers with authority the questions surrounding authorship for ethnic women. That she is also considered a writer in the great American tradition suggests that we need to reevaluate our assumptions and readings of that tradition, alert to the claims of ethnicity and gender on the American identity.

Afterword

Gertrude Stein, an ethnic American woman writer, described her monumental *The Making of Americans* as "an American book an essentially American book."[1] In its attention to ethnicity as the central aspect of the American character, Stein's novel is indeed quintessentially American; it is also an important novel by a woman writer. It becomes necessary to ask what, if anything, makes Stein's ethnic American novel different from novels written by men. Though my concern in this study has been largely the ways in which gender and ethnicity function in American culture, I have focused on women writers, and the issue of difference arises inevitably. There is little question that the experiences of ethnic men and women differed to varying degrees, depending upon cultural expectations within ethnic groups, and that fiction inevitably reflects this difference. It seems obvious, for instance, that marriage is a favorite theme in women immigrants' fiction because marriage was for the most part inevitable, expected, and important for these women. Certain features of American culture—American stories like that of Pocahontas—elicit in important ways different responses from men and women writers, and these I have tried to point out. On the other hand, as mediating ethnic women writers like Mary Antin and Jessie Fauset well knew, it is often as productive to look at similarities as at differences.

Strong similarities, in fact, exist between the male and female ethnic literary traditions; no feature of the ethnic female tradition is exclusively female. If we reconsider ethnic women's problems with authorship, authority, and authentication, it becomes obvious that ethnic men shared many of these problems. There are formal patterns in the development of any literary tradition; it is not surprising that such devices as glossaries, prefaces, and afterwords, or such critical features as generic confusion, dualistic writing styles, or political/aesthetic debates inform any consideration of a male ethnic tradition as well. In fact, it is important to note that, if gender and ethnicity exist as concepts on a continuum, ethnicity will sometimes "outweigh" gender: a male slave's text needs more authentication than Harriet Beecher Stowe's *Uncle Tom's Cabin*. This serves to underscore the point that gender and ethnicity are structurally similar, if also to emphasize that we must consider literary tradition with a historical awareness.

Moreover, thematic concerns of male and female ethnic writers are often related and sometimes identical. Henry Roth's *Call It Sleep* (1934) is as concerned with generational conflict and Americanization as is Martha Ostenso's *Wild Geese* (1927). Anzia Yezierska's *Salome of the Tenements* (1923) is about love and the urban melting-pot; so too is Abraham Cahan's *Yekl* (1896). William Faulkner's *Absalom, Absalom!* (1936) addresses the complexities of miscegenation, incest, and bastardy just as insistently—and far more powerfully—as does Gertrude Atherton's *Senator North* (1900). And male voices of all nationalities—or ethnicities, or eras—have explored the meaning of generations, history, and the family in "generational sagas" whose scope rivals or surpasses that of Gertrude Stein's *The Making of Americans*.

It is important to remember, too, that the "theme" of ethnicity itself has long been an important feature of classic American literature, much of it male-authored, as critics such as Leslie Fiedler have pointed out. Kristin Herzog's *Women, Ethnics, and Exotics* (1983) is a study of the nexus of gender and ethnicity as a locus of power in such mid-nineteenth century authors as Melville and Hawthorne; she claims to find in these authors' "primitives" and female heroines a strength that subverted popular nineteenth-century stereotypes of women and non-Western characters. Critics have long recognized too, for instance, the pervasiveness of the "dark lady" in American fiction, an exoticized and eroticized "ethnic" heroine. There is no question that the issues raised by the women writers considered here have been persistent concerns of all American writers.

But the issue of theme returns us again to difference, for we must acknowledge a difference in emphasis between the concerns of men and women writers. The ethnic woman's novel is more heavily weighted toward the family; each of the thematic concerns cited above is considered ultimately in its domestic sense. If, for Faulkner, incest is a sign of a disruption of history or a disruption of value, for black writer Frances Harper or white writer Gertrude Atherton it begins and ends as disruption of the family, a crime against ancestry. Unlike classic generational sagas, Gertrude Stein's *The Making of Americans* is insistently domestic; it is *only* about the family, about the relationship between the public and private self.

The example of Stein should serve as an assurance that this difference in emphasis in no way lessens the importance of the femininely rendered thematic concern. Harriet Beecher Stowe's intensely domestic *Uncle Tom's Cabin,* we remember, changed the course of history. Many feminist critics have argued that the literature of the home tells us more about the world than does its counterpart, the putative literature of the world. Moreover, the emphasis on female relationships in women's fiction signals another important point of departure in the ethnic female literary tradition. Women's literature about slavery, for instance, far more often addresses the disruption of the mother-child relationship than does that written by men. The insistence on the persistence of these ties contributes to the sense that ethnic women's fiction asserts the matrilinear, recasts ancestry in terms of the mother. Ethnicity—which is fundamentally about the tension between the family and the community, the private and the public—is of central concern to women writers.

In contemporary ethnic writing, these differences in emphasis become still more striking. The works of Toni Morrison, Alice Walker, Maxine Hong Kingston, and E. M. Broner are about relationships within the family and relationships between women—often, mothers and daughters. The insistent female and "ethnic" orientation of much of this fiction suggests that ethnic women are responding to or playing on the ironic logic of a certain radical redemptivism, whereby much of what had earlier excluded women's issues from serious consideration, and women writers from the canon, now clamors to include them by virtue of their prior exclusion. Alice Walker's prize-winning *The Color Purple* (1982) plays every note in the (now exclusively) female range: incest, lesbianism, mother/daughter relationships, sisterhood (in both senses), even the idea of a female God. In her call for a "womanist" ethic in her collection *In Search of Our Mother's Gardens* (1983), Walker cheerfully excludes all but the black female from the ranks of "womanist": the other truly prevails.

More meaningfully, the familial concerns called up by gender and ethnicity have allowed contemporary ethnic women writers to work transformations on what is outside the family, to personalize the public. Gloria Naylor's *The Women of Brewster Place* (1982) is about women and about a place, but the place itself is made animate. "Conceived," in "a damp, smoke-filled room," Brewster Place, Naylor tells us at the outset of her novel, "was the bastard child of several clandestine meetings between the aldermen of the sixth district and the managing director of the Unico Realty Company."[2] Over the course of the novel the women of this community come to constitute a family, contractual if not biological. Naylor's novel is about women and about a place, but by bringing her perspective as a black woman to such objects as an urban dead-end street, Naylor writes about men and women and the world. The best contemporary ethnic women's fiction calls us back to the reasons why gender and ethnicity provide compelling ways to understand American culture; it reminds us of the importance of ancestry within the American community, and it suggests that, however tentative, that community has an ancestry of its own.

If, then, the ethnic female tradition implies difference in emphasis, do other differences exist as well? Is there, for instance, a recognizable difference in stylistic innovation between men's and women's texts? A difference in plot, voice, narrative distance? These are, to be sure, daunting questions for brave critics, and the answers would tell us a lot about gender difference and literary production. I am not certain, however, that these answers would be of great use in understanding gender and ethnicity in American culture. It seems, in fact, counterproductive to talk at great length about what has made this body of fiction "different"—so different, in fact, that with only the recent exceptions of Hurston and Stein, most of it has remained not only outside the canon but unread.

To claim a mysterious "otherness" for the literature of gender and ethnicity is to continue the long and sorry tradition of exoticizing, excluding, and ultimately colonizing Pocahontas. It is time that we reclaim Pocahontas and take a second look at her place in American culture.

This is not to say that ethnic women's fiction should be absorbed into an "American" literary tradition, combed through for Adamic themes and machines in gardens. If there has been consensus in literary criticism that American literature itself reflects consensus, ethnic women's fiction will not comfortably fit in a canon of American literature. However "like" Martha Ostenso's *Wild Geese* is to Henry Roth's *Call It Sleep,* the biologically different generational conflict of Ostenso's novel and the different attendant emotions it evokes set it apart from Roth's; so too does the difference in stylistic approach deserve examination. Furthermore, when ethnic women writers as diverse as Toni Morrison, Pauli Murray, Gayl Jones, and Edna Ferber address in extraordinarily diverse ways the same central American myths and traditions, like the "founding fathers" or the Pocahontas marriage, we must expect that they are aware at once of their place in the American tradition and their place outside it. At a time when notions of *the* canon and *the* American tradition are being rethought, it is useful to look to writers just such as these to see the ways in which they try to rewrite, expand, revise, subvert that tradition and the ways in which they have been excluded from that canon. It is useful, too, to return to Twain and Faulkner, Cahan and Roth, nineteenth-century Indian dramas and twentieth-century Westerns, aware of the sometimes differing versions of gender and ethnicity offered by lesser-known American women writers. If the "other" is always and inevitably a part of culture, it is useful and necessary to listen to what she has to say about that culture. And those ethnic women who followed Pocahontas have insistently reminded us of her presence—and tried to fill her silence with words.

Bibliography

Aaron, Daniel. "The Hyphenate Writer and American Letters." *Smith Alumnae Quarterly*, 55 (1964), 213–17.

———. " 'The Inky Curse': Miscegenation in the White American Literary Imagination." Paper delivered at the Colloquium on National Identity. Miscegenation, and Cultural Expression: A Comparison between the United States and Brazil. Paris, 25–26 March 1982.

Abel, Elizabeth, ed. *Writing and Sexual Difference*. Chicago: University of Chicago Press, 1982.

Abrahams, Roger D. *Deep Down in the Jungle*. Chicago: Aldine, 1970.

Addams, Jane. "The Public School and the Immigrant Child." *NEA Proceedings*, 1908, pp. 99–102.

———. *Twenty Years at Hull-House*. New York: Macmillan, 1910.

Allen, Paula Gunn, ed. *Studies in American Indian Literature: Critical Essays and Course Designs*. New York: MLA, 1983.

Anderson, Barbara. *Southbound*. New York: Farrar, Straus, 1949.

Anderson, Jervis. *This Was Harlem*. New York: Farrar, Straus and Giroux, 1982.

Anderson, Quentin. "John Dewey's American Democrat." *Daedalus*, 108 (1979), 145–59.

Antin, Mary. *At School in the Promised Land or The Story of a Little Immigrant*. New York: Houghton Mifflin, 1912. The Riverside Literature Series.

———. *From Plotzk to Boston*. Boston: W. B. Clarke, 1889.

———. "House of One God." *Common Ground*. Spring 1941, 36–42.

———. "The Lie." *Atlantic Monthly*, 112 (1913), 177–90.

———. *The Promised Land*. Boston: Houghton Mifflin, 1912.

———. *They Who Knock at Our Gates*. Boston: Houghton Mifflin, 1914.

————. "A Woman to Her Fellow-Citizens." *Outlook,* 102 (1912), 482–86.

Ashton, Jean Willoughby. "Harriet Beecher Stowe's Filthy Story: Lord Byron Set Afloat." *Prospects,* 2 (1976), 373–84.

Astrov, Margot, ed. *American Indian Prose and Poetry.* New York: Capricorn, 1962.

Atherton, Gertrude. *Senator North.* New York: John Lane, 1900.

Ault, Nelson, ed. *The Papers of Lucullus Virgil McWhorter.* Seattle: State College of Washington, 1959.

Austern, Nathan. "Israel's Pottage: The Ethnic Mess in John Dos Passos' *U.S.A.*" Master's Essay, Columbia University, 1981.

Baker, Houston A., Jr. *The Journey Back: Issues in Black Literature and Criticism.* Chicago: University of Chicago Press, 1980.

Barron, Milton L., ed. *The Blending Americans: Patterns of Inter-marriage.* Chicago: Quadrangle Books, 1972.

Bataille, Gretchen M., and Kathleen Mullen Sands. *American Indian Women: Telling Their Lives.* Lincoln: University of Nebraska Press, 1984.

Baum, Charlotte, Paula Hyman, and Sonya Michel. *The Jewish Woman in America.* New York: Dial Press, 1976.

Beauvoir, Simone de. *The Second Sex.* trans. H. M. Parshley. 1952; rpt. New York: Alfred A. Knopf, 1975.

Beidler, Peter G., and Marion F. Egge. *The American Indian in Short Fiction.* Metuchen, N.J.: The Scarecrow Press, 1979.

Bennett, Kay. *Kaibah: Recollections of a Navajo Girlhood.* Los Angeles: Westernlore Press, 1964.

Bercovitch, Sacvan. *The American Jeremiad.* Madison: University of Wisconsin Press, 1978.

————. *The Puritan Origins of the American Self.* New Haven: Yale University Press, 1975.

Berkhofer, Robert F., Jr. *The White Man's Indian: Images of the American Indian from Columbus to the Present.* New York: Alfred A. Knopf, 1978.

Berry, Mary Francis. *Black Resistance/White Law: A History of Constitutional Racism in America.* New York: Appleton-Century-Crofts, 1971.

Berzon, Judith. *Neither White Nor Black: The Mulatto Character in American Fiction.* New York: New York University Press, 1978.

Biagi, Shirley. "Forgive Me For Dying." *Antioch Review,* 35 (1977), 224–36.

Bierstadt, Edward Hale. *Aspects of Americanization.* Cincinnati: Stewart Kidd, 1922.

Blackwell, Louise, and Frances Clay. "Lillian Smith, Novelist." *CLAJ,* 15 (1972), 452–58.

Blicksilver, Edith. *The Ethnic American Woman*. Dubuque: Kendall/Hunt Publishing, 1978.

——. "Literature as Social Criticism: The Ethnic Woman Writer." *Modern Language Studies*, 5 (Fall 1975), 46–54.

——. "Traditionalism vs. Modernity: Leslie Silko on American Indian Women." *Southwest Review*, 64 (1979), 144–60.

Boelhower, William. "The Brave New World of Immigrant Autobiography," *MELUS*, 9 (Summer 1982), 5–23.

——. *Immigrant Autobiography in the United States*. Verona, Italy: Essedue Edizioni, 1982.

——. *Through a Glass Darkly: Ethnic Semiosis in American Literature*. Venice, Italy: Edizioni Helvetia, 1984.

Bone, Robert A. *Down Home: A History of Afro-American Short Fiction from Its Beginnings to the End of the Harlem Renaissance*. New York: G. P. Putnam's, 1975.

——. *The Negro Novel in America*. New Haven: Yale University Press, 1958.

Boydston, Jo Ann, ed. *The Poems of John Dewey*. Carbondale: Southern Illinois University Press, 1977.

Braithwaite, William Stanley. "The Novels of Jessie Fauset." *Opportunity*, 12 (1934), 24–28.

Brewer, J. Mason. *American Negro Folklore*. New York: Quadrangle, 1968.

Bridgman, Richard. *Gertrude Stein in Pieces*. New York: Oxford, 1970.

Brinnin, John Malcolm. *The Third Rose: Gertrude Stein and Her Work*. Boston: Little, Brown, 1959.

Brown, Sterling. "A Century of Negro Portraiture in American Literature." *Massachusetts Review*, 7 (1966), 73–96.

Bryan, William Alfred. *George Washington in American Literature*. New York: Columbia University Press, 1952.

Bullock, Penelope. "The Mulatto in American Fiction." *Phylon*, 6 (1945), 78–82.

Bush, Clive. "Toward the Outside: The Quest for Discontinuity in *The Making of Americans*." *Twentieth Century Literature*, 24 (1978), 27–56.

Butts, R. Freeman. *A Cultural History of Education*. New York: McGraw-Hill, 1947.

Cahan, Abraham. *Yekl and the Imported Bridegroom and Other Stories of the New York Ghetto*. 1896; rpt. New York: Dover Books, 1970.

Casey, Daniel J. and Robert E. Rhodes, eds. *Irish-American Fiction: Essays in Criticism*. New York: AMS, 1979.

Cather, Willa. *My Ántonia*. Boston: Houghton Mifflin, 1918.

————. *Sapphira and the Slave Girl*. New York: Alfred A. Knopf, 1940.

Chametzky, Jules. "Our Decentralized Literature: A Consideration of Regional, Ethnic, Racial, and Sexual Factors." *Jahrbuch für Amerikastudien* (Heidelberg), 17 (1972), 56–72.

————. "Regional Literature and Ethnic Realities." *The Antioch Review*, 31 (1971), 385–96.

Chametzky, Jules, and Sidney Kaplan, eds. *Black and White in American Culture*. Amherst, Mass.: University of Massachusetts Press, 1971.

Chesnut, Mary Boykin. *Mary Chesnut's Civil War*. C. Vann Woodward, ed. New Haven: Yale University Press, 1981.

Chodorow, Nancy. *The Reproduction of Mothering: Psychoanalysis and the Sociology of Gender*. Berkeley: University of California Press, 1978.

Chopin, Kate. *Bayou Folk*. 1894; rpt. Ridgewood, N.J.: The Gregg Press, 1967.

Christian, Barbara. *Black Women Novelists: The Development of a Tradition, 1892–1976*. Contributions in Afro-American and African Studies, No. 52. Westport, Conn.: Greenwood Press, 1980.

Clark, William Bedford. "The Letters of Nella Larsen to Carl Van Vechten: A Survey." *Resources for American Literary Study*, 8 (1978), 193–99.

Cooke, Michael G. *Afro-American Literature in the 20th Century: The Achievement of Intimacy*. New Haven: Yale University Press, 1984.

Cremin, Lawrence. *The Transformation of the School: Progressivism in American Education*. New York: Alfred A. Knopf, 1961.

Cuddihy, John. *The Ordeal of Civility: Freud, Marx, Levi-Straus and the Jewish Struggle with Modernity*. New York: Basic Books, 1974.

Dandridge, Rita B. "Male Critics/Black Women's Novels." *CLAJ*, 23 (1979), 1–11.

Davidson, Cathy N. and E. M. Broner, eds. *The Lost Tradition: Mothers and Daughters in Literature*. New York: Frederick Ungar, 1980.

Davis, Arthur P. *From the Dark Tower: Afro-American Writers 1900 to 1960*. Washington: Howard University Press, 1974.

Dean, Sharon, and Erlene Stetson. "Flower-Dust and Springtime: Harlem Renaissance Women." *Radical Teacher*, 18, pp. 1–7.

Diamond, Lynn, and Lee R. Edwards, eds. *The Authority of Experience: Essays in Feminist Criticism*. Amherst: University of Massachusetts Press, 1977.

Dickinson, Anna. *What Answer*. Boston: Ticknor and Fields, 1868.

Dixon, Melvin. "The Teller as Folk Trickster in Chesnutt's *The Conjure Woman*." *CLAJ*, 18 (1974), 186–97.

Dorson, Richard M. *American Negro Folktales*. 1956; rpt. Greenwich, Conn.: Fawcett, 1967.

DuBois, W. E. B. *The Seventh Son: The Thought and Writings of W. E. B. DuBois*, 2 vols. Julius Lester, ed. New York: Vintage Books, 1971.

———. *The Souls of Black Folk*. 1903; rpt. Greenwich, Conn.: Fawcett, 1961.

Dunbar, Olivia. "Teaching the Immigrant Woman." *Harpers Bazaar*, 47 (June 1913), 277–78.

Elder, Arlene. *The "Hindered Hand": Cultural Implications of Early African/American Fiction*. Westport, Conn.: Greenwood Press, 1978.

Ellison, Ralph. *Shadow and Act*. 1953; rpt. New York: Random House, 1964.

Ewen, Stuart. *Captains of Consciousness: Advertising and the Social Roots of the Consumer Culture*. New York: McGraw-Hill, 1976.

Ewen, Stuart and Elizabeth. *Channels of Desire: Mass Images and the Shaping of American Consciousness*. New York: McGraw-Hill, 1982.

Fauset, Jessie. *The Chinaberry Tree*. 1931; rpt. New York: Negro Universities Press, 1961.

———. *Comedy: American Style*. 1933; rpt. College Park, Md.: McGrath Publishing, 1969.

———. "Nostalgia." *Crisis*, 22 (1921), 157–59.

———. *Plum Bun*. New York: Frederick A. Stokes, 1929.

———. *There Is Confusion*. New York: Boni and Liveright, 1924.

Feeney, Joseph. "A Sardonic, Unconventional Jessie Fauset: The Double Structure and Double Vision of Her Novels." *CLAJ*, 22 (1979), 365–82.

Felman, Shoshana, ed. *Literature and Psychoanalysis: The Question of Reading Otherwise*. Baltimore: Johns Hopkins University Press, 1982.

Ferber, Edna. *Cimarron*. 1929; rpt. New York: Bantam Books, 1963.

———. *Great Son*. New York: Doubleday, 1945.

———. *Ice Palace*. 1958; rpt. New York: Macfadden Books, 1964.

———. *A Peculiar Treasure*. 1938; rpt. New York: Lancer Books, 1960.

———. *Saratoga Trunk*. New York: Doubleday, 1941.

———. *Showboat*. Garden City, New York: Doubleday, 1926.

Fiedler, Leslie. *An End to Innocence: Essays on Culture and Politics*. Boston: Beacon Press, 1955.

————. *The Inadvertent Epic from* Uncle Tom's Cabin *to* Roots. New York: Simon and Schuster, 1979.

————. *Love and Death in the American Novel.* 1960; rev. ed. New York: Stein and Day, 1975.

————. *The Return of the Vanishing American.* New York: Stein and Day, 1968.

Fifer, Elizabeth. "Is Flesh Advisable? The Interior Theatre of Gertrude Stein." *Signs,* 4 (1979), 472–83.

Fine, David F. *The City, the Immigrant, and American Fiction, 1880–1920.* Metuchen, N.J.: The Scarecrow Press, 1977.

Fisher, Dexter, and Robert Stepto, eds. *Afro-American Literature: The Reconstruction of Instruction.* New York: MLA, 1979.

Fleming, E. McClung. "Symbols of the United States: From Indian Queen to Uncle Sam." In Ray B. Browne et al. eds. *Frontiers of American Culture.* Lafayette, Ind.: Purdue University Studies, 1968.

Forgie, George. *Patricide in the House Divided: A Psychological Interpretation of Lincoln and His Age.* New York: W. W. Norton, 1979.

Frazier, E. Franklin. *Black Bourgeoisie.* Glencoe, Ill.: Free Press, 1957.

Frederickson, George. *The Black Image in the White Mind: The Debate on Afro-American Character and Destiny, 1817–1914.* New York: Harper and Row, 1971.

Friedman, Lawrence J. *The White Savage: Racial Fantasies in the Postbellum South.* Englewood Cliffs, N.J.: Prentice-Hall, 1970.

Gaither, Frances. *Double Muscadine.* New York: MacMillan, 1949.

Gallup, Donald. "The Making of *The Making of Americans.*" *New Colophon,* 3 (1950), 54–74.

Gans, Herbert J. "Symbolic Ethnicity: The Future of Ethnic Groups and Cultures in America." In Gans, et al., eds. *On the Making of Americans: Essays in Honor of David Reisman.* Philadelphia: University of Pennsylvania Press, 1979, pp. 193–219.

————. *The Urban Villagers: Group and Class in the Life of Italian Americans.* New York: Free Press, 1962.

Gates, Henry Louis. "Introduction." In Harriet E. Wilson, *Our Nig.* 1859; rpt. New York: Vintage Books, 1983.

Gayle, Addison. *The Way of the New World: The Black Novel in America.* Garden City, New York: Anchor Press, 1975.

Gelfant, Blanche. "Sister to Faust: The City's 'Hungry Woman' as Heroine." *Novel,* 15 (1981), 23–28.

Genovese, Eugene D. *Roll, Jordan, Roll: The World the Slaves Made.* New York: Pantheon, 1974.

Gibbs, Anna. "Hélène Cixous and Gertrude Stein: New Directions in Feminist Criticism." *Meanjin,* 38 (1979), 281–93.

Gilbert, Julie Goldsmith. *Ferber: A Biography.* Garden City, New York: Doubleday, 1978.

Gilbert, Mercedes. *Aunt Sara's Wooden God.* 1938; rpt. College Park, Md.: McGrath Publishing, 1969.

Gilbert, Sandra M., and Susan Gubar. *The Madwoman in the Attic: The Woman Writer and the Nineteenth-Century Imagination.* New Haven: Yale University Press, 1979.

Glazer, Nathan, and Daniel P. Moynihan, eds. *Ethnicity: Theory and Experience.* Cambridge: Harvard University Press, 1975.

Gleason, Philip. "American Identity and Americanization." In Stephan Thernstrom, ed. *Harvard Encyclopedia of American Ethnic Groups.* Cambridge: Harvard University Press, 1980.

———. "Confusion Compounded: The Melting Pot in the 1960s and 1970s." *Ethnicity,* 6 (1979), 10–17.

———. "The Melting Pot: Symbol of Fusion or Confusion." *American Quarterly,* 16 (1964), 20–46.

Gloster, Hugh. *Negro Voices in American Fiction.* Chapel Hill: University of North Carolina Press, 1948.

Goldman, Emma. *Living My Life.* 2 vols. 1931; rpt. New York: Dover, 1970.

Gordon, Milton M. *Assimilation in American Life: The Role of Race, Religion, and National Origins.* New York: Oxford University Press, 1964.

———. *Human Nature, Class, and Ethnicity.* New York: Oxford University Press, 1978.

Gorer, Geoffrey. *The American People: A Study in National Character.* New York: W. W. Norton, 1948.

Goulder, Nancy. "Demon Lovers and 'Unquiet Slumbers': The Female Gothic in *Wuthering Heights.*" Unpublished ms., Columbia University, 1982.

Grau, Shirley Ann. *The Keepers of the House.* New York: Alfred A. Knopf, 1964.

Green, Rayna. "The Pocahontas Perplex: The Image of Indian Women in American Culture." *Massachusetts Review,* 16 (1975), 698–714.

Green, Rose Basile. *The Italian-American Novel: A Document of the Interaction of Two Cultures.* Rutherford, N.J.: Fairleigh Dickinson University Press, 1973.

Greer, Colin. *The Great School Legend: A Revisionist Interpretation of American Public Education.* New York: Basic Books, 1972.

Gross, Seymour L. and John Edward Hardy. *Images of the Negro in American Literature*. Chicago: University of Chicago Press, 1966.

Gutman, Herbert G. *The Black Family in Slavery and Freedom, 1750–1925*. New York: Pantheon, 1976.

Guttman, Allen. *The Jewish Writer in America: Assimilation and the Crisis of Identity*. New York: Oxford University Press, 1971.

Guy, Rosa. *Ruby*. New York: Viking, 1976.

Haley, Alex. *Roots*. Garden City, New York: Doubleday, 1976.

Handlin, Oscar, ed. *Children of the Uprooted*. New York: Grosset and Dunlap, 1968.

———. *Race and Nationality in American Life*. New York: Little, Brown, 1957.

———. *The Uprooted: The Epic Story of the Great Migrations That Made the American People*. Boston: Little, Brown, 1952.

Hansen, Chadwick. "The Metamorphosis of Tituba, or Why American Intellectuals Can't Tell an Indian Witch from a Negro." *New England Quarterly*, 47 (1974), 3–12.

Harper, Frances. *Iola Leroy; or Shadows Uplifted*. 1892; rpt. College Park, Md.: McGrath Publishing, 1969.

Harper, Michael S., and Robert B. Stepto, eds. *Chant of Saints: A Gathering of Afro-American Literature, Art, and Scholarship*. Urbana: University of Illinois Press, 1979.

Hartmann, George. *The Movement to Americanize the Immigrant*. 1948; rpt. New York: AMS Press, 1967.

Heilbrun, Carolyn. *Reinventing Womanhood*. New York: W. W. Norton, 1979.

Hemenway, Robert. *Zora Neale Hurston: A Literary Biography*. Urbana: University of Illinois Press, 1977.

Herskovits, Melville J. *The Myth of the Negro Past*. 1941; rpt. Boston: Beacon Press, 1958.

Herzog, Kristin. *Women, Ethnics, and Exotics: Images of Power in Mid-Nineteenth Century Fiction*. Knoxville: University of Tennessee Press, 1983.

Higham, John. *Send These To Me: Jews and Other Immigrants in Urban America*. New York: Atheneum, 1975.

———. *Strangers in the Land: Patterns of American Nativism 1860–1925*. New York: Atheneum, 1963.

Hijiya, James A. "Roots: Family and Ethnicity in the 1970s." *American Quarterly*, 30 (1978), 548–56.

Hines, Donald M., ed. *Tales of the Okanogans*. Fairfield, Wash.: Ye Galleon Press, 1976.

Hopkins, Pauline. *Contending Forces; A Romance Illustrative of Negro Life North and South*. Boston: Colored Co-operative Publishing, 1900.

————. "General Washington, A Christmas Story." *Colored American Magazine*, 2 (November 1900), 95–104.

————. "Of One Blood, Or the Hidden Self." *Colored American Magazine*, 6 (November 1902–November 1903).

[Hopkins, Pauline]. "Winona: A Tale of Negro Life in the South and Southwest." *Colored American Magazine*, 5 (May 1902–October 1902).

Hopkins, Sarah Winnemucca. *Life Among the Piutes: Their Wrongs and Claims*. Boston: Cupples and Upham, 1883.

Hirschfelder, Arlene B. *American Indian and Eskimo Authors*. New York: Association on American Indian Affairs, 1973.

Howard, Harold P. *Sacajawea*. Norman, Ok.: University of Oklahoma Press, 1971.

Howe, Irving. *World of Our Fathers: The Journey of the East European Jews to America and the Life They Found and Made*. New York: Simon and Schuster, 1976.

Howe, M. A. De Wolfe, ed. *Barrett Wendell and His Letters*. Boston: Atlantic Monthly Press, 1924.

Hubbell, Jay. "The Smith-Pocahontas Story in Literature." *The Virginia Magazine of History and Biography*, 65 (1957), 275–300.

Huggins, Nathan. *Harlem Renaissance*. New York: Oxford University Press, 1971.

————. "National Character and Community." *The Center Magazine*, 7 (July/August 1974), pp. 51–66.

Hughes, John Milton Charles. *The Negro Novelist: A Discussion of the Writings of American Negro Novelists 1940–1950*. Freeport, New York: Books for Libraries Press, 1953.

Hull, Gloria T., Patricia Bell Scott, and Barbara Smith, eds., *But Some of Us Are Brave: Black Women's Studies*. Old Westbury, N.Y.: Feminist Press, 1972.

Hum-Ishu-Ma [Mourning Dove]. *Co-ge-we-a: The Half Blood: A Depiction of the Great Montana Cattle Range*. Boston: Four Seas, 1927.

Hurst, Fannie. *Back Street*. New York: Holt, Rinehart, and Winston, 1932.

————. *Imitation of Life*. New York: Harper, 1933.

Hurston, Zora Neale. *Dust Tracks on a Road*. Philadelphia: Lippincott, 1942.

————. "High John de Conquer." *American Mercury*, 57 (1943), 450–58.

————. *I Love Myself When I Am Laughing*. Alice Walker, ed. Old Westbury, N.Y.: Feminist Press, 1979.

————. *Jonah's Gourd Vine*. 1934; rpt. Philadelphia: Lippincott, 1971.

————. *Moses, Man of the Mountain*. 1939; rpt. Chatham, N.J.: The Chatham Bookseller, 1967.

————. *Mules and Men*. 1935; rpt. Bloomington: Indiana University Press, 1963.

————. *Seraph on the Sewanee*. Philadelphia: Lippincott, 1948.

————. *Their Eyes Were Watching God*. 1937, rpt. Urbana: University of Illinois Press, 1978.

Hyman, Stanley Edgar. "Negro Literature and Folk Tradition." In *The Promised End*. Cleveland: World Publishing, 1963.

Inglehart, Babette. "Daughters of Loneliness: Anzia Yezierska and the Immigrant Woman Writer," *Studies in American Jewish Literature,* 1 (Winter 1975), 1–10.

Inglehart, Babette, and Anthony Mangione. *The Image of Pluralism in American Literature: An Annotated Bibliography on the American Experience of European Ethnic Groups*. New York: Institute on Pluralism and Group Identity, 1974.

Irwin, John. *Doubling and Incest/Repetition and Revenge*. Baltimore: Johns Hopkins University Press, 1975.

Jackson, Helen Hunt. *Ramona*. 1884; rpt. Boston: Little, Brown, 1911.

James, Edward T., ed. *Notable American Women 1607–1950: A Biographical Dictionary*. 3 vols. Cambridge: Harvard University Press, 1971.

Janeway, Elizabeth. *The Powers of the Weak*. New York: Alfred A. Knopf, 1980.

Jellinek, Estelle, ed. *Women's Autobiography: Essays in Criticism*. Bloomington: University of Indiana Press, 1980.

Johnson, Abby A. "Literary Midwife: Jessie Redmon Fauset and the Harlem Renaissance." *Phylon,* 21 (June 1978), 143–53.

Johnson, James Weldon. "The Dilemma of the Negro Author." *American Mercury,* 15 (1928), 477–81.

Johnston, James Hugo. *Race Relations in Virginia and Miscegenation in the South, 1776–1860*. Amherst: University of Massachusetts Press, 1970.

Jones, Gayl. *Corregidora*. New York: Random House, 1975.

————. *Eva's Man*. New York: Random House, 1976.

Jones, LeRoi. *Home: Social Essays*. New York: William Morrow, 1966.

Jordan, Winthrop D. *White Over Black: American Attitudes Toward the Negro, 1550–1812*. 1968; rpt. Baltimore: Penguin Books, 1973.

Kapai, Leela. "Dominant Themes and Technique in Paule Marshall's Fiction." *CLAJ,* 16 (1972), 49–59.

Karier, Clarence, Paul C. Violas, and Joel Spring. *Roots of Crisis:*

American Education in the Twentieth Century. Chicago: Rand McNally, 1973.

Katz, Leon. "The First Making of *The Making of Americans:* A Study Based on Gertrude Stein's Notebooks and Early Versions of Her Novel." Ph.D. diss.; Columbia University, 1963.

————. "Weininger and *The Making of Americans*." *Twentieth Century Literature*, 24 (1978), 8–26.

Katz, Michael B., ed. *Education in American History: Readings on The Social Issues*. New York: Praeger, 1973.

Kaye-Smith, Sheila. "Mrs. Adis." *Century*, 103 (1922), 321–26.

Keiser, Albert. *The Indian in American Literature*. New York: Oxford University Press, 1933.

Kellner, Bruce. *Carl Van Vechten and the Irreverent Decades*. Norman, Ok.: University of Oklahoma Press, 1968.

Kellor, Frances. "The Immigrant Woman." *Atlantic Monthly*, 100 (1907), 401–7.

————. "The Protection of Immigrant Women." *Atlantic Monthly*, 101 (1908), 246–55.

Kemble, Frances. *Journal of a Residence on a Georgian Plantation in 1838–1839*. New York: Harper and Bros., 1863.

King, Grace. *Balcony Stories*. New York: The Century Company, 1893.

Kingston, Maxine Hong. *The Woman Warrior: Memoirs of a Childhood Among Ghosts*. New York: Vintage Books, 1977.

Klein, Marcus. *Foreigners: The Making of American Literature 1900–1940*. Chicago: University of Chicago Press, 1981.

Kolodny, Annette. *The Lay of the Land: Metaphor as Experience and History in American Life and Letters*. Chapel Hill: University of North Carolina Press, 1975.

Koltun, Elizabeth, ed. *The Jewish Woman: New Perspectives*. New York: Schocken Books, 1976.

Kovel, Joel. *White Racism: A Psychohistory*. New York: Pantheon, 1971.

Kretzoi, Charlotte. "Gertrude Stein's Attempt at 'The Great American Novel.' " *Studies in English and American* (Budapest, Hungary), 4 (1978), 7–34.

Krupat, Arnold. "An Approach to Native American Texts." *Critical Inquiry*, 9 (1982), 323–38.

Lang, Lucy Robins. *Tomorrow is Beautiful*. New York: MacMillan, 1948.

Larsen, Nella. *Passing*. 1929; rpt. New York: Negro Universities Press, 1969.

————. *Quicksand*. 1928; rpt. New York: Negro Universities Press, 1969.

————. "Sanctuary." *Forum*, 83 (1930), 15–18.

Larson, Charles R. *American Indian Fiction*. Albuquerque, N.M.: University of New Mexico Press, 1978.

Lee, Harper. *To Kill A Mockingbird*. New York: J. P. Lippincott, 1960.

Lerner, Gerda. "Black and White Women in Interaction and Confrontation." *Prospects*, 2 (1976), 193–208.

Levine, Lawrence. *Black Culture and Black Consciousness: Afro-American Folk Thought From Slavery to Fiction*. New York: Oxford University Press, 1977.

Lewis, David Levering. "The Politics of Art: The New Negro, 1920–1935." *Prospects*, 3 (1977), 237–62.

————. *When Harlem Was in Vogue*. New York: Vintage, 1982.

Littlefield, David, and James W. Parins. *A Bibliography of Native American Writers 1722–1924*. Metuchen, N.J.: Scarecrow Press, 1981.

Lowry, Annie. *Karnee: A Paiute Narrative*. Lalla Scott, ed. Reno: University of Nevada Press, 1966.

Luhan, Mabel Dodge. *Intimate Memories*. 4 vols. New York: Harcourt, Brace, 1933–1937.

Lurie, Nancy Oestreich, ed. *Mountain Wolf Woman, Sister of Crashing Thunder: The Autobiography of a Winnebago Woman*. Ann Arbor: University of Michigan Press, 1961.

McCarthy, Mary. *Memories of a Catholic Girlhood*. New York: Harcourt, Brace, 1957.

McClymer, John F. "The Federal Government and the Americanization Movement." *Prologue*, 10 (1978), 23–41.

MacShane, Frank. "American Indians, Peruvian Jews." *New York Times Book Review*, 12 June 1977, p. 15.

Mainiero, Lina, ed. *American Women Writers*. 4 vols. New York: Frederick Ungar, 1982.

Manners, Ande. *Poor Cousins*. New York: Coward, McCann, and Geoghegan, 1972.

Marshall, Paule. *Brown Girl, Brownstones*. 1959; rpt. Old Westbury, N.Y.: Feminist Press, 1981.

————. *The Chosen Place, The Timeless People*. New York: Harcourt, Brace, 1969.

Mead, Margaret. *And Keep Your Powder Dry*. New York: W. W. Morrow, 1942.

Mechling, Joy. "Playing Indian and the Search for Authenticity in Modern White America." *Prospects*, 5 (1980), 17–33.

Mellow, James. *A Charmed Circle: Gertrude Stein and Company*. New York: Praeger, 1974.

Mencke, John G. *Mulattoes and Race Mixture: American Attitudes and Images.* Studies in American History and Culture no. 4. Ann Arbor: University of Michigan Research Press, 1979.

Meriwether, Louise. *Daddy Was a Numbers Runner.* New York: Jove, 1970.

Miller, Nancy. "Emphasis Added: Plots and Plausibilities in Women's Fiction." *PMLA,* 96 (1981), 36–48.

————. "The Text's Heroine: A Feminist Critic and Her Fictions." *Diacritics,* 12 (1982), 48–53.

Moore, Debra Dash. *At Home in America: Second Generation New York Jews.* New York: Columbia University Press, 1981.

Moore, Marianne. "The Spare American Emotion." *Dial,* 80 (1926), 153–56.

Morrison, Toni. *The Bluest Eye.* New York: Simon and Schuster, 1972.

————. *Song of Solomon.* New York: New American Library, 1977.

————. *Sula.* New York: Alfred A. Knopf, 1973.

Morton, Leah [Elizabeth Stern]. *I Am A Woman—and a Jew.* 1926; rpt. New York: Arno Press, 1969.

Mosberger, Robert. "The Further Transformation of Tituba." *New England Quarterly,* 47 (1974), 456–58.

Mossiker, Frances. *Pocahontas: The Life and the Legend.* New York: Alfred A. Knopf, 1976.

Murray, Albert. *The Omni-Americans: New Perspectives on Black Experience and American Culture.* New York: Avon, 1970.

Murray, Pauli. *Proud Shoes: The Story of an American Family.* New York: Harper and Bros., 1956.

Musgrave, Marian E. "Triangles in Black and White." *CLAJ,* 14 (1971), 444–51.

Myrdal, Gunnar. *An American Dilemma: The Negro Problem and Modern Democracy.* New York: Harper, 1944.

Nasaw, David. *Schooled to Order: A Social History of Public Schooling in the United States.* New York: Oxford University Press, 1979.

Naylor, Gloria. *The Women of Brewster Place.* New York: Penguin, 1983.

Olneck, Michael R., and Marvin Lazerson. "Education." In Stephan Thernstrom, ed., *Harvard Encyclopedia of American Ethnic Groups.* Cambridge: Harvard University Press, 1980.

Ostenso, Martha. *The Mad Carews.* New York: Dodd, Mead, 1927.

————. *The Waters Under the Earth.* New York: Dodd, Mead, 1930.

————. *Wild Geese.* New York: Dodd, Mead, 1925.

Pearce, Roy Harvey. *Savagism and Civilization: A Study of the In-*

dian and the American Mind. Baltimore: Johns Hopkins Press, 1965.

Perkinson, Henry J. *The Imperfect Panacea: American Faith in Education 1865–1965*. New York: Random House, 1968.

Pesotta, Rose. *Bread Upon the Waters*. New York: Dodd, Mead, 1944.

Peterkin, Julia. *Black April*. Indianapolis, Ind.: Bobbs Merrill, 1927.

————. *Bright Skin*. Indianapolis, Ind.: Bobbs Merrill, 1932.

Petry, Ann. *Country Place*. 1947; rpt. Chatham, N.J.: The Chatham Bookseller, 1971.

————. *The Narrows*. Boston: Houghton Mifflin, 1953.

————. *The Street*. Boston: Houghton Mifflin, 1946.

Phillips, Leon. *First Lady of America: A Romanticized Biography of Pocahontas*. Richmond, Va.: Westover Publishing, 1973.

[Pinzer, Maimie]. *The Maimie Papers*. Ruth Rosen and Sue Davidson, eds. Old Westbury, N.Y.: Feminist Press, 1971.

Plain, Belva. *Evergreen*. New York: Dell, 1978.

Plath, Sylvia. "America! America!" in *Johnny Panic and the Bible of Dreams*. New York: Harper and Row, 1980.

Pope, Edith. *Colcorton*. New York: Charles Scribners Sons, 1944.

Pratt, Norma Fain. "Jewish Women through the 1930's." *American Quarterly*, 30 (1978), 681–702.

Prucha, Francis Paul. *Americanizing the American Indians: Writings by "Friends of the Indian" 1880–1900*. Cambridge: Harvard University Press, 1973.

Qoyawayma, Polingaysi [Elizabeth Q. White] (as told to Vada S. Carlson). *No Turning Back: A Hopi Indian Woman's Struggle To Live in Two Worlds*. Albuquerque: University of New Mexico Press, 1964.

Radin, Paul. *The Trickster*. 1956; rpt. New York: Shocken Books, 1973.

Repplier, Agnes. "Americanism." *Atlantic Monthly*, 117 (1916), 289–97.

————. *Counter-Currents*. Boston: Houghton Mifflin, 1916.

Rich, Adrienne. *Of Woman Born: Motherhood as Experience and Institution*. New York: Norton, 1976.

Ridgely, J. V. *Nineteenth-Century Southern Literature*. Lexington: University Press of Kentucky, 1980.

Rogin, Michael Paul. *Fathers and Children: Andrew Jackson and the Subjugation of the American Indian*. New York: Alfred A. Knopf, 1975.

Rollins, Alice Wellington. *Uncle Tom's Tenement*. Boston: Wm. E. Smythe, 1888.

Rose, Peter I., ed. *The Ghetto and Beyond: Essays on Jewish Life in America*. New York: Random House, 1969.

Rosenblatt, Roger. *Black Fiction.* Cambridge: Harvard University Press, 1974.

Rourke, Constance. *American Humor: A Study of the National Character.* 1931; rpt. New York: Harcourt Brace Jovanovich, 1959.

Sales, Raoul de Roussy de. "Love in America." In Warren Susman, ed. *Culture and Commitment 1929–1945.* New York: Geo. Braziler, 1973, pp. 93–101.

Sato, Hiroko. "Under the Harlem Shadow: A Study of Jessie Fauset and Nella Larsen." In Arna Bontemps, ed. *The Harlem Renaissance Remembered.* New York: Dodd, Mead, 1972.

Scheick, William J. *The Half-Blood: A Cultural Symbol in 19th Century American Fiction.* Lexington: University Press of Kentucky, 1979.

Schwartz, Barry N., and Robert Disch, eds. *White Racism: Its History, Pathology, and Practice.* New York: Dell, 1970.

Scott, Anne Firor. *The Southern Lady: From Pedestal to Politics 1830–1930.* Chicago: University of Chicago Press, 1970.

———. "Women's Perspective of the Patriarchy in the 1850s." *The Journal of American History,* 61 (1974), 55–60.

Scudder, Vida D. *A Listener in Babel.* Boston: Houghton Mifflin, 1903.

Sekaquaptewa, Helen (as told to Louise Udall). *Me and Mine: The Life Story of Helen Sekaquaptewa.* Tucson: University of Arizona Press, 1969.

Seller, Maxine Schwartz, ed. *Immigrant Women.* Philadelphia: Temple University Press, 1981.

Shockley, Ann. *Loving Her.* New York: Avon, 1978.

———. "Pauline Elizabeth Hopkins: A Biographical Excursion into Obscurity." *Phylon,* 33 (Spring 1972), 22–26.

Sicherman, Barbara and Carol Hurd Green. *Notable American Women: The Modern Period.* New York: Harvard University Press, 1980.

Sigourney, Lydia Huntley. *Pocahontas and Other Poems.* New York: Harper, 1841.

Silko, Leslie Marmon. *Ceremony.* New York: Viking, 1977.

Sinclair, Jo. *Wasteland.* New York: Harper and Bros., 1946.

Singh, Amritjit. *The Novels of the Harlem Renaissance: Twelve Black Writers 1923–1933.* University Park: Pennsylvania State University Press, 1976.

Slesinger, Tess. *Time: The Present.* New York: Simon and Schuster, 1935.

Smith, Betty. *Maggie-Now.* New York: Harper, 1958.

———. *A Tree Grows in Brooklyn.* New York: Harper, 1947.

Smith, Lillian. *Killers of the Dream.* New York: W. W. Norton, 1949.

————. *Strange Fruit*. New York: Reynal and Hitchcock, 1944.

Sollors, Werner. *Amiri Baraka/LeRoi Jones: The Quest for a "Populist Modernism."* New York: Columbia University Press, 1978.

————. "Between Consent and Descent: Studying Ethnic Literature in the U.S.A." New York Institute for the Humanities *Intellectual History Group Newsletter*, 4 (Spring 1982), 13–19.

————. "A Defense of the Melting Pot." In Rob Kroes, ed. *The American Identity. Fusion and Fragmentation*. Amsterdam: European Contributions to American Studies III, 1980, pp. 181–214.

————. "First Generation, Second Generation, Third Generation: Metaphorical Thinking in America." Unpublished ms., Columbia University, 1981.

————. "Literature and Ethnicity." In Stephan Thernstrom, ed. *Harvard Encyclopedia of American Ethnic Groups*. Cambridge: Harvard University Press, 1980, pp. 647–65.

————. "Theory of American Ethnicity." *American Quarterly*, 33 (1981), 257–83.

Stein, Gertrude. *Alphabets and Birthdays*. New Haven: Yale University Press, 1957.

————. *The Autobiography of Alice B. Toklas*. New York: Harcourt, Brace, 1933.

————. *Bee Time Vine, and Other Pieces 1913–1927*. Freeport, New York: Books for Libraries Press, 1969.

————. *Everybody's Autobiography*. New York: Random House, 1937.

————. *Fernhurst, Q.E.D., and Other Early Writings*. New York: Liveright, 1971.

————. *Four in America*. New Haven: Yale University Press, 1947.

————. *The Geographical History of America; or, the Relation of Human Nature to the Human Mind*. New York: Random House, 1936.

————. *Geography and Plays*. Boston: Four Seas, 1922.

————. *How To Write*. Paris: Plain Edition, 1931.

————. *How Writing is Written*. Robert Bartlett Haas, ed. Los Angeles: Black Sparrow Press, 1974.

————. *Lectures in America*. 1935; rpt. New York: Vintage Books, 1975.

————. *The Making of Americans*. 1925; rpt. New York: Harcourt, Brace, 1934.

————. *Narration*. Chicago: University of Chicago Press, 1935.

————. *Picasso*. London: B. T. Batsford, 1958.

————. *Three Lives: Stories of the Good Anna, Melanctha, and the Gentle Lena*. New York: Grafton Press, 1909.

————. *What are Masterpieces*. 1940; rpt. New York, Pitman, 1970.

Stepto, Robert B. *From Behind the Veil: A Study of Afro-American Narrative*. Urbana: University of Illinois Press, 1979.

Stern, E[lizabeth] G. *My Mother and I*. New York: MacMillan, 1917.

Stewart, Allegra. *Gertrude Stein and the Present*. Cambridge: Harvard University Press, 1967.

Stonequist, Eugene V. *The Marginal Man: A Study in Personality and Culture Conflict*. 1937; rpt. New York: Russell and Russell, 1961.

Suckow, Ruth. *The Folks*. New York: Farrar and Rinehart, 1934.

Sutherland, Donald. *Gertrude Stein: A Biography of Her Work*. Westport, Conn.: Greenwood Press, 1951.

Sykes, Hope. *Second Hoeing*. New York: G. P. Putnam's, 1935.

Sylvander, Carolyn Wedin. *Jessie Redmon Fauset, Black American Writer*. Troy, N.Y.: Whitston Publishing, 1981.

Tanner, Tony. *Adultery in the Novel: Contract and Transgression*. Baltimore: Johns Hopkins University Press, 1979.

————. *The Reign of Wonder: Naivety and Reality in American Literature*. Cambridge, Eng.: University Press, 1975.

Tarry, Ellen. *The Third Door: The Autobiography of an American Negro Woman*. New York: David McKay, 1955.

Tate, Claudia. "Nella Larsen's *Passing:* A Problem of Interpretation." *BALF*, 14 (1980), 142–46.

Tax, Meredith. *Rivington Street*. New York: W. W. Morrow, 1982.

Theisz, R. D. "The Critical Collaboration: Introductions as a Gateway to the Study of Native American Bi-Autobiography," *American Indian Culture and Research Journal*, 5 (1981), 65–80.

Thernstrom, Stephan, ed. *The Harvard Encyclopedia of American Ethnic Groups*. Cambridge: Harvard University Press, 1980.

Thornton, Hortense. "Sexism as Quagmire: Nella Larsen's *Quicksand*." *CLAJ*, 16 (1973), 285–301.

Toomer, Jean. *Cane*. New York: Boni and Liveright, 1923.

Trollope, Frances. *Domestic Manners of the Americans*. 1831; rpt. New York: Alfred A. Knopf, 1949.

Turner, Darwin T., comp. *Afro-American Writers*. Northbrook, Ill.: AHM, 1970.

————. *In a Minor Chord: Three Afro-American Writers and Their Search for Identity*. Carbondale: Southern Illinois University Press, 1971.

Vauthier, Simone. "(Non)-famille romanesque, famille socio-historique, famille fantasmatique: l'exemple *d'Oran the Outcast* (1833)." *Ranam*, 8 (1975), 163–81.

————. "Textualité et Stereotypes: Of African Queens and Afro-American Princes and Princesses: Miscegenation in *Old Hepsy*."

Paris: Publications du Consel Scientifique de la Sorbonne Nouvelle, [n.d.].

Walker, Alice. *The Color Purple*. New York: Simon and Schuster, 1982.

————. *Meridian*. New York: Pocket Books, 1976.

Walker, Margaret. *Jubilee*. 1966; rpt. New York: Bantam Books, 1977.

Walters, Ronald G. *The Anti-Slavery Appeal: American Abolitionism After 1830*. Baltimore: Johns Hopkins University Press, 1976.

Warfel, Harry. *American Novelists of Today*. New York: American Book, 1951.

Washington, Booker T. *Up From Slavery*. In Louis Harlan, ed. *The Booker T. Washington Papers*, Vol. 1. Urbana: University of Illinois Press, 1972.

Washington, Mary Helen, ed. *Black-eyed Susans: Classic Stories By and About Black Women*. Garden City, N.Y.: Anchor, 1975.

————. "Nella Larsen: Mystery Woman of the Harlem Renaissance." *MS.,* 9 (December 1980), 44–50.

Washington, Joseph R. *Marriage in Black and White*. Boston: Beacon Press, 1970.

Weinstein, Norman. *Gertrude Stein and the Literature of Modern Consciousness*. New York: Frederick Ungar, 1970.

West, Dorothy. *The Living is Easy*. 1948; rpt. Old Westbury, N.Y.: Feminist Press, 1982.

Whitlow, Roger. *Black American Literature: A Critical History*. Chicago: Nelson Hall, 1973.

Wiggins, William H., Jr. "The Trickster as Literary Hero: Cecil Brown's *The Life and Loves of Mr. Jiveass Nigger*." *New York Folklore Quarterly,* 29 (1973), 269–86.

Williams, Ora. "A Bibliography of Works Written by American Black Women." *CLAJ,* 15 (1972), 354–77.

Williams, William Carlos. *In the American Grain*. 1933; rpt. New York: New Directions, 1956.

Wilson, Edmund. *Axel's Castle: A Study in the Imaginative Literature of 1870–1930*. New York: Scribner's, 1950.

[Wilson, Harriet E.] *Our Nig; or, Sketches from the Life of a Free Black, in a Two-Story White House, North. Showing That Slavery's Shadows Fall Even There*. Introd. Henry Louis Gates. 1859; rpt. New York: Vintage Books, 1983.

Wilson, James D. "Incest and American Romantic Fiction." *Studies in the American Literary Imagination,* 7 (Spring 1974), 31–50.

[Wirt, William]. *The Letters of the British Spy*. 1811; rpt. Upper Saddle River, N.J.: Literature House, 1970.

Yans McLaughlin, Virginia. *Family and Community: Italian Immigrants in Buffalo, 1880–1930*. Ithaca, N.Y.: Cornell University Press, 1977.

Yezierska, Anzia. *Arrogant Beggar*. Garden City, N.Y.: Doubleday, 1927.

———. *Bread Givers*. 1925; rpt. New York: Persea Books, 1975.

———. *Hungry Hearts*. New York: Grosset and Dunlap, 1920.

———. *The Open Cage*. Alice Kessler-Harris, ed. New York: Persea Books, 1979.

———. "Prophets of Democracy." *The Bookman*, 52 (1921), 497–98.

———. *Red Ribbon on a White Horse*. New York: Scribner's, 1950.

———. *Salome of the Tenements*. New York: Boni and Liveright, 1923.

———. "Wild Winter Wind." *Century*, 113 (1927), 485–91.

Youman, Mary Mabel. "Nella Larsen's *Passing:* A Study in Irony." *CLAJ*, 18 (1974), 235–41.

Young, James O. *Black Writers of the Thirties*. Baton Rouge: Louisiana State University Press, 1973.

Young, Philip. "The Mother of Us All." *Kenyon Review*, 24 (1962), 391–441.

Zafar, Rafia. " 'Colored people gettin' more like white folks every day': Color and Morality in the Novels of Jessie Fauset." Master's Essay, Columbia University, 1982.

Zanger, Jules. "The Tragic Octoroon in Pre-Civil War Fiction." *American Quarterly*, 18 (1966), 63–70.

Zangwill, Israel: *The Melting-Pot*. New York: Macmillan, 1923.

Notes

Introduction

1. Oscar Handlin, *The Uprooted: The Epic Story of the Great Migrations That Made the American People* (New York: Grosset and Dunlap, 1951), 3.
2. Jules Chametzky, in "Our Decentralized Literature: A Consideration of Regional, Ethnic, Racial, and Sexual Factors," *Jahrbuch für Amerikastudien* (Heidelberg), 17 (1972), discusses Howells's comments in a context that takes into account gender and ethnicity in a useful way.
3. Werner Sollors, "Literature and Ethnicity," in Stephan Thernstrom, ed., *Harvard Encyclopedia of American Ethnic Groups* (Cambridge: Harvard University Press, 1980), 648.
4. Simone de Beauvoir, *The Second Sex*, trans. H. M. Parshley (1952; rpt. New York: Alfred A. Knopf, 1975), xvi–xvii.
5. Carolyn Heilbrun, *Reinventing Womanhood* (New York: W. W. Norton, 1979), in Chapter 2, "Woman as Outsider," 37–70, also discusses Virginia Woolf's recommendation of a "Society of Outsiders" for women in her 1938 *Three Guineas*.
6. Myrdal, in Appendix 5, "A Parallel to the Negro Problem," in *An American Dilemma* (New York: Harper and Bros., 1944), was responding to a long tradition, with its roots in the abolitionist movement, of equating women's plight with blacks'. William Chafe, in *Women and Equality* (New York: Oxford University Press, 1977) expands on the formulation of this parallel; Gerda Lerner, in her review of Chafe's book in *Reviews in American History*, 6 (1978), defends the theory's historical usefulness against criticisms made by, for instance, Catherine Stimpson, "Thy Neighbor's Wife, Thy Neighbor's Servants: Women's Libera-

tion and Black Civil Rights," in Vivian Gornick and Barbara K. Moran, eds., *Woman in Sexist Society* (New York: Basic Books, 1971), 452–79. The parallel has problems in theory but some practical usefulness.

7. The reader should consult my bibliography for citation of works noted. The general bibliographies on ethnicity I found most useful for this study are Jean Fagin Yellin's essay, "Afro-American Women, 1800–1910: Excerpts from a Working Bibliography," in Gloria T. Hull, Patricia Bell Scott, Barbara Smith, eds., *But Some of Us Are Brave: Black Women's Studies* (Old Westbury, N.Y. The Feminist Press, 1982), 221–44; Maxine Schwartz Seller, "Bibliographical Essay," in Seller, ed., *Immigrant Women* (Philadelphia: Temple University Press, 1981), 329–40; Werner Sollors's bibliographical essay, "Theory of Ethnicity," *American Quarterly*, 33 (1981), 257–83 (in a special bibliographical issue on ethnicity). In selecting fiction for study, I relied most heavily on Babette Inglehart and Anthony Mangione, *The Image of Pluralism in American Literature: An Annotated Bibliography of the American Experience of European Ethnic Groups* (New York: Institute on Pluralism and Group Identity, 1974); Ora Williams, "A Bibliography of Works Written by American Black Women," *CLAJ*, 15 (1972), 354–77; and Lina Mainiero, ed., *American Women Writers*, 4 vols. (New York: Frederick Ungar, 1982), which provides biographical and bibliographical sketches of women writers.

8. Smith quoted in Philip Young, "The Mother of Us All," *Kenyon Review*, 24 (1962), 395.

9. See Sollors, "Literature and Ethnicity," 647–65.

Chapter 1

1. A source that gathers cultural representations of Pocahontas, and concentrates on these representations as symbols is E. McClung Fleming, "Symbols of the United States: From Indian Queen to Uncle Sam," in Ray B. Browne, ed., *Frontiers of American Culture* (Lafayette: Purdue University Studies, 1968), 1–24. Rayna Green, in her "The Pocahontas Perplex: The Image of Indian Women in American Culture," *Massachusetts Review*, 16 (1975), 698–714, provides some reproductions of the cultural iconography of Pocahontas.

2. Edith Blicksilver, "Leslie Marmon Silko," in *American Women Writers*, Vol. 4, Lina Mainiero, ed. (New York: Frederick Ungar, 1982), 82. Silko is also the author of a book of stories, *Laguna*

(1974), and a prose poem, *Storyteller* (1981). Blicksilver also has an article that discusses Silko's stories, "Traditionalism vs. Modernity: Leslie Silko on American Indian Women," *Southwest Review*, 64 (1979), 149–60. *American Indian Quarterly*, 5, i (1979) is a special issue on Silko. For biographical information see Russell Martin, "Writers of the Purple Sage," *New York Times Magazine*, 27 December 1981, p. 22.

3. Frank MacShane, "American Indians, Peruvian Jews," [rev. of Silko's *Ceremony*] *New York Times Book Review*, 12 June 1977, p. 15. Robert Sayre, in his review in *Studies in American Indian Literatures*, New Series 2 (1978), 8–12, suggests that *Ceremony* is a romance, and provides "what had been missing from the male-dominated literature of myth, history, and realism" (12).

4. Leslie Marmon Silko, *Ceremony* (New York: Viking, 1977), 4.

5. Silko, *Ceremony*, 35–36.

6. Many critics are exploring the relationship of biography and autobiography to fiction; a representative work is the collection of essays in Estelle Jellinek, ed., *Women's Autobiography: Essays in Criticism* (Bloomington: Indiana University Press, 1980). Recent ethnic literary scholarship, which pays close attention to folk elements in ethnic fiction, seldom addresses the problem of genre. One notable exception is Robert Hemenway; in his biography, *Zora Neale Hurston: A Literary Biography* (Urbana: University of Illinois, 1977), and in a critical study of Hurston's *Jonah's Gourd Vine*, "Are You a Flying Lark or a Setting Dove?" in Dexter Fisher and Robert B. Stepto, eds., *Afro-American Literature: The Reconstruction of Instruction* (New York: Modern Language Assn., 1979), 122–52, he gives some consideration to the fictiveness of folklore. It is not accidental that the question comes up in the case of Hurston, because she used folklore so extensively in her novels, and also wrote "non-fictional" folklore.

7. Werner Sollors, "Literature and Ethnicity," *Harvard Encyclopedia of American Ethnic Groups*, Stephan Thernstrom, ed. (Cambridge: Harvard University Press, 1980), 648.

8. Theory of ethnicity is a field unto itself, embracing the disciplines of history, political science, sociology, anthropology, statistics, and literature. A competent introduction to the "field" is William Petersen's essay, "Concepts of Ethnicity," 234–42 in the *Harvard Encyclopedia* cited above (*HEAEG*). The editors of *HEAEG*, the most valuable recent source on ethnicity, provide a brief introduction which has most directly informed my conception of what is "ethnic." Werner Sollors's bibliographical essay, "Theory of American Ethnicity," *American Quarterly*, 33 (1981), 257–83

(in a special bibliographical issue on ethnicity) is the most thorough and insightful recent overview of the field.

9. Daniel F. Littlefield and James W. Parins, *A Bibliography of Native American Writers 1772–1924* (Metuchen, N.J.: Scarecrow Press, 1981), xi.

10. See A. LaVaonne Ruoff's review of *No Turning Back* in *Studies in American Indian Literature,* New Series 1, Number 2 supplement (1977), 22–24.

11. See Gretchen Bataille and Kathleen Mullen Sands, *American Indian Women: Telling Their Lives* (Lincoln: University of Nebraska Press, 1984); and R. D. Theisz, "The Critical Collaboration: Introductions as a Gateway to the Study of Native-American Bi-Autobiography," *American Indian* Culture and Research Journal, 5 (1981), 65–80.

12. On this issue, I endorse what feminist critic Nancy Miller has concluded in what at first would seem a far removed context. Discussing the "institutionalization" of the feminist literary critic in "The Text's Heroine: A Feminist Critic and Her Fictions," *Diacritics,* 12 (1982), 48–53, Miller closes by discussing Foucault's questions about authorship in his 1980 "What Is an Author?" in *Language, Counter-Memory, Practice.* Foucault imagines a society that no longer asks "tiresome repetitions" like "Who is the real author?" and "Have we proof of his authenticity and originality?" asking instead, "What matter who's speaking?" "What matter who's speaking?" repeats Miller. "I would answer that it matters, for example, to women who have lost and still routinely lose their proper name in marriage, and whose signature—not merely their voice—has not been worth the paper it was written on; women for whom the signature—by virtue of its power in the world of circulation—is *not* immaterial. Only those who have it can play with not having it" (53). On the "textuality" of Indian literature, an excellent essay is Arnold Krupat, "An Approach to Native American Texts," *Critical Inquiry,* 9 (1982), 323–38.

13. I have relied heavily on the catalogue of McWhorter's papers at the State College of Washington in Seattle. Nelson Ault, *The Papers of Lucullus Virgil McWhorter* (Seattle: State College of Washington, 1959). Of all the "items" in Ault's catalogue, close to two hundred include material relating to Mourning Dove, ranging from photographs to correspondence about "domestic concerns." "Mourning Dove" is the name she is most commonly called.

14. Ault, Introduction, 7.

15. Lucullus McWhorter, "Biographical Sketch," in Hum-Ishu-Ma

[Mourning Dove], *Co-ge-we-a: The Half Blood: A Depiction of the Great Montana Cattle Range* (Boston: Four Seas, 1927). Further references in this chapter will be made parenthetically within the text.

16. McWhorter, "Biographical Sketch," 12.

17. The authorship of *Coyote Tales,* originally published in Caldwell, Idaho in 1933, is further obscured by its having been reprinted in 1976, by Donald M. Hines, as *Tales of the Okanogans* (Fairfield, Wash.: Ye Galleon Press, 1976). I am indebted to Karl Kroeber for directing me to and providing me a copy of this book.

18. Ault, 7.

19. Charles E. Larson discusses *Co-ge-we-a* in Appendix 1, pp. 173–80, of his useful study *American Indian Fiction* (Albuquerque University of New Mexico Press, 1978). It is important to note, too, that the title page of *Co-ge-we-a* also indicates that the book is "given through Sho-pow-tan," which I do not know what to make of.

20. Biographical information about McWhorter is provided in Ault's introduction.

21. Like Mourning Dove, Cogewea writes in order to preserve the ways of the Indians. Cogewea, "recognizing the new order of things . . . realized that these threads in the woof of her people's philosophy, must be irretrievably lost unless speedily placed on record" (33). R. D. Theisz points out that "the most common rationale [of the collaborated Indian text] revolves around 'The Vanishing Red Man' theme. On the premise that the curtain has closed on a 'formerly great culture,' we will be provided one last look at the disappearing actors" (70).

22. Hines, Foreword, 7.

23. Hines, 13–14.

24. Hines, 64.

25. Margot Astrov quoted in Gerald Haslam, "Literature of *The People:* Native American Voices," *CLAJ,* 15 (1971), 156. In African culture, from which the trickster tale is also derived, the power of the word has similar noted importance. Melvin Dixon, in "The Teller as Folk Trickster in Chesnutt's *The Conjure Woman,*" *CLAJ,* 18 (1974), 186–97, relates the trickster tradition back to *Nommo,* the magic power of the word. He quotes Janheinz Jahn's 1961 *Muntu: The New African Culture:* "Through Nommo, the word, man establishes his mastery over things . . . the word itself is force, . . . According to African philosophy, man has by force of his word, dominion over 'things': he can change them, make them work for him, and command them. But

to command things with words is to practice magic, and to practice magic is to write poetry." (191, ellipses Dixon's)

26. The works I have consulted regarding the trickster are Paul Radin, *The Trickster* (1956; rpt. New York: Schocken Books, 1973), an analysis of the Winnebago trickster cycle with essays by Jung and Karl Kerenyi; Roger D. Abrahams's *Deep Down in the Jungle* (Chicago: Aldine, 1970), a study of the folk culture of Philadelphia street gangs; Zora Neale Hurston's "High John de Conquer," *American Mercury,* 57 (1943), 450–58, a study of a trickster important to Hurston's fiction; Henry Louis Gates, "Binary Oppositions in Chapter One of *Narrative of the Life of Frederick Douglass an American Slave Written by Himself,*" in Dexter Fisher and Robert Stepto, eds., *Afro-American Literature: The Reconstruction of Instruction,* 212–32, a study of oppositions set up and subverted by Douglass, a trickster/mediator; William H. Wiggins, Jr., "The Trickster as Literary Hero: Cecil Brown's *The Life and Loves of Mr. Jiveass Nigger,*" *NY Folklore Quarterly,* 29 (1973), 269–86, an analysis of the John/Efan trickster cycle in a recent black novel; J. Mason Brewer, *American Negro Folklore* (New York: Quadrangle Books, 1968), particularly the "John" stories in the "Tales" section, 3–104; Richard M. Dorson, *American Negro Folktales* (1956; rpt. Greenwich, Conn.: Fawcett, 1967), which contains the most extensive collection of tales involving a trickster figure; Sterling A. Brown, "A Century of Negro Portraiture in American Literature," *Massachusetts Review,* 7 (Winter 1966), [pp. 73–96], which discusses "strategies of evasion" in black texts; and Lawrence Levine, *Black Culture and Black Consciousness: Afro-American Folk Thought from Slavery to Freedom* (New York: Oxford, 1977), the single most important work on the subject. In connection with Mourning Dove's novel, it is interesting to note Levine's comments on the tradition of "greenhorns and tenderfeet . . . pricked by falsifying narratives and dialogs" which he links to the selling to greenhorns of gold bricks, Grant's Tomb, the Brooklyn Bridge, etc. (360).

27. Their debate appears in final form in Ralph Ellison, "Change the Joke and Slip the Yoke," *Shadow and Act* (New York: Random House, 1953), and Stanley Edgar Hyman, "Negro Literature and Folk Tradition," *The Promised End* (Cleveland, World Publishing Co., 1963). Hyman first advanced the idea, pointing out an interesting connection between the trickster and language in James Baldwin's "Autobiographical Notes" in *Notes of a Native Son;* the author sees himself as a black Caliban telling a white Prospero,

"You taught me language, and my profit on't is I know how to curse" (303). Ellison cites "the strategy of a smart man playing dumb" which "grows out of our awareness of the joke at the center of the American identity" (54) in order to argue the archetypal universality of the trickster.

28. Abrahams, 65.
29. Quoted in Abrahams, 63.
30. Levine, 105–6.
31. Elizabeth Janeway, *Powers of the Weak* (New York: Knopf, 1980), 145.

Chapter 2

1. Leslie Bennetts, "An 1859 Black Literary Landmark Is Discovered," *New York Times,* 8 November 1982, p. C13.
2. "Our Nig" [Harriet E. Wilson], *Our Nig; or, Sketches from the Life of a Free Black, In a Two-Story White House, North. Showing That Slavery's Shadows Fall Even There* (Boston: George C. Rand and Avery, 1859), n.p.
3. Harriet E. Wilson, *Our Nig; or, Sketches from the Life of a Free Black,* with an Introduction and Notes by Henry Louis Gates, Jr. (New York: Vintage Books, 1983). Gates's excellent introduction elaborates further on some of the bibliographical and theoretical issues surrounding Wilson's authorship that I have discussed briefly here.
4. The most complete biography of Mary Antin can be assembled through reading *The Promised Land* (Boston: Houghton Mifflin, 1912) and *From Plotzk to Boston* (Boston: W. B. Clarke, 1889). (Antin's village, Polotzk, was misspelled throughout.) An article in the *Outlook,* 102 (1912), 482–86, "A Woman to her Fellow-Citizens," provides a sense of Antin's political views; her "The Soundless Trumpet," *Atlantic Monthly,* 159 (1937), 560–69, represents Antin's later thinking, as does "House of One God," *Common Ground* (Spring 1941), 36–42. See Oscar Handlin's entry in *Notable American Women,* Vol. 1, Edward T. James et al., eds. (Cambridge: Harvard University Press, 1971), 57–59, and the entry in *The National Cyclopedia of American Biography,* Vol. 39 (New York: James T. White, 1954), 40. Reviews of *The Promised Land* that provide biographical information are: *The Nation,* 94 (1912), 517; "The Immigrant," *New York Times,* 14 April 1912, p. 228; William H. Maxwell, "Mary Antin's 'The Promised Land,'" *Literary Digest,* 44 (1912), 1261–62; "How One Immigrant Girl Discovered America," *The Dial,* 52 (1912),

348–50; George Middleton, "Mary Antin's 'The Promised Land,' "
Bookman, 35 (1912), 419–21. [Maimie Pinzer], *The Maimie
Papers,* Ruth Rosen and Sue Davidson, eds. (Old Westbury, N.Y.:
The Feminist Press, 1977), 158–67, a collection of letters written
by a former prostitute, Maimie Pinzer, to Fanny Quincy Howe,
presents a valuable portrait of Antin, whom Maimie did not much
like.

5. Antin, *The Promised Land,* 211–12.
6. Antin, *The Promised Land,* 237.
7. Antin, *The Promised Land,* 345. Barrett Wendell describes his
friendship with Antin in a letter to Sir Robert White-Thompson,
collected in M. A. De Wolfe Howe, *Barrett Wendell and His
Letters* (Boston: Atlantic Monthly Press, 1924), 281–82. Wendell
wrote, "She has developed an irritating habit of describing herself
and her people as Americans, in distinction from such folks as
[my wife] and me, who have been here for three hundred years"
(282).
8. Interestingly, however, the writing of *The Promised Land* was
motivated by Antin's friendship with a woman, Josephine Lazarus,
the sister of the Statue of Liberty poem's Emma Lazarus, who
urged Antin to write and whose death inspired Antin to do so.
Lazarus does not appear in *The Promised Land*—except in the
dedication. This aspect of the mediation of Antin's authorship is
to recur with some frequency in the ethnic literary tradition. Somewhat fancifully, one could posit the culmination of this tradition,
in which other ethnic women "sponsor" other ethnic female texts,
in the contemporary institution in the publishing trade of an
editor imprint. Black writer Gayl Jones's *Corregidora* (1975),
published by Random House, bears the imprint, "A Toni Morrison
Book"; it is edited, with all that entails, by another ethnic woman
novelist.
9. Jules Chametzky, "Our Decentralized Literature: A Consideration
of Regional, Ethnic, Racial, and Sexual Factors," *Jahrbuch für
Amerikastudien* (Heidelberg), 17 (1972), 56–72. Chametzky's
important article also discusses George Washington Cable's interaction with the New England literary establishment, as well as
Charles Chesnutt and Kate Chopin. See also his "Regional Literature and Ethnic Realities," *The Antioch Review,* 31 (1971),
385–96.
10. The most thorough discussion of Yezierska's relationship with
Dewey is provided by Jo Ann Boydston in her introduction to
The Poems of John Dewey, Jo Ann Boydston, ed. (Carbondale:
Southern Illinois University Press, 1977), ix–lxvii.

11. James Mellow, *A Charmed Circle: Gertrude Stein and Company* (New York: Praeger, 1974), 193. Van Vechten is a particularly interesting figure in the context of this study; of the writers I consider he was acquainted with Gertrude Atherton, Willa Cather, Mabel Dodge Luhan, Edna Ferber, Ellen Glasgow, Fannie Hurst, Zora Neale Hurston, Nella Larsen, Gertrude Stein, and Alice Toklas. Nathan Huggins, in his *Harlem Renaissance* (New York: Oxford University Press, 1971), 93–116, provides an excellent account of Van Vechten's role in promoting the authors of the Renaissance; through his publisher, Knopf, Van Vechten arranged the publication of the works of James Weldon Johnson, Nella Larsen, Rudolph Fisher, Chester Himes, and Langston Hughes. A close friend of Johnson, Hughes, and Countee Cullen, Van Vechten was also responsible for assembling the important James Weldon Johnson collection of black manuscripts at Yale. Nella Larsen's first novel is dedicated to Van Vechten and his wife. In his role of promoter of Harlem artists, Van Vechten has come under considerable criticism, both from Huggins and David Levering Lewis in his *When Harlem Was In Vogue* (New York: Vintage, 1982). Van Vechten's encouragement and promotion of Stein's work, on the other hand, is seldom questioned. From his first introduction to Stein's work, which generated his arrangement for the publication of her 1914 *Tender Buttons,* Van Vechten was Stein's most vigorous supporter, writing enthusiastic reviews and prefaces and promoting editions of her work. In 1951, with the help of Donald Gallup, Donald Sutherland, and Thornton Wilder, the Stein collection was established at Yale and her works began to be published posthumously by the Yale Press; Van Vechten was Stein's literary executor until he was eighty. See Bruce Kellner's biography, *Carl Van Vechten and the Irreverent Decades* (Norman: University of Oklahoma Press, 1968).

12. Antin, *The Promised Land,* 367–73. To cite just two further examples of the use of glossaries or appended texts in ethnic women's novels: Zora Neale Hurston's 1934 *Jonah's Gourd Vine* contains a glossary translating dialect forms and explaining folk expression; a more extreme example of annotation is her 1935 *Mules and Men,* which has four appendices, one of which contains detailed recipes for cures of gonorrhea and lockjaw.

13. Frances Harper, *Iola Leroy; or Shadows Uplifted* (1892; rpt. College Park, Md.: McGrath Publishing, 1969), 1–3.

14. Margaret Walker, *Jubilee* (1966; rpt. New York: Bantam Books, 1977), n.p.

15. Robert B. Stepto, "Narration, Authentication, and Authorial Con-

trol in Frederick Douglass's *Narrative* of 1845," in Dexter Fisher and Robert B. Stepto, eds., *Afro-American Literature: The Reconstruction of Instruction* (New York: Modern Language Assn., 1979), 181.

16. *Roots* itself, it should be added, was a text that seemed to demand authentication—and got it, both from Haley himself, always attesting the truth of his ancestry, and from historians like Oscar Handlin, who "vouched" for it. Haley was also accused of plagiarizing from Harold Courlander's *The African* (1967). See the account in the *New York Times,* 20 November 1978, 126–27; and "Uprooted," *Newsweek,* 93 (22 January 1979), 10. Walker's and Courlander's suits were dismissed.

17. Two recent articles have given consideration to this problem, and to the question of sexism in the criticism of black women's novels: Rita B. Dandridge, "Male Critics/Black Women's Novels," *CLAJ,* 23 (1979), 1–11; and Barbara Smith, "Toward a Black Feminist Criticism," in Gloria T. Hull, Patricia Bell Scott, and Barbara Smith, eds., *But Some of Us Are Brave: Black Women's Studies* (Old Westbury, N.Y.: The Feminist Press, 1982), 157–75.

18. Antin, *The Promised Land,* 260.

19. Antin, *They Who Knock At Our Gates* (Boston: Houghton Mifflin, 1914), 63.

20. Antin, *They Who Knock At Our Gates,* 98. See Werner Sollors, "Literature and Ethnicity," in Stephan Thernstrom, ed. *Harvard Encyclopedia of American Ethnic Groups* (Cambridge: Harvard University Press, 1980), 647–65; and "A Defense of the Melting Pot" in Rob Kroes, ed., *Fusion and Fragmentation: The American Identity* (Amsterdam: European Contributions to American Studies III, 1980), 181–214.

21. Agnes Repplier's "The Modest Immigrant" was reprinted in a collection of her essays, *Counter-Currents* (Boston: Houghton Mifflin, 1916), 197–232. For biographical information, see George Stewart Stokes's entry in *Notable American Women,* Vol. 3, pp. 137–39. Compare Repplier's comment to Barrett Wendell's, cited above.

22. Antin, *The Promised Land,* 17.

23. Antin, *The Promised Land,* 87–88.

24. Anzia Yezierska, *Red Ribbon on a White Horse* (New York: Scribner's, 1950), 207.

25. Yezierska, "America and I," in *The Open Cage,* Alice Kessler-Harris, ed. (New York: Persea Books, 1979), 33.

26. Elizabeth G. Stern, *My Mother and I* (New York: Macmillan, 1917), 112.

27. Review of *My Mother and I, Nation,* 105 (1917), 225.

28. Babette Inglehart, in "Daughters of Loneliness: Anzia Yezierska and the Immigrant Woman Writer," *Studies in American Jewish Literature,* 1 (Winter 1975), 1–10, quotes contemporary reviews of Yezierska's work. The best sources for Yezierska's life are her *Red Ribbon on a White Horse;* Carol B. Schoen, *Anzia Yezierska* (Boston: Twayne, 1982); Jules Chametzky's entry in *Notable American Women: The Modern Period* (Cambridge: Harvard University Press, 1980), 753–54; Alice Kessler-Harris's introduction to *Bread Givers* (1925; rpt. New York: Persea Books, 1975), v–xiii; her introduction to *The Open Cage,* v–xiii; and an afterword by Louise Levitas Henriksen, Yezierska's daughter, to *The Open Cage,* 253–62.

29. This is an unfortunate oversight, and one in which I am aware I participate. Often the "ethnic" novelist can explore areas of significant psychological complexity and meanings by writing about "nonethnics." Just as James Baldwin chose to write about homosexuality using white characters in *Giovanni's Room,* so Petry and Hurston explore the complexities of female sexuality in their respective "white" novels.

30. Barbara Christian, *Black Women Novelists: The Development of a Tradition* (Westport, Conn.: Greenwood Press, 1980), 19.

31. Robert Bone's *The Negro Novel in America* (New Haven: Yale University Press, 1958) is the best source on Reconstruction black fiction. Arlene Elder, *The "Hindered Hand": Cultural Implications of Early African/American Fiction* (Westport, Conn.: Greenwood Press, 1978), discusses this period at length. See also Addison Gayle, *The Way of the New World: The Black Novel in America* (Garden City, N.Y.: Anchor Press, 1975), esp. 1–58; Barbara Christian, 3–34; Hugh Gloster, *Negro Voices in American Fiction* (Chapel Hill, N.C.: University of North Carolina Press, 1948). E. Franklin Frazier's *Black Bourgeoisie* (Glencoe, Ill.: The Free Press, 1957), is indispensable for a study of this period.

32. Bone, *The Negro Novel,* 20.

33. A later black writer, James Weldon Johnson, addressed the problem of the "divided audience" at length in "The Dilemma of the Negro Author," *American Mercury* 15 (1928), 477–81. Johnson wrote that the black author's audience "is more than a double audience; it is a divided audience, an audience made up of two elements with differing and often opposite and antagonistic points of view" (477).

34. Harper, 9.

35. Harper, 16.

36. Harper, 250–51.
37. Harper, 282.

Chapter 3

1. Nathan Huggins, *Harlem Renaissance* (New York: Oxford University Press, 1971), 9. The sources I have used for the following discussion of the period are Huggins and David Levering Lewis, *When Harlem Was in Vogue* (New York: Vintage, 1982, as well as Jervis Anderson, *This Was Harlem: A Cultural Portrait 1900–1950* (New York: Farrar, Straus, Giroux, 1982).
2. Lewis, *When Harlem Was in Vogue*, 296.
3. I am indebted in my discussion of Fauset to Carolyn Wedin Sylvander's thorough critical biography, *Jessie Redmon Fauset, Black American Writer* (Troy, N.Y.: Whitston Publishing, 1981). See also Cheryl A. Wall's entry in *Notable American Women: The Modern Period*, Barbara Sicherman and Carol Hurd Green, eds. (Cambridge: Harvard University Press, 1980), 225–27. Hiroko Sato's "Under the Harlem Shadow: A Study of Jessie Fauset and Nella Larsen," in Arna Bontemps, ed., *The Harlem Renaissance Remembered* (New York: Dodd, Mead, 1972), 63–89, is a useful study of Fauset, as is Rafia Zafar's " 'Colored people gettin' more like white folks every day': Color and Morality in the Novels of Jessie Fauset" (Master's essay, Columbia University, 1982). Joseph Feeney, "A Sardonic, Unconventional Jessie Fauset: The Double Structure and Double Vision of Her Novels," *CLAJ*, 22 (1979), 365–82, as the title suggests, attempts a formalist salvage of Fauset's work. For more traditional assessments of Fauset, see Arthur P. Davis, *From The Dark Tower: Afro–American Writers 1900 to 1960* (Washington: Howard University Press, 1974), 90–94; Robert Bone, *The Negro Novel in America* (New Haven: Yale University Press, 1958), 101–2; Amritjit Singh, *The Novels of the Harlem Renaissance: Twelve Black Writers, 1923–1933* (University Park, Pa.: Pennsylvania State University Press, 1976); Barbara Christian, *Black Women Novelists: The Development of a Tradition* (Westport, Conn.: Greenwood Press, 1980), 41–47; Addison Gayle, *The Way of the New World: The Black Novel in America* (Garden City, N.Y.: Anchor Press, 1975), 115–23.
4. Quoted in Sato, 68. Another valuable contemporary assessment is William Stanley Braithwaite, "The Novels of Jessie Fauset," *Opportunity*, 12 (1934), 24–28. For citation and discussion of other contemporary responses and for an excellent historical account of Fauset's career, see Lewis, *When Harlem Was in Vogue*, 121–25.

5. Bone, *The Negro Novel in America*, 102.
6. Lewis feels that Fauset's characters "reflect faithfully a significant class of black life." *When Harlem Was in Vogue*, 124.
7. Quoted in Sato, 67.
8. Jessie Fauset, *The Chinaberry Tree* (1931: rpt. New York: Negro Universities Press, 1961), x.
9. Fauset, *There is Confusion* (New York: Boni and Liveright, 1924), 232.
10. Fauset, *The Chinaberry Tree*, 36.
11. Huggins, *Harlem Renaissance*, 195. As recently as 1962, Leroi Jones (Amiri Baraka) suggested this connection between civilization and civility, culture and cultivation. "Literature, for the Negro writer, was always an example of 'culture.' Not in the sense of the more impressive philosophical characteristics of a particular social group, but in the narrow sense of 'cultivation' or 'sophistication' by an individual within that group. . . . To be a writer was to be 'cultivated,' in the stunted bourgeois sense of the word." Leroi Jones, "The Myth of a Negro Literature," *Home* (New York: William Morrow, 1966), 107–8.
12. Huggins writes, "Whatever its exoticism, the 'renaissance' echoed American progressivism in its faith in democratic reform, in its extraordinarily high evaluation of art and literature as agents of change, and in its almost uncritical belief in itself and its future. . . . Harlemites could believe in the future of the 'New Negro' because they accepted the system without question." *Harlem Renaissance* (303).
13. William Stanley Braithwaite, "The Novels of Jessie Fauset," *Opportunity*, 12 (1934), 24–28.
14. See Lewis, *When Harlem Was in Vogue*, 121–25 and 177. Langston Hughes, quoted in Lewis (121), also named Charles S. Johnson at *Opportunity*—whom Lewis foregrounds of "The Six"—and Alain Locke.
15. Huggins, *Harlem Renaissance*, 228.
16. Fauset, "Nostalgia," *Crisis*, 22 (1921), 157.
17. For contemporary critical responses to Larsen, see Lewis, *When Harlem Was in Vogue*, 231–32. He quotes DuBois's *Crisis* comment; DuBois thought *Quicksand* "on the whole, the best piece of fiction that Negro America has produced since the heyday of Chesnutt, and stands easily with Jessie Fauset's *There is Confusion* in its subtle comprehension of the curious cross currents that swirl about the black Americans." For biographical details of Larsen's life, see Lewis, 231–33, and Mary Helen Washington, "Nella Larsen: Mystery Woman of the Harlem Renaissance," *Ms.*, 9 (De-

cember 1980), 44–50, which contains minor inaccuracies but is otherwise very thorough.

18. Mary Helen Washington relates the fact but not the details of the plagiarism charge, "Nella Larsen," 46. Larsen's "Sanctuary" appeared in *Forum*, 83 (1930), 15–18, and Sheila Kaye-Smith's "Mrs. Adis" in *Century*, 103 (1922), 321–26. The exchange of letters appeared in *Forum*, 83 (1930), April supplement, xli–xlii.

19. William Bedford Clark's description of these letters is very useful in reconstructing Larsen's life and views. "The Letters of Nella Larsen to Carl Van Vechten: A Survey," *Resources for American Literary Study*, 8 (1978), 193–99.

20. Washington quotes Larsen as saying in an interview, "I don't see my family much now. It might make it awkward for them, particularly my half-sister." "Nella Larsen," 45.

21. Larsen's letters quoted in Clark, 196–98.

22. In her letters to Van Vechten, Clark recounts, Larsen describes a quarrel with Walter White over her reference to "propaganda" in her discussion of black art.

23. Quoted in Mary Mabel Youman, "Nella Larsen's *Passing: A Study in Irony, CLAJ*, 18 (1974), 236.

24. Lewis, *When Harlem Was in Vogue*, 238.

25. Nella Larsen, *Passing* (1929; rpt. New York: Negro Universities Press, 1969), 70.

26. Robert Bone, *The Negro Novel in America*, 102–6, praises Larsen's novel as inferior only to Toomer's *Cane*, but his discussion of the novel is perfunctory, and he places Larsen in the "Rear Guard" of the Renaissance.

27. Hortense Thornton, "Sexism as Quagmire: Nella Larsen's *Quicksand,*" *CLAJ*, 16 (1973), 285–301.

28. Sato's discussion of Larsen treats her fiction in some critical depth, as does Youman's; see also Claudia Tate, "Nella Larsen's *Passing:* A Problem of Interpretation," *BALF*, 14 (1980), 142–46; and Sharon Dean and Erlene Stetson, "Flower-Dust and Springtime: Harlem Renaissance Women," *Radical Teacher*, 18, pp. 1–7.

29. Barbara Christian, *Black Women Novelists: The Development of a Tradition, 1892–1976*, Contributions in Afro-American and African Studies, No. 52 (Westport, Conn.: Greenwood Press, 1980), 53.

30. Dorothy West's novel has not received the attention it deserves, nor have the facts of her authorship. Bone provides an excellent analysis, *The Negro Novel in America*, 187–91, but the novel is not even mentioned in, for instance, Christian's *Black Women Novelists*. In the recent re-issue of *The Living is Easy* by the

Feminist Press, Adelaide M. Cromwell, in an afterword, suggests many interesting areas for study; an influential 1930s figure, West edited *Challenge* and *New Challenge,* black journals which sought to encourage the work of "newer Negroes." A close friend of Van Vechten's, West was a figure of controversy to rival Fauset or Larsen: Zora Neale Hurston called her "audacious," Wallace Thurman found her magazines "too pink tea and la de da" (quoted in Cromwell, "Afterword," in Dorothy West, *The Living is Easy* (1948; rpt. Old Westbury, N.Y.: The Feminist Press, 1982), 354–55).

31. Petry's work has received some critical response, presumably because *The Street* is an important novel of a definable school. See Christian, 63–68, and also Bone, *The Negro Novel in America,* 180–85, who curiously most admires Petry's *Country Place,* calling it "the best of the assimilationist novels." Petry, out of Fauset, West, and Larsen, seems to be the one writer who truly did grow up in the middle class.

A fact of Petry's career that I find of particular interest is that she was instrumental in mythologizing the slave woman Tituba as a black in her 1964 children's book, *Tituba of Salem Village.* Tituba, in fact, seems to have been a West Indian. Two articles discuss this interesting ethnic transformation: Chadwick Hansen, "The Metamorphosis of Tituba, or Why American Intellectuals Can't Tell an Indian Witch from a Negro," *New England Quarterly,* 47 (1974), 3–12; and Robert Mosberger, "The Further Transformation of Tituba," *New England Quarterly,* 47 (1974), 456–58. Tituba as Indian is a kind of anti-Pocahontas because she supposedly incited witchcraft in the Salem community. Perhaps this is why legend has blackened her.

32. Alice Walker, the author of *Meridian* (1976) and *The Color Purple* (1982), has told and retold the dramatic story of her search for Hurston's grave, in the foreword to Robert Hemenway's biography, *Zora Neale Hurston: A Literary Biography* (Urbana: University of Illinois Press, 1977), xi–xviii, and the anthology of Hurston's work, *I Love Myself When I Am Laughing,* Alice Walker, ed. (Old Westbury, N.Y.: The Feminist Press, 1979). Gayl Jones, the author of *Corregidora* (1975) and *Eva's Man* (1976), has some interesting comments on Hurston's influence in an interview with Michael Harper published in *Chant of Saints: A Gathering of Afro-American Literature, Art, and Scholarship,* Michael S. Harper and Robert B. Stepto, eds. (Urbana: University of Illinois Press, 1979), 362–75.

33. Hemenway, 65. I am extremely indebted to Hemenway's thorough

biography; the details of Hurston's life that I discuss are, unless otherwise cited, from his study of Hurston. Lewis's account of her relationship with her patron is valuable, 152–53, and Huggins's brief consideration of her, 130–33, places her in the Harlem Renaissance context. Robert A. Bone, in *Down Home: A History of Afro-American Short Fiction from Its Beginnings to the End of the Harlem Renaissance* (New York: G. P. Putnam's, 1975) was the first critic to consider fully Mrs. Osgood Mason's role in the Harlem Renaissance, although his focus is primarily on her relationship with Langston Hughes.

34. Hemenway, 78. Hemenway interprets Hurston's reuse of her material to an unconscious wish to get out of the rigorous folklore business.

35. Reviews quoted and discussed in Hemenway, 241–42. Wright and Hurston, perhaps because they were vying for a potentially large readership they saw as turf, took on adversary positions in reviewing each other's work. Reviewing his *Uncle Tom's Children* (1938), Hurston criticized Wright's dialect and his political message, writing, "This is a book about hatreds. Mr. Wright serves notice . . . that he speaks of people in revolt, and his stories are so grim that the Dismal Swamp of race hatred must be where they live." "Stories of Conflict," *Saturday Review of Literature,* 17 (2 April, 1938), 32. Wright criticized Hurston's "facile sensuality," concluding, "In the main, her novel is not addressed to the Negro, but to a white audience whose facile tastes she knows how to satisfy. She exploits that phase of Negro life which is 'quaint,' the phrase which evokes a piteous smile on the lips of the 'superior' race." "Between Laughter and Tears," *New Masses,* 24 (5 October, 1937), 25.

36. See Hemenway, 101. Hurston and Hughes hoped to develop a new black theatre; their efforts led to a disastrous collaboration on a play called "Mule Bone" in 1930, which in turn led to a notorious quarrel.

37. Quoted in Hemenway, 228.

38. Lewis, 154.

39. Quoted in Huggins, *Harlem Renaissance,* 130–31.

40. Hurston, "High John de Conquer," *American Mercury,* 57 (1943), 451–52.

41. Hurston, *Moses, Man of the Mountain* (1939; rpt. Chatham, N.J.: The Chatham Bookseller, 1967), 171. Hurston's version of Moses' story is interesting in the special importance she gives to Miriam's role, questioning whether the Exodus would have occurred without her.

42. Hemenway, 286–87.
43. Hemenway, 116.
44. Hemenway, 139.
45. Hemenway, 129.
46. Hemenway, 109.
47. Hemenway, 17. Her mother's death marked, wrote Hurston, "the end of a phase in my life."
48. Hemenway, 282.
49. Hemenway, 203–4.
50. Hurston, *Their Eyes Were Watching God* (1937; rpt. Urbana: University of Illinois Press, 1978), 19.
51. Hurston, *Their Eyes Were Watching God*, 284.

Chapter 4

1. Werner Sollors discusses the problems associated with the use of the term "generations" and such issues as Hansen's Law in "First Generation, Second Generation, Third Generation: Metaphorical Thinking in America" (Unpublished ms., Columbia University, 1981). The discussion of American rhetoric and ideology in this chapter is informed by Sacvan Bercovitch, *The Puritan Origins of the American Self* (New Haven: Yale University Press, 1975) and *The American Jeremiad* (Madison: University of Wisconsin Press, 1978); and Werner Sollors, "Literature and Ethnicity," *Harvard Encyclopedia of American Ethnic Groups,* ed. Stephan Thernstrom (Cambridge: Harvard University Press, 1980), 647–55.
2. Blanche Gelfant's "Sister to Faust: The City's 'Hungry Woman' as Heroine," *Novel,* 15 (1981), 23–28, a suggestive study of hungry heroines in American fiction, including many novels by ethnic women, has been an important source for this chapter.
3. For discussions of Jewish immigrant fathers and daughters and the patriarchal dimensions of Judaism, see Charlotte Baum, Paula Hyman, and Sonya Michel, *The Jewish Woman in America* (New York: Dial Press, 1976); E. Koltun, ed., *The Jewish Woman: New Perspectives* (New York: Schocken Books, 1976); Carolyn Heilbrun, *Reinventing Womanhood* (New York: W. W. Norton, 1979); and Norma Fain Pratt, "Jewish Women through the 1930's," *American Quarterly,* 30 (1978), 681–703.
4. Anzia Yezierska, *Bread Givers* (1925; rpt. New York: Persea Books, 1975), 11. Further references in this chapter will be made parenthetically in the text.

5. Yezierska, *Red Ribbon on a White Horse* (New York: Scribner's, 1950), 72.

6. Martha Ostenso, *Wild Geese* (New York: Dodd, Mead, 1925), 71. Further references in this chapter will be made parenthetically within the text. Ostenso was a first-generation Norwegian-American who authored about thirty novels, of which *Wild Geese* is considered the best.

7. A doomed sister in a later Ostenso novel, *The Waters Under the Earth* (1930) becomes wheelchair-bound and devoted to her father after an accident cuts short her attempt to elope; her father thanks God daily that she is home again. In Hope Sykes's *Second Hoeing* (New York: G. P. Putnam's, 1935), the heroine, Hannah Schreismiller, is doomed to stay at work on the beet fields under her tyrannical father, because, her sister pregnant and forced to marry and her mother dead from too many pregnancies, she must stay to take care of the children. Still, Hannah resolves, " 'Inside of me, I gotta be something. I gotta do it. I won't get no more schooling, but I gotta learn how to live. I gotta live like I was somebody and I'm going to!' " (215).

8. See Gelfant, who writes, "In American novels women's hunger reveals itself in unexpected places and in unexpected ways. We are accustomed to seeing fictional heroines in a bedroom, hungering for love, but we have conveniently overlooked their regular appearance in a library, wanting knowledge" (26). Other "hungry heroines" Gelfant cites include Pynchon's Oedipa Maas, Dreiser's Sister Carrie, Maxine Hong Kingston's Woman Warrior, Thomas Wolfe's Helen Gant.

9. Yezierska, "How I Found America," *Hungry Hearts* (New York: Grosset and Dunlap, 1920), 261–62.

10. Mary Antin, *The Promised Land* (Boston: Houghton Mifflin, 1912), 199.

11. Pauli Murray, *Proud Shoes: The Story of an American Family* (New York: Harper and Bros., 1956), 169.

12. Elizabeth G. Stern, *My Mother and I* (New York: Macmillan, 1917), 14.

13. Stern, 31.

14. Antin, *The Promised Land*, p. xi.

15. Antin, *The Promised Land*, 180–81.

16. See Sollors's discussion of the typology of the "promised land" and rebirth in the melting pot in "Literature and Ethnicity," esp. 649–53. On similar features in immigrant autobiography, see William Boelhower, "The Brave New World of Immigrant Autobiography," *MELUS*, 9 (Summer 1982), 5–23; and Boelhower's

book, *Immigrant Autobiography in the United States* (Verona, Italy: Essedue Edizioni, 1982).

17. Yezierska, *Bread Givers,* 76. Sollors, in "First Generation," cites Ernest Jones's description of the grandfather complex, by which the child wants to parent his own parents, as reminiscent of generational conflict in America (25).

18. Antin, *The Promised Land,* xx.

19. Stern, 109.

20. Stern, 76.

21. Stern, 140.

22. Leah Morton [Elizabeth G. Stern], *I Am a Woman—and a Jew* (1926; rpt. New York: Arno Press, 1969), 1.

23. Antin, *The Promised Land,* xiii.

24. Yezierska, *Bread Givers,* 207.

25. Yezierska, "The Fat of the Land," *Hungry Hearts,* 209.

26. Colin Greer, in *The Great School Legend: A Revisionist Interpretation of American Public Education* (New York: Basic Books, 1972), has vigorously questioned the success of Americanization, calling it part of "the great school legend." In a representative argument, he suggests that the "myth" of Americanization "has meant that the existing problem of black poverty in inner cities is explained by the experience of slavery or the deprivations of poverty itself. If blacks don't yet make it and it isn't their fault exactly, it is—in the optimism of our most enlightened policymakers and the social scientists who served them—the fault of something in Negro history made manifest in public school" (82).

27. Yezierska, "The Miracle," *Hungry Hearts,* 45.

28. Antin, *The Promised Land,* 204–5.

29. Antin, *The Promised Land,* 271. For a discussion of the expectations of immigrant parents for their children, see Timothy Smith, "Immigrant Social Aspirations and American Education 1880–1930," in Michael B. Katz, ed., *Education in American History: Readings on the Social Issues* (New York: Praeger, 1973), 236–50. He cites three major factors in the parents' concern: the desire to earn a better living, "the need to shape a structure of family and communal life that would fit the requirements of mobile and urban existence," and "the quest for a national identity that would fulfill the sense of duty to their homeland or to their people that memory inspired and still not contradict their new allegiance to America" (288).

30. Riis quoted in Henry J. Perkinson, *The Imperfect Panacea: American Faith in Education, 1865–1965* (New York: Random House, 1968), 68. A particularly useful account of the role education

played in the Americanization movement is provided by Marcus Klein, *Foreigners: The Making of American Literature 1900– 1940* (Chicago: University of Chicago Press, 1981), 21–32. Klein discusses "the sense of a *necessary* inversion of parent-child relationship" (25, his emphasis), which I discuss above. See Michael R. Olneck and Marvin Lazerson, "Education," in *HEAEG*, 303–19.

31. General histories of education I found helpful in this area are Lawrence Cremin, *The Transformation of the School: Progressivism in American Education* (New York: Knopf, 1961); David Nasaw, *Schooled to Order: A Social History of Public Schooling in the United States* (New York: Oxford, 1979); R. Freeman Butts, *A Cultural History of Education* (New York: McGraw Hill, 1947).

32. Cremin, 66.

33. The best analysis of Americanization according to an Anglo-Saxon ideal is provided by Milton M. Gordon, *Assimilation in American Life: The Role of Race, Religion, and National Origins* (New York: Oxford, 1964) in Chapter 4, "Theories of Assimilation Part I: Introduction and Anglo-Conformity," 84–114. See also Philip Gleason, "American Identity and Americanization," *HEAEG*, 31–58.

34. Quoted in Cremin, 68.

35. On the Americanization movement in general, a thorough overview is provided by Philip Gleason, "American Identity and Americanization." Other works consulted include Edward George Hartmann, *The Movement to Americanize the Immigrant* (1948; rpt. New York: AMS Press, 1967); John F. McClymer, "The Federal Government and the Americanization Movement," *Prologue,* 10 (1978), 23–41; Edward Hale Bierstadt, *Aspects of Americanization* (Cincinnati: Stewart Kidd, 1922). Primary sources that discuss women and the Americanization movement or that discuss the movement from a woman's point of view include Jane Addams, "The Public School and the Immigrant Child," *NEA Proceedings,* 1908, pp. 99–102; Olivia Dunbar, "Teaching the Immigrant Woman," *Harpers Bazaar,* 47 (June 1913), 277–78; Frances Kellor, "The Immigrant Woman," *Atlantic Monthly,* 100 (1907), 401–7 and "The Protection of Immigrant Women," *Atlantic Monthly,* 101 (1908), 246–55; Agnes Repplier, "Americanism," *Atlantic Monthly,* 117 (1916), 286–97.

36. Gordon, 127–28.

37. Antin, *The Promised Land,* 223–24.

38. Antin, *The Promised Land,* 225.

39. Antin, *The Promised Land,* 229. Phyllis Wheatley's "To His Ex-
    cellency George Washington" was written in 1775. William Al-
    fred Bryan, *George Washington in American Literature* (New
    York: Columbia University Press, 1952) is a valuable source
    concerning the ways in which Washington has been invoked and
    described in pre-Civil War literature. Werner Sollors, in "Litera-
    ture and Ethnicity," 650, discusses Wheatley's "typological
    deliverance."

40. Antin, *The Promised Land,* 238.

41. Sylvia Plath, "America! America!" in *Johnny Panic and the Bible
    of Dreams* (New York: Harper and Row, 1980), 52–53.

42. Ann Petry, *The Street* (Boston: Houghton Mifflin, 1946), 63–64.

43. See George Forgie, *Patricide in the House Divided: A Psychologi-
    cal Interpretation of Lincoln and His Age* (New York: W. W.
    Norton, 1979), esp. 40–53 for a discussion of the emotional
    meaning of the founding fathers. Forgie's thesis is based on "the
    proposition that the prevalent use of familial metaphors in public
    discourse reflected the increasingly deep and strong emotional
    bonds that joined Americans to each other and to their past" (29).

44. Bercovitch, *The American Jeremiad,* 26. Bercovitch argues that
    with the Revolution, "a new era had begun with the discovery of
    the New World, . . . and the Revolution confirmed it, precisely
    as Christ had confirmed the new era of faith" (128). Bercovitch's
    account of the jeremiad places the Revolution as part of an Amer-
    ican typology of mission, with Washington "enshrined as savior,
    his mighty deeds expounded, his apostles ranked, the Judas in
    their midst identified, the Declaration of Independence adequately
    compared to the Sermon on the Mount, the sacred places and ob-
    jects (Bunker Hill, Valley Forge, the Liberty Bell) properly
    labeled, the Constitution duly ordained (in Emerson's words) as
    'the best book in the world' next to the New Testament, and the
    Revolution, summarily, 'indissolubly linked' (as John Quincy
    Adams put it) with the 'birthday . . . of the Savior,' as being
    the social, moral, and political correlative of 'the Redeemer's mis-
    sion on earth,' and thus 'the first irrevocable pledge of the ful-
    fillment of the prophecies, announced directly from Heaven' "
    (129).

45. Antin, "A Woman to Her Fellow-Citizens," *Outlook,* 102 (1912),
    482.

46. Margaret Mead, "We Are All Third Generation," in *And Keep
    Your Powder Dry* (New York: W. W. Morrow, 1942), 49–50.

47. Mead, 53. Werner Sollors cites Perry Miller in *Nature's Nation*
    on the same issue: "Being an American is not something to be

inherited so much as something to be achieved. . . . Then, why are we so nervous? Why do we so worry about our identity?" Quoted in "Between Consent and Descent: Studying Ethnic Literature in the U.S.A.," *Intellectual History Group Newsletter*, New York Institute for the Humanities, 4 (Spring 1982), 13.

48. Bercovitch cites the example of Margaret Fuller, who asked in *Woman in the Nineteenth Century* that the language of the Declaration of Independence be extended to include women. Rhetoric is enlarged, no alternative rhetoric set forth. So, argues Bercovitch, "the American consensus could absorb feminism, so long as that would lead into the middle-class American way. Blacks and Indians too could learn to be True Americans, when in the fullness of time they could adopt the tenets of black and red capitalism. John Brown could join Adams, Franklin, and Jefferson in the pantheon of Revolutionary heroes when it was understood that he wanted to fulfill (rather than undermine) the American dream. On that provision, Jews and even Catholics could eventually become sons and daughters of the American Revolution" (*The American Jeremiad*, 159–60).

49. Pauli Murray, 271.

50. Pauli Murray, 275–76.

51. Yezierska, "Wild Winter Wind," *Century*, 113 (1927), 486.

52. Forgie, 185. See Pauline Hopkins, "General Washington, A Christmas Story," *Colored American Magazine*, 2 (November 1900), 95–104.

53. Eugene Genovese, *Roll, Jordan, Roll: The World the Slaves Made* (New York: Pantheon, 1974), 446.

54. Genovese, 450.

55. Ralph Ellison, "Hidden Name and Complex Fate," in *Shadow and Act* (1953; rpt. New York: Random House, 1964), 147–48. In this context, Booker T. Washington's vivid account of his choosing his own surname on the first day of school is also of interest. Washington commented, "I think there are not many men in our country who have had the privilege of naming themselves in the way that I have." *Up From Slavery*, in *The Booker T. Washington Papers*, Vol. 1, Louis R. Harlan, ed. (Urbana: University of Illinois Press, 1972), 232. Washington later learned that his mother had named him Booker Taliaferro at birth, so he added that in, and his name is a nice representation of an ancestrally derived and self-made American ethnic identity.

56. Petry, *The Narrows* (Boston: Houghton Mifflin, 1953), 67. The characters in Petry's novel are extremely conscious of names, A black woman, Mamie Powther, has three children: J.C. (Mamie

reasons, " 'When he gets old enough, he can pick a name for him-self, to match up with the initials' ") (18), and the twins, Kelly and Shapiro, transethnically named and transethnically referred to as "the starving Armenians." Mamaluke Hill, whose full name is Matthew Mark Luke John Acts-of-the-Apostles Son-of-Zebedee Garden-of-Gethsemane Hill, is called by his "basket name," which is "a kind of pet name that they give an infant until such time as he's baptized and his christened name is officially fastened to him. They use his pet name lest an evil spirit learn his real name and turn him into a changeling" (69–70).

57. Toni Morrison, *Song of Solomon* (New York: New American Library, 1977), 53–54. The epigram attached to the novel is, "The fathers may soar/ And the children may know their names."

58. Morrison, *Song of Solomon*, 76.

59. Morrison, *Song of Solomon*, 333.

Chapter 5

1. Philip Young, "The Mother of Us All," *Kenyon Review*, 24 (1962), 414.

2. Lydia Huntley Sigourney, in "Pocahontas" in *Pocahontas and Other Poems* (New York: Harper, 1841), celebrates Pocahontas's sacrifice: "Whose generous hand vouchsafed its tireless aid/ To guard a nation's gem? Thine, thine heroic maid!" (20). Mary Webster Mosby in her long poem *Pocahontas* (Philadelphia: Henry Hooker, 1840), provides a heroic Pocahontas with an-cestors among the Vikings and the ten lost tribes of Israel.

3. Rayna Green, "The Pocahontas Perplex: The Image of Indian Women in American Culture," *Massachusetts Review*, 16 (1975), 714.

4. Rayna Green, 703.

5. Rayna Green, 711–12. Leslie Fiedler, *The Return of the Vanish-ing American* (New York: Stein and Day, 1968), especially 63–83, "The Basic Myths, II: Love in the Woods." Fiedler discusses the ways in which cultural expressions of the Pocahontas myth have served to de-eroticize their subject.

6. DuBois quoted in Eugene Genovese, *Roll Jordan Roll: The World the Slaves Made* (New York: Pantheon, 1974), 413; DuBois does not refer specifically to relations between black women and white men. For historical evidence, see, for example, James Hugo John-ston, *Race Relations in Virginia and Miscegenation in the South* (Amherst: University of Massachusetts Press, 1970). He writes,

"The mulatto was in most cases, it seems certain, the descendant of the white man and the Negro woman" (217).

7. Werner Sollors, "Theory of American Ethnicity," *American Quarterly,* 33 (1981), 271.

8. Winthrop D. Jordan, *White Over Black: American Attitudes Toward the Negro, 1550–1812* (1968; rpt. Baltimore: Penguin Books, 1973), 137–38.

9. Simone Vauthier, "Textualité et Stereotypes: Of African Queens and Afro-American Princes and Princesses: Miscegenation in *Old Hepsy*" (Paris: Publications du Consel Scientifique de la Sorbonne Nouvelle, [n.d.]), 89.

10. The term is also problematic when applied to Indian women. Pocahontas's legal marriage aside, in most of their relations with white men, Indian women were not legally wives, or were wives who shared their husbands with a number of other women. Consider a latter-day Pocahontas, Sacagawea, whose white husband Charbonneau had so many wives that historians cannot separate out her life from theirs.

11. Relevant here is the dubious legal status accorded to some marriages even *among* blacks under slavery.

12. Sollors, "A Defense of the Melting Pot," in *The American Identity: Fusion and Fragmentation,* ed. Rob Kroes (Amsterdam: European Contributions to American Studies III, 1980), 189. Annette Kolodny, *The Lay of the Land: Metaphor as Experience and History in American Life and Letters* (Chapel Hill: University of North Carolina Press, 1975) is a persuasive cultural history of the ambivalence of Americans toward a land metaphorized as a woman.

13. Philip Gleason provides thorough analyses of the melting-pot and its attributes in "The Melting Pot: Symbol of Fusion or Confusion," *American Quarterly,* 16 (1964), 20–46; and "Confusion Compounded: The Melting Pot in the 1860s and 1970s," *Ethnicity,* 6 (1979), 10–17.

14. Gleason, "The Melting Pot," 41. See also Albert Murray, who uses the language of intermarriage to describe the American identity: "American culture, even in its most rigidly segregated precincts, is patently and irrevocably composite. It is, regardless of the hysterical protests of those who would have it otherwise, incontestably mulatto." *The Omni-Americans: New Perspectives on Black Experience and American Culture* (New York: Avon, 1970), 39.

15. Anzia Yezierska, *Salome of the Tenements* (New York: Boni and

Liveright, 1923), 51. Further references in this chapter will be made parenthetically within the text.

16. Yezierska, "The Miracle," *Hungry Hearts* (New York: Grosset and Dunlap, 1920), 115. She continues, "In America millionaires fall in love with poorest girls. Matchmakers are out of style, and a girl can get herself married to a man without the worries for a dowry."

17. Quoted in Charlotte Baum, Paula Hyman, Sonya Michel, *The Jewish Woman in America* (New York: Dial Press, 1976), 63. Of considerable interest here are John Cuddihy's observations on Freud and the role of love in the Jewish experience. Cuddihy, in *The Ordeal of Civility: Freud, Marx, Levi-Strauss and the Jewish Struggle with Modernity* (New York: Basic Books, 1974) analyzes the Jewishness of Freud and Marx in the particular context of their rejection of romantic love as "courtly," "refined," "un-Jewish." Cuddihy writes, "For Freud *courteosie* is a decoration of sexual intercourse in the same way that courtesy decorates social intercourse. His deepest urge was to strip both of their courtliness. He experienced both as a hypocritical disguise—analogous to Marx's superstructure—that must be stripped away, like any 'appearance,' exposing the 'reality' beneath" (72). Cuddihy's thesis—often provocative and more convincing in the case of Freud than of Marx or Levi-Strauss—is directly relevant to the metaphor of intermarriage as I set it forth in these chapters. Couched in the rhetoric of romance, advertised by the language of courtly love, the intermarriage metaphor is of course fundamentally "about" sexuality—as women writers repeatedly insisted.

18. Quoted in Baum, Hyman, and Michel, 221.

19. Stuart and Elizabeth Ewen, *Channels of Desire: Mass Images and the Shaping of American Consciousness* (New York: McGraw Hill, 1982), 102. The Ewens discuss the movies of Cecil B. de-Mille, particularly *Old Wives for New* (1918), *Male and Female* (1919), and *Forbidden Fruit* (1920), which "created a fantasy world where sex, romance, marriage, and money were intertwined to create a new frame of reference" and which "gave voice to a crucial myth of modern culture: metamorphosis through consumption" (100).

20. Raoul de Roussy de Sales, "Love in America," *Atlantic Monthly*, 161 (May 1938); rpt. in Warren Susman, ed., *Culture and Commitment 1929–1945* (New York: Geo. Braziler, 1973), 95.

21. Tess Slesinger, "The Times So Unsettled Are," *Time: The Present* (New York: Simon and Schuster, 1935), 69. Slesinger was the daughter of immigrants, her father a Hungarian and her mother a

Russian Jew. For biographical information see Shirley Biagi, "Forgive Me For Dying," *Antioch Review,* 35 (1977), 224–36.

22. Slesinger, 76.

23. Slesinger, 86.

24. Quoted in Ande Manners, *Poor Cousins* (New York: Coward, McCann, and Geoghegan, 1972), 139.

25. Representative press accounts are "A Ghetto Romance," *N-Y Tribune Illustrated Supplement,* 16 April 1905; and "J.G. Phelps to Wed Young Jewess," *New York Times,* 6 April 1905. The Stokes did not live the storybook lives readers may have imagined; they lived frugally and devoted their energies to socialist causes. Mrs. Stokes became more radical as Mr. Stokes became less so, and the couple divorced in 1925.

26. Ann Petry, *The Narrows* (Boston: Houghton Mifflin, 1953), 164. Petry's novel, discussed in another chapter, has as its subject an affair between a black man and a white woman. In the light of the context in which the butler's remark is made, it is interesting to note the persistence of Cinderella-derived mistress/maid themes in ethnic women's fiction. Implicit in this subgenre—best exemplified in Yezierska's 1927 *Arrogant Beggar,* Slesinger's 1930 "The Friedman's Annie," and Betty Smith's 1958 *Maggie-Now*—is the notion that the maid/heroine can marry her employer's son. Usually, the heroine is disillusioned in her efforts and returns to an ethnic suitor. Again, of course, this is the story of *Pamela,* with ethnicity perhaps replacing class.

27. Robert K. Merton, "Intermarriage and the Social Structure: Fact and Theory," in *The Blending Americans: Patterns of Intermarriage,* ed. Milton L. Barron (Chicago: Quadrangle Books, 1972), 20.

28. "The Miracle," *Hungry Hearts,* 137.

29. "Hunger," *Hungry Hearts,* 46–47.

30. "Wings," *Hungry Hearts,* 34.

31. "Hunger," *Hungry Hearts,* 57.

32. Jo Ann Boydston, "Introduction," *The Poems of John Dewey,* ed. Jo Ann Boydston (Carbondale: Southern Illinois University Press, 1977), ix–lxvii. Dewey's poems, many of which were written for or about Yezierska, provide valuable supplementary evidence for the contours of the Yezierska/Dewey relationship.

33. Yezierska, *Red Ribbon on a White Horse* (New York: Scribner's, 1950), 112.

34. Quoted in Boydston, xxxii.

35. Babette Inglehart, "Daughters of Loneliness: Anzia Yezierska and the Immigrant Woman Writer," *Studies in American Jewish Literature,* 1 (Winter 1975), 4.

36. *Red Ribbon on a White Horse,* 116.
37. Gleason, "The Melting Pot," 40.
38. Quentin Anderson, "John Dewey's American Democrat," *Daedalus,* 108 (1979), 149.
39. Boydston, 4–5.
40. Some of Dewey's poems were retrieved from the wastebasket of his office by M. Halsey Thomas, a neighbor of Dewey's in Butler Library at Columbia who describes himself as "addicted to Boswelling"; others were discovered in 1939 when Herbert Schneider took over Dewey's office and threw the desk's contents into a wastebasket, from which Thomas salvaged more poems. Dewey's poems remained in the Columbiana Collection at Columbia until 1957, until they were transferred to Dewey's wife. In 1970 the John Dewey Foundation began its attempts to examine the collection, determine authorship, and publish: this is where Boydston came in. See Boydston, ix–xiv.
41. Boydston, xlv.
42. Yezierska, "Prophets of Democracy," *The Bookman,* 52 (1921), 497. Even the praise of Dewey as an American Tolstoy is undercut elsewhere in Yezierska's works. In *Salome of the Tenements,* Jacques Hollins scoffs at the heroine's comparison of her Deweyesque lover to Tolstoy: "Wasn't [Tolstoy] a faker pretending to make himself for a coarse peasant when he had back of him culture—education—art, and all that money can buy? Wasn't he faking when he preached the gospel of celibacy after having nine children of his own?" (55).
43. Smith and Strachey quoted in Young, 395.
44. The fullest bibliography of cultural representations can be assembled by synthesizing the findings of Philip Young and Rayna Green with Jay Hubbell, "The Smith-Pocahontas Story in Literature," *The Virginia Magazine of History and Biography,* 65 (1957), 275–300. See also Frances Mossiker, *Pocahontas: The Life and the Legend* (New York: Knopf, 1976).
45. The quotations from Crane are from *The Complete Poems and Selected Letters of Hart Crane,* ed. Brom Weber (Garden City, New York: Anchor Books, 1966). Crane refers to his conception of Pocahontas's symbolic value in a letter to Otto H. Kahn, 248–55.
46. George Frederickson, *The Black Image in the White Mind: The Debate on Afro-American Character and Destiny, 1817–1914* (New York: Harper and Row, 1971), and Joel Kovel, *White Racism: A Psychohistory* (New York: Pantheon, 1971) are primarily concerned with white perceptions of black male sexuality. Lawrence J. Friedman, *The White Savage: Racial Fantasies*

in the Postbellum South (Englewood Cliffs, N.J.: Prentice-Hall, 1970), 140–42, discusses Reconstruction black activists' efforts to protect black women from white aggression and to "elevate the purity" of the black woman. Winthrop Jordan, 136–78, discusses notions of black female sexuality. A DuBois essay on black women is also valuable: "The Damnation of Women," in *The Seventh Son: The Thought and Writings of W. E. B. DuBois,* ed. Julius Lester (New York: Vintage Books, 1971), Vol. 1, pp. 511–26. Ronald G. Walters, in his study of 19th-century social reform, *The Antislavery Appeal: American Abolitionism After 1830* (Baltimore: Johns Hopkins University Press, 1976), provides a very interesting analysis of sexuality and slavery. In Chapter 5, "Control: Sexual Attitudes, Self-Mastery, and Civilization," 70–87, Walters suggests that the eroticization not only of blacks but of the entire South was a powerful and problematic weapon in the antislavery arsenal. Walters draws connections between power and sexuality that are especially relevant here.

47. Johnston, 217.
48. Genovese, 428.
49. Quotations are from Jordan, 150–51. Similar stereotypes, ones I feel sure one would discover upon further investigation, have been applied to Indian women. Werner Sollors, "Literature and Ethnicity," in *The Harvard Encyclopedia of American Ethnic Groups,* ed. Stephan Thernstrom (Cambridge: Harvard University Press, 1980), 654, cites Cotton Mather's appreciation in the "Life of John Eliot" of Indian women's "extraordinary Ease in Childbirth."
50. Lillian Smith, *Strange Fruit* (New York: Reynal and Hitchcock, 1944), 73.
51. See Smith's *Killers of the Dream* (New York: W. W. Norton, 1949).
52. Smith, *Strange Fruit,* 127.
53. *Killers of the Dream* is an important exploration of the critical nexus of race and sexuality, and provides one of the best considerations of the role the black Mammy has played in Southern male perceptions of black and white female sexuality. In a different context, Smith explained her reasons for writing *Strange Fruit:* it was "intended to be a hard-hitting Naturalistic novel that would place blame for the South's inhuman treatment of black people. And the blame lay . . . with the segregated structure of Southern society . . . [and] with the various Southern myths, involving white womanhood and the superiority of white males, . . . with the ignorance, fear, and poverty of many whites, and with the

warped and obsessive notions of whites about sex" (quoted in Louise Blackwell and Frances Clay, "Lillian Smith, Novelist," *CLAJ*, 15 (1972), 456).

54. Leah Morton [Elizabeth Stern] *I Am A Woman—And A Jew* (1926; rpt. New York: Arno Press, 1969), 61.

55. Stern is a staunch defender of intermarriage, but her own marriage to a non-Jew engendered painful generational conflicts between Stern and her parents and Stern and her children; her husband's attitude toward her Jewishness and her writing about it seems to have been at best ambivalent.

56. Robert Bone, who otherwise admires Larsen's novel, believes that "Helga's tragedy, in Larsen's eyes, is that she allows herself to be declassed by her sexuality" and thinks Larsen reveals "a prudish attitude toward sex." *The Negro Novel in America* (New Haven: Yale University Press, 1958), 105–6. Most critics have dismissed *Quicksand* as something of an anomaly, a psychological case study. Nathan Huggins, in *Harlem Renaissance* (New York: Oxford University Press, 1971), 157–61, is an exception. Recent critics have turned their attention to Larsen's view of black female sexuality in *Quicksand* and *Passing*. See Sharon Dean and Erlene Stetson, "Flower-Dust and Springtime: Harlem Renaissance Women," *Radical Teacher*, 18 pp. 1–8; Hortense Thornton, "Sexism as Quagmire: Nella Larsen's *Quicksand*," *CLAJ*, 16 (1973), 285–301; Barbara Christian, *Black Women Novelists: The Development of a Tradition, 1892–1976*, Contributions in Afro-American and African Studies, No. 52 (Westport, Conn.: Greenwood Press, 1980), 48–53. Christian states, a little simplistically, that Helga is "destroyed by her womb" (53).

57. Nella Larsen, *Quicksand* (1928; rpt. New York: Negro Universities Press, 1969), 163. Further references in this chapter will be made parenthetically within the text.

58. Helga anticipates Olsen's rejection of her, suggesting to him, " 'We can't tell, you know; if we were married, you might come to hate all dark people. My mother did that' " (196).

59. Hum-Ishu-Ma [Mourning Dove], *Co-ge-we-a: The Half Blood: A Depiction of the Great Montana Cattle Range* (Boston: Four Seasons, 1927), 17. Further references in this chapter will be made parenthetically within the text.

60. Jessie Fauset, *Plum Bun* (New York: Frederick A. Stokes, 1929), 143–44.

61. Fauset, *Plum Bun,* 135.

62. Angela witnesses Fielding angrily demanding that black customers

be thrown out of a restaurant; Clare Kendry's husband nicknames her "Nig."

63. The heroine of *Salome* asks herself, "How did Rose Pastor catch on to Graham Stokes?" (134).

64. The language of this question evokes another strand in the ethnic literary tradition: that of presenting characters who, in dialogue with each other, represent the idea of a divided self—each character representing a half of a dichotomy within the self. Werner Sollors has located this tradition in, for instance, Amiri Baraka's *Dutchman* (1964) and *The Motion of History* (1978) as well as in the "Bona and Paul" section of Toomer's *Cane*. See *Amiri Baraka/LeRoi Jones, The Quest for a Populist Modernism* (New York: Columbia University Press, 1978).

65. Quoted in Milton M. Gordon, *Human Nature, Class, and Ethnicity* (New York: Oxford University Press, 1978), 187.

66. Sacvan Bercovitch has definitively located this aspect of American rhetoric. See *The Puritan Origins of the American Self* (New Haven: Yale University Press, 1975) and *The American Jeremiad* (Madison: University of Wisconsin Press, 1978).

67. Werner Sollors, in his essay "Literature and Ethnicity," 647–55, analyzes the nature of the rhetoric of Americanization in American literature. For a thorough overview of the meanings of Americanization in American culture, see Philip Gleason's essay, "American Identity and Americanization," also in *HEAEG*, 31–58.

68. Morton, 186.

69. Stern, *My Mother and I* (New York: Macmillan, 1917), 169.

70. Quoted in Genovese, 413.

71. Ferber's 1926 *Showboat* contains an incident of miscegenation that reveals a more serious dimension of Ferber's ethnic consciousness, and that functions in the novel as a powerful protest against the absurdity of the antimiscegenation laws. The incident, magnified in all musical and cinematic versions of the novel, concerns the marriage of Julie and Steve, two showboat performers. Julie, dark-haired, dark-eyed, and of a suitably tragic demeanor, passes for white; her fair-haired husband knows her secret. A sheriff, tipped off by Steve's rival, attempts to arrest the pair for violation of antimiscegenation laws. In a dramatic scene that shocked and titillated Broadway audiences, Steve cuts his wife's finger and drinks her blood, thereby asserting the legality of their marriage on the grounds that he now has at least one drop of black blood in him. Ferber protests not only antimiscegenation laws but notions of racial distinction.

72. Edna Ferber, *Cimarron* (1929; rpt. New York: Bantam Books, 1963), 275.
73. Ferber, *Cimarron*, 276–77.
74. Ferber, *Cimarron*, 287.
75. Ferber's tone in *Cimarron* is ironic, but in fairness it should be stated that Ferber took her novel very seriously. In her first autobiography, *A Peculiar Treasure* (1938; rpt. New York: Lancer Books, 1960), 302, Ferber explains, *"Cimarron* had been written with a hard and ruthless purpose. It was, and is, a malevolent picture of what is known of American womanhood and American sentimentality. It contains paragraphs and even chapters of satire, and, I am afraid, bitterness, but I doubt that more than a dozen people ever knew this. All the critics and hundreds and thousands of readers took *Cimarron* as a colorful romantic Western American novel."
76. Ferber, *Cimarron*, 285.
77. Ferber, *Cimarron*, 297.
78. Ferber, *Cimarron*, 298.

Chapter 6

1. Gayl Jones, *Corregidora* (New York: Random House, 1975), 9.
2. Jones, *Corregidora*, 77. Jones, in an interview with black poet Michael Harper, "Gayl Jones: An Interview" in *Chant of Saints: A Gathering of Afro-American Literature, Art, and Scholarship,* ed. Michael Harper and Robert Stepto (Urbana: University of Illinois Press, 1979), 352–75, has interesting comments about *Corregidora* and about the black literary tradition which indicate her concern with identity and inheritance. About Zora Neale Hurston, she says, "It has to do with legacy. We have to solve the problems she couldn't solve. . . . And we have to keep her, you know. . . . I feel that [Alice Walker] is doing that. You know, keeping and taking things further. That's what legacy is" (365).
3. Simone Vauthier, "(Non)-famille romanesque, famille sociohistorique, famille fantasmatique: l'exemple d'*Oran the Outcast* (1833)," *Ranam,* 8 (1975), 163. Tony Tanner, *Adultery in the Novel: Contract and Transgression* (Baltimore: Johns Hopkins University Press, 1979).
4. John Irwin, *Doubling and Incest/Repetition and Revenge* (Baltimore: Johns Hopkins University Press, 1975), 33. Irwin's impressionistic and psychoanalytic reading of Faulkner is extremely provocative in terms of the quality of the uncanny in mulatto fiction, which I discuss later.

5. Simone Vauthier writes that the mulatto "designates the moment of origins, when black and white met on a footing of sexual equality, and ultimately the *humanity* of the black partner. Chocolate brown or honey colored, he disproves the myth of two races separated by an "impassable gulf.' " "Textualité et Stereotypes: Of African Queens and Afro-American Princes: Miscegenation in *Old Hepsy*" (Paris: Publications du Consel Scientifique de la Sorbonne Nouvelle, [n.d.], 88 (Vauthier's emphasis). Pauli Murray, in her autobiographical *Proud Shoes: The Story of an American Family* (New York: Harper and Bros., 1956), in relating the confusion over mulattos reflected in the census, comments on the " 'lost boundaries' " of her own family (66). Race differentiation itself was threatened by the existence of the mulatto. See Winthrop D. Jordan, *White Over Black: American Attitudes Toward the Negro, 1550–1812* (1968; rpt. Baltimore: Penguin Books, 1973), esp. Chap. 3, "Fruits of Passion: The Dynamics of Interracial Sex," 136–78, which concludes, "Interracial propagation was a constant reproach that [the white male] was failing to be true to himself. Sexual intimacy strikingly symbolized a union he wished to avoid. . . . Continued racial intermixture would eventually undermine the logic of the racial slavery on which his society was based" (177–78).

   In the critical literature on the theory of ethnicity, the notion of boundaries is an important concept. In fact, some scholars have suggested that boundaries alone define ethnic groups, and that the areas within those boundaries are inconsequential or irrelevant. For an overview of the literature on this idea, see Werner Sollors, "Theory of American Ethnicity," *American Quarterly*, 33 (1981), 257–83.

6. For laws regarding miscegenation and the mulatto, see Jordan, 167–78; James Hugo Johnston, *Race Relations in Virginia and Miscegenation in the South, 1776–1860* (Amherst: University of Massachusetts Press, 1970), particularly 165–314; and Mary Francis Berry, *Black Resistance/White Law: A History of Constitutional Racism in America* (New York: Appleton Century Crofts, 1971).

7. Mary Boykin Chesnut, *Mary Chesnut's Civil War*, ed. C. Vann Woodward (New Haven: Yale University Press, 1981), 30. For white female responses to slavery, other primary sources include Frances Kemble, *Journal of a Residence on a Georgian Plantation in 1838–1839* (New York: Harper and Bros., 1863); and, from an Englishwoman's perspective, Frances Trollope, *Domestic Manners of the Americans* (1831; rpt. New York: Alfred A.

Knopf, 1949). There is a vast secondary literature on this subject; one useful work is Anne Firor Scott, *The Southern Lady: From Pedestal to Politics 1830–1930* (Chicago: University of Chicago Press, 1970). Scott turns her attention more directly to the question of Southern white women and sexuality in "Women's Perspective of the Patriarchy in the 1850s," *The Journal of American History*, 61 (1974), 55–60.

8. Eugene Genovese, *Roll, Jordan, Roll: The World the Slaves Made* (New York: Pantheon, 1974), 419.

9. Genovese, 344–46.

10. Pauli Murray, 46.

11. Pauli Murray, 52.

12. Jordan, 164.

13. Genovese, 74.

14. The mulatto child was, of course, usually raised not in his white father's family, but in his black mother's.

15. Genovese, 415, points out that most free blacks, in fact, were products of miscegenation; but the converse is not necessarily true. In fiction this aspect of denied inheritance informs the plot of black writer Margaret Walker's 1966 *Jubilee*. *Jubilee*'s heroine, Vyry, is a mulatto slave whose white father and master repeatedly promises to free her but dies with no provision for her freedom in his will. In white writer Frances Gaither's 1949 *Double Muscadine*, the mulatto slave Lethe, freed in her master's will, is denied her legacy and remains a slave; this disruption of inheritance generates the events of the novel.

16. Frances Harper, *Iola Leroy; or, Shadows Uplifted* (1892; rpt. College Park, Md.: McGrath Publishing, 1969), 66–67.

17. Harper, 77.

18. Herbert G. Gutman, *The Black Family in Slavery and Freedom, 1750–1925* (New York: Pantheon, 1976).

19. Vauthier, "Textualité et Stereotypes," 90. Vauthier examines a similar theme in Charles James Cannon's 1833 *Oran the Outcast* in her "(Non)-famille romanesque." Oran plays out the crime of the bastard's parricide. James D. Wilson also mentions Oran in his "Incest and American Romantic Fiction," *Studies in the American Literary Imagination*, 7 (Spring 1974), 31–50, though he does not make the important connection between incest and unknown ancestry, and sees incest rather as a culmination of "solipsism." It is interesting to note that Harriet Beecher Stowe herself seems to have had an interest in incest, publishing in the *Atlantic Monthly* an article about Lord Byron's incest with his half-sister. Mark Twain came to Stowe's defense in the furor that ensued the

article's publication; he attempted to use the incident humorously, but reported that incest was a "situation so tremendous" that he could not. See Jean Willoughby Ashton, "Harriet Stowe's Filthy Story: Lord Byron Set Afloat," *Prospects*, 2 (1976), 373–84.

20. Gutman, 89.

21. Robert Bone, *The Negro Novel in America* (New Haven: Yale University Press, 1958), 24. The early black novelist was also attracted to melodrama because it solved problems of characterization that inevitably arose in an era of black stereotyping, and by the fact that melodrama, Bone adds somewhat cryptically, is "a literature of social aspiration" (25).

22. The best analysis of mulattoes in American fiction is Judith Berzon's *Neither White Nor Black: The Mulatto Character in American Fiction* (New York: New York University Press, 1978). More specialized works include Jules Zanger, "The Tragic Octoroon in Pre-Civil War Fiction," *American Quarterly*, 18 (1966), 63–70; Penelope Bullock, "The Mulatto in American Fiction," *Phylon*, 6 (1945), 78–82; and William J. Scheick, *The Half-Blood: A Cultural Symbol in 19th Century American Fiction* (Lexington: University Press of Kentucky, 1979), a study of half-blood Indians.

23. Berzon, 99.

24. Sterling Brown, "A Century of Negro Portraiture in American Literature," *Massachusetts Review*, 7 (1966), [p. 79].

25. Brown, [p. 79].

26. Hugh Gloster, in *Negro Voices in American Fiction* (Chapel Hill: University of North Carolina Press, 1948) writes that in this "counter-propaganda," "educated and well-mannered colored characters . . . often engage in long discussions of racial and political issues" (98). Critical attempts to view the literature of a single ethnic group in terms of organic development often acknowledge a stage in which "discussion novels" predominate. Rose Basile Green, for instance, in her history of Italian-American fiction, *The Italian-American Novel: A Document of the Interaction of Two Cultures* (Rutherford, N.J.: Fairleigh Dickinson University Press, 1973) suggests that the early works written by members of an emergent ethnic group are explanatory reports or autobiographies which attempt to define the group's unfavorable position socially and economically. The move to "pure" fiction is imperceptible and inevitable. Of course, a similar pattern characterizes the development of "American literature."

27. Harper, 228.

28. [Pauline Hopkins], "Winona: A Tale of Negro Life in the South and Southwest," *Colored American Magazine*, 5 (May 1902–October 1902), 183.

29. Nancy Goulder, "Demon Lovers and 'Unquiet Slumbers,': The Female Gothic in *Wuthering Heights*" (Unpublished ms., Columbia University, 1982), 5. Goulder applies Freud's notion of the uncanny to the Gothic. See Sigmund Freud, "The 'Uncanny,'" in *On Creativity and the Unconscious* (1919; rpt. New York: Harper and Row, 1958), 122–61. The notion of the uncanny is particularly relevant here in light of its German sense of unhome-like, which both Freud and Goulder discuss. The anxiety over boundaries that black/white relations call up is precisely related to its threat to the *home*.

    Leslie Fiedler was probably the first critic to suggest a connection between texts about miscegenation and the Gothic genre, in his discussion of Twain's *Pudd'nhead Wilson* as a Gothic novel in *Love and Death in the American Novel* (1960; rev. ed. New York: Stein and Day, 1975), 403–9.

30. Pauline Hopkins, "Of One Blood, Or the Hidden Self," *Colored American Magazine*, 6 (November 1902–November 1903), 102.

31. Quoted in Ann Shockley, "Pauline Hopkins: A Biographical Excursion into Obscurity," *Phylon*, 33 (1972), 25. In connection with Hopkins and the Freudian notion of the uncanny, it is interesting that Bone quotes Hopkins as exhorting her fellow blacks, "We must guard ourselves against the growth of any sinful appetite" (14).

32. Grace King, "The Little Convent Girl," *Balcony Stories* (New York: Century, 1893), 149.

33. King, 161.

34. King, 161.

35. Bone, *The Negro Novel in America*, 97.

36. Gutman's comments on naming practices in the black family are especially relevant in understanding the notion of two Bye families. See especially Chapter 6, "Somebody Knows My Name," 230–56. The Bible Peter cherishes carries a complicated but important inscription: the signature of his great-grandmother, Judy Bye, and that of her husband, an African slave named Cezar Bye, which is crossed out. Peter's grandfather, a mulatto, had written in Cezar's name, and Cezar, who hated all white men, crossed it out. As such, the inscription represents simultaneously denial and affirmation of inheritance. The Bye family motto is, significantly, "By their fruits shall ye know them."

37. Jessie Fauset, *Plum Bun* (New York: Frederick A. Stokes, 1929), 168. *Plum Bun* is subtitled "A Novel Without a Moral," which seems to belie critical assessments of Fauset that characterize her work as didactic, inspirational, or moralistic.

38. Fauset, *The Chinaberry Tree* (1931; rpt. New York: Negro Universities Press, 1969), 2.

39. Holloway's white daughters, however, in what seems to be a gesture of female bonding in the face of threatened inheritance, provide for Laurentine's training as a seamstress.

40. Fauset, *The Chinaberry Tree*, 157–58. Ethnic women's fiction commonly questions whether the Biblical injunction applies to the mothers too.

41. Fauset, *The Chinaberry Tree*, 121.

42. Fauset, *The Chinaberry Tree*, 161 (ellipsis in original).

43. The mask's mouth is "distorted to its fullest, reviling words issuing from those eternally open lips" (185). This grotesque and even Gothic vision of the *comic* mask gives new weight to the title of Fauset's *Comedy: American Style*, and lends support to Joseph Feeney's assessment of her ironic vision.

44. Pope seems to displace her own guilt about writing Abby's "life" onto Clement Johnson. Johnson wants to buy Colcorton, fascinated by its pegged floorboards, neglected Chippendales, and Sheraton kitchen chairs. Pope, in effect, shows Abby the notes Johnson—and, by extension, Pope herself—is keeping on Abby with the end of novelizing her. The notes contain such judgements as "American as corn cob pipe . . . dry humour indicated mostly by inflection." Edith Pope, *Colcorton* (New York: Charles Scribner's Sons, 1944), 129.

45. Pope, 245.

46. Pope, 258–9.

47. Pope, 260–61.

48. Pope, 297.

49. Pope, 284. Pope writes, "[Abby's] sorrow would be personal and would end. It would not be handed down over the years; she had *dispossessed* Jad of all that. The Clanghearnes' errors would be paid for by herself" (323, my emphasis). Abby does strange things not only to inheritance but to history itself.

50. Barbara Anderson, *Southbound* (New York: Farrar, Strauss, 1949), 172 and 229.

51. Vauthier, "Textualité et Stereotypes," 98.

52. Sigmund Freud, "Taboo and Emotional Ambivalence" in *Totem and Taboo*, trans. James Strachey (1913; rpt. New York: Norton, 1950), 22. The recurrence of the mulatto suggests Freud's con-

cept of the repetition compulsion principle, which he sets forth
most definitively in his 1920 *Beyond the Pleasure Principle,* and
which is of course central to the idea of the uncanny discussed
above.

53. See John G. Mencke, *Mulattoes and Race Mixture: American
Attitudes and Images,* Studies in American History and Culture,
no. 4 (Ann Arbor: University of Michigan Research Press, 1979),
41–44; and George M. Frederickson, *The Black Image in the
White Mind* (New York: Harper and Row, 1971). For studies of
white racist thought, Barry N. Schwartz and Robert Disch's anthology, *White Racism: Its History, Pathology, and Practice* (New
York: Dell, 1970) is valuable, and Joel Kovel's *White Racism: A
Psychohistory* (New York: Pantheon, 1971), is provocative.

54. Quoted in Genovese, 418.

55. Frances Gaither, *Double Muscadine* (New York: MacMillan,
1949), 135.

56. Gaither, 81.

57. Louise Blackwell and Frances Clay, "Lillian Smith, Novelist,"
CLAJ, 15 (1972), 452–53.

58. Berzon, 31. For a less simplistic account of the uses of primitivism, see Robert Bone's discussion of the "myth of primitivism" in
the Harlem Renaissance in *Down Home: A History of Afro-
American Short Fiction from Its Beginnings to the End of the
Harlem Renaissance* (New York: G. P. Putnam's, 1975), 124–30.

59. For a definition of romantic racialism, see George Frederickson,
101–2.

60. Anna Dickinson, *What Answer* (Boston: Ticknor and Fields,
1868), 75.

61. In the 1934 film version of *Imitation of Life,* starring Claudette
Colbert, Fredi Washington's Peola does not have herself sterilized;
in fact, the specter of her marriage to a white man is never raised.
Presumably, passing was strong enough stuff for contemporary
audiences without the threat of miscegenation made explicit.

62. Gertrude Atherton, *Senator North* (New York: John Lane, 1900),
161.

63. Atherton, 95.

64. Atherton, 243.

65. Atherton, 15.

66. Atherton, 79–80.

67. Atherton, 88.

68. Margaret Walker, *Jubilee* (1966; rpt. New York: Bantam Books,
1977), 425.

69. Nella Larsen, *Passing* (1929; rpt. New York: Negro Universities Press, 1969), 97–98.

70. For critical responses to Larsen's *Passing*, see the notes and discussion in Chapter 2.

71. The lines are from Countee Cullen's significantly entitled "Heritage," from his 1925 collection *Color*.

72. Larsen, *Passing*, 188.

73. Larsen, *Passing*, 120.

74. Mary Mabel Youman, "Nella Larsen's *Passing*: A Study in Irony." *CLAJ*, 18 (1974), 235. Youman concludes, "Though Clare is the literal 'passer' she returns to her birthright: Irene who remains 'Black' has sold her soul and 'passes' into white inhumanity" (241).

75. Larsen, *Passing*, 118.

76. Sollors, "Between Consent and Descent: Studying Ethnic Literature in the U.S.A.," New York Institute for the Humanities *Intellectual History Group Newsletter*, 4 (Spring 1982), 13–19. Sollors writes that writers and critics have expressed and perpetuated this conflict by "hovering between contractual and hereditary, self-made and ancestral definitions of their own as well as of American identity" (16).

77. Jordan, 167.

78. Shirley Ann Grau, *The Keepers of the House* (New York: Alfred A. Knopf, 1964), 85.

Chapter 7

1. Leaving aside the question of the "generational saga" aspect of world literature, it is not difficult to trace the rise of this specific genre following the publication of Alex Haley's *Roots* in 1976. *Roots* touched off a surge of interest in ancestry, and self-definition through ancestry. An excellent analysis of this phenomenon is provided by James A. Hijiya in a review essay, "Roots, Family and Ethnicity in the 1970s," *American Quarterly*, 30 (1978), 548–56. Hijiya discusses popular novels like Jack Shepherd's 1975 *The Adams Chronicles: Four Generations of Greatness* and Louis Auchincloss's 1976 *The Winthrop Covenant* (which follows generations of Winthrops, descendants of John, down to a draft dodger who keeps revealing the Puritan origins of his American self). Clearly, the "generational saga" has its "roots" here, though the genre—like Americans—cannot be entirely ancestrally defined. As a female genre, it borrows heavily from the best-selling com-

munity, particularly historical romances and so-called bodice-rippers. The difficulty in locating the genre's identity is exemplified by the publication of an explanatory article in *Publisher's Weekly,* Kathryn Falk and Elaine Kolb's "Telling the Romance Styles Apart," 220 (13 November 1981), 39. The lack of distinction within the genre is represented by the fact that the "generational saga" author often writes books in other genres. Belva Plain followed her 1978 pure "generational saga" *Evergreen* with *Random Winds* in 1980, a novel that spans generations but is not a true generational saga in that it does not begin in the Old World. Cynthia Freeman's 1979 *Portraits* is a generational saga, her 1981 *Come Pour the Wine* is a historical romance, and her 1981 *No Time for Tears* is a contemporary romance. A true generational saga which expands the limits of the genre is Meredith Tax's 1982 *Rivington Street.* Written by a feminist labor historian, the novel consciously follows formula but strives for a historical grounding and literary merit. Other generational sagas, of very little merit, are Gay Coulter's 1981 *Midwife,* Gloria Goldreich's 1982 *This Promised Land,* and Sharon Steener's 1982 *The Jews.*

2. Marianne Moore, "The Spare American Emotion," [review of *The Making of Americans*] *Dial,* 80 (February 1926), 153–56. Moore's review concludes, "As Bunyan's Christian is English yet universal, this sober, tender-hearted, very searching history of a family's progress, comprehends in its picture of life which is distinctly American, a psychology which is universal" (156). John Malcolm Brinnin, in *The Third Rose: Gertrude Stein and Her Work* (Boston: Little, Brown, 1959), also places the novel as a generational saga. He writes that the novel, "for all its attenuations and repetitions and vermiculations, can still be regarded as a novel having a discernible relation to many other chronicles of family history which appeared in the late nineteenth and early twentieth centuries" (124).

3. Gertrude Stein, *What Are Masterpieces* (1940; rpt. New York: Pitman, 1970), 68–69. Ann Douglas pointed out this important aspect of Stein's ethnicity to me.

4. Edmund Wilson, *Axel's Castle: A Study in the Imaginative Literature of 1870–1930* (New York: Scribner's, 1950), 240. Wilson sees "a sort of fatty degeneration of her imagination and style" in Stein's development from *Three Lives* to *The Making of Americans.*

5. The original version of *The Making of Americans* was published as one of Robert McAlmon's Contact Editions in Paris in 1925; it was 925 pages long. Portions of the novel were serialized in the

transatlantic review in 1924. After the success of *The Autobiography of Alice B. Toklas,* Stein abridged the novel to 416 pages; it was published by Harcourt, Brace in 1934. In spite of the protests of readers like Katherine Anne Porter, Stein seems to have been satisfied with the abridged version. Although no reading experience compares to that of reading the original long version, I have found the 1934 edition adequate for citation purposes. For accounts of the novel's various publications, see James Mellow, *A Charmed Circle: Gertrude Stein and Company* (New York: Praeger, 1974), 267–70 and 318–20; Richard Bridgman, *Gertrude Stein in Pieces* (New York: Oxford, 1970), 59–60; and Donald Gallup, "The Making of *The Making of Americans,*" *New Colophon,* 3 (1950), 54–74.

6. Quoted in Bridgman, 59.

7. Gertrude Stein, "The Gradual Making of The Making of Americans," in *Lectures in America* (1935; rpt. New York: Vintage, 1975), 153.

8. A great deal of ink has been spilled on the subject of the dates of Stein's composition, much of it in interesting speculation. The single most useful assessment of this matter is Leon Katz's unpublished doctoral dissertation, "The First Making of *The Making of Americans:* A Study Based on Gertrude Stein's Notebooks and Early Version of Her Novel" (Columbia University, 1963). Katz has definitely fixed the dates of composition at 1902–1911. See also Katz's "Weininger and *The Making of Americans,*" *Twentieth Century Literature,* 24 (1978), 8–26. Stein said in her lecture on the novel that the writing of it took her "almost three years" but the "preparation" may have taken longer. "I made [the novel] gradually and it took me almost three years to make it, but that is not what I mean by gradual. What I mean by gradual is the way preparation was made inside of me" (195). The reader of Stein quickly learns that most of Stein's statements about her work require liberal interpretation.

9. Bridgman, 60–61, considers *The Making of Americans* an apprentice work, "psychologically liberating" for Stein. There is no denying that it was such, but this assessment implies a judgment of the novel's quality that I disagree with. I am extremely indebted to Bridgman's analysis of the novel, 59–116, and to his overall consideration of Stein's career. Although I consider his the single most important critical work on Stein, no Stein reader can overlook Donald Sutherland's *Gertrude Stein: A Biography of Her Work* (Westport, Conn.: Greenwood Press, 1951); Norman Weinstein's *Gertrude Stein and the Literature of Modern Consciousness* (New York: Ungar, 1970); and Allegra Stewart's *Gertrude Stein and*

the Present (Cambridge: Harvard University Press, 1967). The best biographical understanding of Stein can be gained from using Bridgman's critical study with Mellow and Brinnin. I found other critical works extremely useful, among them Anna Gibbs, "Hélène Cixous and Gertrude Stein: New Directions in Feminist Criticism," *Meanjin,* 38 (1979), 281–93; Elizabeth Fifer, "Is Flesh Advisable? The Interior Theatre of Gertrude Stein," *Signs* 4 (1979), 472–83; Tony Tanner's chapter on Gertrude Stein, "Gertrude Stein and the Complete Actual Present," in *The Reign of Wonder: Naivety and Reality in American Literature* (Cambridge, Eng.: University Press, 1975); and, particularly, Charlotte Kretzoi, "Gertrude Stein's Attempt at 'The Great American Novel,'" *Studies in English and American Literature* (Budapest, Hungary), 4 (1978), 7–34. *Twentieth Century Literature* 24 (1978) is a special issue on Stein, but of two essays on *The Making of Americans,* only the Katz essay cited above is of real value, Clive Bush's "Toward the Outside: The Quest for Discontinuity in *The Making of Americans,*" 27–56, being interesting but needlessly difficult, a quality much Stein criticism shares.

10. Stein's use of the triangle as a structural arrangement in her early fiction (including her 1901 "Melanctha" in *Three Lives*) is based not only on her relationship with May Bookstaver but also on the so-called "Hodder episode," concerning Alfred Hodder's relationship with Miss Guinn, a friend o' M. Carey Thomas at Bryn Mawr—which in fact appears in *The Making of Americans* as the Philip Redfern/Martha/Cora Dounor grouping. Katz's dissertation provides the most thorough discussion of the Bookstaver and Hodder affairs and the biographical/fictional correspondences, but see also Mellow, 50–77.

11. Katz, "The First Making," 75. Charlotte Kretzoi writes, *"The Making of Americans* belongs mainly to the nineteenth century with occasional glimpses even into the eighteenth century," citing the social and moral values of the book, the author's addresses to the reader, and the influence of George Eliot (10–11).

12. Bridgman, 74, provides the clearest explanation of the classification system.

13. Stein quotes her own essay in "The Gradual Making of The Making of Americans," 138.

14. See Katz, "Weininger and *The Making of Americans.*" A further area of inquiry might be the ways in which Stein's homosexuality, and her life-long interest in gender distinctions, affected her response to Weininger's rigidly schematic assignation of character according to gender.

15. As do Anna Gibbs and Elizabeth Fifer in the articles cited above.

The pieces collected in Stein's 1922 *Geography and Plays,* and in
the Yale Edition's *Bee Time Vine* and *Alphabets and Birthdays,*
many of which were written in 1915–1917 in Mallorca during
what seems to have been an idyllic interlude in Stein's relationship with Toklas, contain vividly erotic references to and dialogues
with Toklas. Representative poems are "A Sonatina" and "Lifting
Belly," both in *Bee Time Vine.* Bridgman, 137–59, provides a good
account of this phase, but the subtext of eroticism throughout
Stein's other works remains an important and underexplored area.

16. This statement appears, for example, on p. 229 of *The Making of
Americans* (New York: Harcourt, Brace, 1934). Further references to this novel in this chapter will be made parenthetically
within the text.

17. The beginning of the Martha Hersland section sets forth this notion. Critics have done much with this statement, biographically
(the withdrawal of Leo) and otherwise. A far more poignant statement is made in the Alfred Hersland section about the ways in
which Stein writes for herself and for strangers: "Disillusionment
in living is the finding out nobody agrees with you not those that
are and were fighting with you. . . . not those that are fighting
for you. Complete disillusionment is when you realise that no one
can for they can't change. The amount they agree is important to
you until the amount they do not agree with you is completely
realised by you. Then you say you will write for yourself and for
strangers" (282).

18. Bridgman, 61. The analogy is particularly nice in light of Stein's
fondness for the automobile, in which she apparently cut a very
stately figure. Another notable metaphor for the novel is Donald
Sutherland's; he compares it to the Pentagon, which "is or was a
self-contained labyrinth of simple essential abstractions" (56).

19. "The Gradual Making of The Making of Americans," 160.

20. Bernard Fäy, "Preface," *The Making of Americans,* xx.

21. Of all the critics of the novel, only Charlotte Kretzoi, 13–14, gives
some consideration to this central point. She writes, "the most
central American experience is that of the immigrant—shared by
all Americans except the Indians: the process of adjusting themselves to the new land's requirements and customs in the first generation, the family reminiscences about them handed down to the
second and third generation, becoming dimmer and dimmer in
subsequent generations" (13).

22. Leon Katz provides the most thorough discussion of Stein's Jewishness, "The First Making of *The Making of Americans,*" 203–8.
In the 1930s Stein chose to see herself as "oriental" (quoted in

Katz, 204). The families in *The Making of Americans,* originally Jewish, became in later versions German and then middle class. See also Bridgman, 160–61.

23. Aristotle, in his *Nichomachean Ethics* (Book vii, Chapter 6), uses the story to show that passions are accepted only insofar as they are not expressed excessively, and that the exercise of "unnatural" passions—he cites unnatural forms of sexual intercourse—is less acceptable than circumscribed "natural" behavior. Stein, who might have had some personal interest in this interpretation, then moves interestingly to interpret the story to allow acceptance of one's own harmless "sins." The story and Stein's interpretation of it have an interesting psychosexual link, which Bridgman acknowledges but does not fully consider, 66–67.

24. Mellow, 20–22, provides the fullest discussion of Stein's ancestors.

25. The difficulty in addressing the amount of time in which a generation "passeth away" suggests the formidable problems associated with the use of the concept of "generations" in interpreting American culture and immigrant history. Werner Sollors's "First Generation, Second Generation, Third Generation: Metaphorical Thinking in America" (Unpublished ms., Columbia University, 1981), a broad study of generations in American culture, traces a generational imagery in American rhetoric from John Higginson's descriptive account in his 1697 "Attestation" to Cotton Mather's *Magnalia Christi Americana,* through Marcus Lee Hansen's Law ("What the son forgets the grandchild wishes to remember") to Mel Brooks's generational analysis of the Frankenstein story, arguing that generational imagery supports jeremiadic and moralistic renditions of American backsliding and progress. Sollors points out that the idea of generations is used widely without attention to the meaning of the idea.

26. Stein, "Portraits and Repetition," *Lectures in America,* 165. Stein sees the "current generation" as so filled with movement that it does not have to be seen against a background in order that its movement be perceived. She writes, "A motor goes inside of an automobile and the car goes. In short this generation has conceived an intensity of movement so great that it has not to be seen against something else to be known, and therefore, this generation does not connect itself with anything, that is what makes this generation what it is and that is why it is American" (166).

27. Stein, "Portraits and Repetition," 177.

28. Bridgman, 71. Think of the triangular affairs in *The Making of Americans, Q.E.D, Melanctha; Three Lives,* etc.

29. Margaret Mead, *And Keep Your Powder Dry: An Anthropologist*

Looks at America (New York: W. Morrow, 1942). The statement
is the title of Mead's third chapter. As Sollors points out, "No
method of generational counting can validate her verdict" (22),
and Mead's statement functions as a metaphor from which it is
problematic to draw empirical conclusions.

30. This concept, whether it is voiced in its classic the-child-is-father-
of-the-man phrasing or not, seems to pop up repeatedly in Stein
criticism. Clive Bush, in an unintelligible context, states it directly,
p. 40. The concept is central to Stein's philosophy. It is an interesting notion in connection with Ernest Jones's formulation of the
"grandfather complex," which Sollors points out, p. 25, and which
I discuss earlier, under the terms of which the child wishes to become her grandparents in order to parent her parents.

31. Bridgman, 10. Mellow, however, finds David Hersland far more
complex than Daniel Stein seems to have been. Much of Stein
herself went into David Hersland, and she is not entirely unsympathetic toward her fictional father.

32. As Stein asserts in The Autobiography of Alice B. Toklas (New
York: Harcourt, Brace, 1933), 138. Bridgman, 86, discusses the
notion of David Hersland (III) as hero. He feels that the young
Hersland is analogous to Leo, although he acknowledges that
Brinnin's candidate is Leon Solomon, a Harvard friend. Of course
David Hersland (III) bears resemblance to Stein; Stein is auto-
biographically invested in each character in The Making of Ameri-
cans, including the servants.

33. David Hersland keeps up with the second governess after her marriage to the baker, always giving her advice, particularly "whether
she was getting fatter or thinner" and "what was the right way for
her to do to content her husband." "[H]e mostly talked to her
about eating and marrying," writes Stein (185–86). The overtones
of oral eroticism are unmistakable here.

34. See Bridgman, 342.

35. The Geographical History of America (New York: Random
House, 1936), 23.

36. Werner Sollors, who considers Stein an ethnic writer in "Literature and Ethnicity," in The Harvard Encyclopedia of American
Ethnic Groups, ed. Stephan Thernstrom (Cambridge: Harvard
University Press, 1980), 6, points out the connection to Washington in this passage.

37. Stein, Four in America (New Haven: Yale, 1947), 168.

38. Four in America, 169.

39. Representative statements of Stein's interest in the name George
are: "What is the difference between George Washington and
George Hawkins?" (Four in America, 167); and "George Wash-

ington is a name a pleasant name and all the same it is a name" (*Four in America,* 169). Stein liked the name George. The seventh chapter of *How To Write* (Paris: Plain Edition, 1931), titled "Finally George a Vocabulary," radiates out from her play on that name.

40. *Four in America,* 183.

41. *Four in America,* 192. Is it possible that "Martha Hersland"—the first name that of George's wife, the second signalling her possession of the land—is another comment on forefathers?

42. Quoted in Bridgman, 11.

43. Stein, *Picasso* (London: B. T. Batsford, 1938), 14–15.

44. *Picasso,* 18.

45. *The Making of Americans,* 49. Stein writes that grandmothers are "always old women or as little children to us the generation of grandchildren."

Tony Tanner, in his chapter on Gertrude Stein in *The Reign of Wonder,* places Stein in what he sees as an "American interest in a recovered naivety of vision" (190). He believes that Stein's "ideal of what we may call seeing without remembering, without associating, without thinking" follows Thoreau's ideal of "seeing without looking" and Whitman's "first step," and anticipates Anderson's and Hemingway's "reality hunger" (190).

46. Bridgman, 267. See Stein, *The Geographical History of America,* esp. 200–207. Anna Gibbs discusses entity and identity writing, concluding that there is little difference between them (288).

47. Editor Robert Bartlett Haas, *How Writing is Written* (Los Angeles: Black Sparrow Press, 1974), makes an editorial division between some of Stein's "entity" and "identity" works.

48. Stein, *Narration* (Chicago: University of Chicago Press, 1935), 25.

49. *Narration,* 24.

50. Bridgman, 97.

51. *Narration,* 24.

52. This technique, of "occasionally decelerating time to emphasize select action," Nathan Weinstein suggests, is consistent with Stein's affection for *Clarissa,* which she claimed was her favorite novel (Weinstein, 38). The two novels have interesting similarities in technique. Weinstein also refers to Martha and her umbrella, relating Stein's use of the incident to Henri Bergson's sense of psychological time. A useful study on repetition and narrative is Peter Brooks, "Freud's Masterplot," in *Literature and Psychoanalysis,* ed. Shoshana Felman (Baltimore: Johns Hopkins University Press, 1982), 280–300.

53. "The Gradual Making of The Making of Americans," 157.

Afterword

1. "The Gradual Making of The Making of Americans," *Lectures in America* (1935; rpt. New York: Vintage, 1975), 160.
2. Gloria Naylor, *The Women of Brewster Place* (New York: Viking, 1982), 1.

Index

Abrahams, Roger, 28
Addams, Jane, 84
American identity, 157–58; ancestral definition of, 3; experience of migration and, 3, 165–67; generational conflict and, 88–90; rhetoric and, 71–73, 89–92, 126; as shared difference, 3, 252 n. 76. *See also* Americanization *and* Ethnic female identity
American Indian women's writing, 9, 12–30; bibliographic problems and, 15, 17–18; storytelling, 14–15; tricksters and, 26–30, *See also individual authors*
Americanization, 10, 71–96, 125–26, 234 n. 35; Founding Fathers and, 86–96; generational conflict, 72–78; intermarriage and, 100–101, 105–8; Oedipus complex and, 88–89; as rebirth, 10, 80–83, 126; rhetoric of, 126. *See also* Ethnic female identity; Melting pot
Anderson, Barbara, 149
Anderson, Quentin, 111
Anderson, Sherwood, 178
Antin, Mary, 10, 37, 42, 44, 83–84; Founding Fathers and, 86–87; *From Plotzk to Boston,* 34; generational conflict in, 82; Jeremiad and, 89–90; as mediated text, 36;

as mediator, 33–34; 38–40; 222 nn. 7, 8; *The Promised Land,* 10, 33–34, 40, 42, 81, 82, 86–87; role of education in, 80, 83–84; *They Who Knock At Our Gates,* 38–39; mentioned, 51, 71, 88, 96, 161, 189
Aristotle: *Nichomachean Ethics,* 166
Astrov, Margaret, 27
Atherton, Gertrude, 11, 152–53, 190, 191
Authentication of texts, 36–38. *See also* Mediation

Barth, John, 113
Bataille, Gretchen, 17
Beauvoir, Simone de, 5
Bercovitch, Sacvan, 89, 235 n. 44, 236 n. 48
Berzon, Judith, 140, 157, 158
Black genteel tradition, 9, 43–47, 60–61. *See also* Reconstruction novelists
Black women writers: and approaches to Pocahontas marriage, 103–4; and folklore, 57; and literacy, 45, 54; subversive power of language, 45–47; tricksterism, 58, 66. *See also individual authors;* Harlem Renaissance; Reconstruction novelists